John Ogilvie

Philosophical and Critical Observations on the Nature, Characters, and Various Species of Composition

Vol. I

John Ogilvie

Philosophical and Critical Observations on the Nature, Characters, and Various Species of Composition
Composition
Vol. I

ISBN/EAN: 9783337086350

Printed in Europe, USA, Canada, Australia, Japan

Cover: Foto ©Thomas Meinert / pixelio.de

More available books at **www.hansebooks.com**

PHILOSOPHICAL and CRITICAL

OBSERVATIONS

ON THE

NATURE, CHARACTERS,

AND

VARIOUS SPECIES

OF

COMPOSITION.

By JOHN OGILVIE, D.D.

IN TWO VOLUMES.

VOL. I.

Η πως αν αλλως συιςη τοδι ΤΟ ΠΑΝ, ει μη ΡΥΘΜΩ τινι και
ΤΑΞΕΙ διεκεκοσμητο. Και τα υφ' ημων κατασκευαζομενα οργαια
ΜΕΤΡΩ ΠΑΝΤΑ γιγνονται. Ει δε ΠΑΝΤΑ αλλα, πολλω γε
μαλλον Ο ΛΟΓΟΣ, ατι και ΠΕΡΙΕΚΤΙΚΟΣ ΑΠΑΝΤΩΝ ΩΝ.
ΛΟΝΓΙΝ. ΑΠΟΣΠΑΣ.

Of all the arts in which mankind excel,
Nature's chief master-piece is WRITING WELL.
BUCKINGHAM.

LONDON,
Printed for G. ROBINSON, in Paternoster-Row.
MDCCLXXIV.

ADVERTISEMENT.

IN the moſt flouriſhing ages of Greece and Rome, the various branches of the ſub-ject of this Eſſay employed the pens of authors, whoſe works every ſucceeding age has contemplated with admiration. In the preſent enlightened æra, to whatever frivo-lous objects the public taſte may have been ſometimes directed, the author cannot ſuppoſe that ſuch a ſubject can fail of being in itſelf univerſally agreeable, as it naturally draws the attention as well of thoſe who occupy the different departments of the Art, as of the reader who hath peruſed their writings with emolument or pleaſure.——With regard to the execution in the preſent inſtance, every reader will judge for himſelf. The author will neither attempt to raiſe his eſteem of it, by enlarging on the approbation with which it has been honoured by ſome reſpectable critics ; nor to repreſs juſt cenſure by mean acknow-ledgments of timidity. He will take the li-berty only to obſerve, that though the works of the moſt eminent ancient and modern wri-

ters

ters on the subject of Composition have been consulted, and are often referred to in the present, yet far from following their track with servility, he has, upon some occasions, differed from them in opinion, and has even exposed their blemishes with freedom. This conduct will displease no reader who observes that it was necessary to give examples of the faults, as well as of the beauties of Composition; and that both are most clearly discerned, when contrasted properly with each other. Opinions which he judged exceptionable, he will likewise be excused for having attempted to refute, by those who acquit him of the only charges that render this conduct inexcusable—petulance, or malignity. Where the writers whom he consulted either suggested to his mind a certain train of observation, or served to confirm and illustrate such as occurred to him, he has never failed either to quote the passage from their works, or to throw it into the notes; which last, in a work of this kind, have been rendered unavoidably numerous and protracted. That this coincidence of sentiment did not occur more frequently, the author can only ascribe to the extensive view which he was led to take of his subject. His tract in the first part of the work (in which the intellectual powers

are

are considered as influencing Composition) he was left to chalk out for himself*. The lights thrown upon the other branches of it, particularly by the ancient critics, are stronger, and more diversified. He has therefore endeavoured at the same time to confirm his own observations by a variety of examples drawn from their writings, (the most striking of which are made intelligible to the English reader), and to relax the mind from rigid disquisition, by placing before it some capital strokes of the most consummate masters of the art. There is still another, and an important branch of the subject that remains to be treated; in which it is proposed to consider this divine Art as a principal means of promoting the civilization and the happiness of mankind. This view of it is necessary to complete the Author's original plan; though the critical part is fully comprised in what is now offered to the public. In so large a compass as is here taken, and on themes in canvassing which freedom of thought is not subjected to censure, there must be a corresponding variety of opinions. The writer does not form so idle an expectation, as that every reader will think in the

---

* See the two first Notes of Sect. I.

same

same manner as himself on each of these sub-jects. To the question therefore,—" By what standard would you have your perform-ance to be tried?"—he replies,—Let the same degree of candour and impartiality *be employed in judging of the merit or de-fects of the following observations, which the author himself has applied to those of every author, ancient or modern, which in the pro-secution of this attempt he hath had occasion to investigate.*

N. B. The reader will observe that the terms Understanding, Judgment, Reason, are used to signify the same intellectual power, though the first of these, strictly speaking, is of larger import. This liberty the author took in order to avoid repetitions.

CONTENTS.

BOOK I.

Of Compofition as it regards the Faculties of the Mind.

SEC-

vi CONTENTS.

The following ERRORS were occasioned by the AUTHOR's distance from the Press.

Page 29. line 6. of the note, *for* throw *read* thrown. P. 133. l. 7. *for* conflux *read* conflict. P. 149. l. 24 of the note, *for* in *read* of. P. 176. l. 11. *for* abstains *read* obtains. P. 202. l. 24. *read* in the art, &c. P. 209. l. 22. *for* a while *read* and while. P. 230. l. 8. of the note, *for* in concluding *read* to conclude. P. 238. l. 21. *place the* (;) *after the word* whatever. P. 247. l. 6, of the note, *for* Cinzas *read* Cineas. P. 271. l. 9. *for* or *read* for. l. 10. *for* mild *read* wild. P. 317. l. 3. of the note, *dele* the. P. 368. l. 12, 13. *for* perspicacity *read* perspicuity. P. 412. l. 9. *after* venture *add* to propose.

PHILOSOPHICAL AND CRITICAL

OBSERVATIONS

ON

COMPOSITION.

BOOK I.

Of Compofition as it regards the Faculties of the Mind.

SECTION I.

Introductory Obfervations on the Nature of Compofition.

COMPOSITION will probably be contemplated by a mind that reflects on its nature, importance, and tendency, in the two following general lights. It will be confidered in one view as the refult of a peculiar combination, and propenfity of the faculties of the mind: in another, as *an art*, diftinguifhed by par-

ticular

ticular characters, divided into various fpecies; and producing effects of the greateft
importance to the civilization and happinefs
of mankind. It is propofed, in the prefent
Effay, to examine this copious fubject under thefe general heads: in the profecution
of which, after having endeavoured to point
out the fpheres of the intellectual powers
in this art, to mark the fignatures by
which each is difcriminated; to difplay
their diverfified combinations, and to lay
down fuch rules as tend to bring thefe
moft nearly to an equipoife, when found
to have been originally difproportioned;
we propofe to confider, in feparate fections,
the principal characters of claffical compofition; to take a view of its various fpecies, as formed by the union of thefe characters; and to conclude the work by making fome obfervations on the defign, importance, and tendency of the art.

As it will be obvious to any perfon who
hath read on this fubject, that we muft
here underftand the term Compofition
(thus comprehenfively viewed) in a larger
fenfe than hath formerly been affigned to
it,

it*, we shall make a few remarks, in the
present section, on the powers that occupy

its

---

* Our meaning will be greatly mistaken, if it is supposed that any general censure is implied here on the
authors who have examined this subject; as if their
views of it had been contracted and defective. Far
otherwise. By saying that the term Composition is
taken in this Essay in a larger sense, or includes a greater
variety of parts than these assign to it, we intend only
to point out the difference betwixt a general definition,
including every branch of a comprehensive art; and
one adapted more immediately to some detached field,
or department of it. The philosophical critic, it is
obvious, may take a view of the present theme suffi-
ciently adequate as far as this science is concerned,
though propriety will require that it should extend to
nothing beyond it. The same remark may be applied to poetry, eloquence, history, considered as species of one comprehensive art. In each it is obvious
that the definition of this term, when applied to any
of these separately, must necessarily include fewer objects, and take in a much less compass upon the whole,
than when it is viewed as relating to all. It happens
indeed frequently, that in consequence of that natural
propensity, which every writer feels to place his own
subject in as important a light as possible, and to make
it comprehend the most various assemblage, accounts
of these are pompously given, which dispassionate reason may reject as exaggerated. In this manner the
different provinces of this art, instead of being properly discriminated, are promiscuously blended together,

B 2 and

its various departments; as necessary to place before the mind a full and appropriated idea of the subject *.

The

---

and the mind, after having considered what different writers have advanced on each, finds itself wholly at a loss to determine its bounds with precision. It is this circumstance principally which renders it a matter of so much difficulty to select, in treating particular subjects, the composition that it is best adapted to its nature. Hence the philosopher, either assuming too often the dress of the orator, or laying it aside altogether, in a sphere where he meets with models of each kind, is in hazard, according to the particular biass of his mind, of making too much, or too little use of the ornaments of discourse, by which means his expression is rendered either florid, or enervated and uninterest-ing. The observation hath equal force when applied to the other branches abovementioned. A general view of the art, in which we consider not only what constitutes the perfection of each character contemplated by itself, but in what manner the concurrence of all ought to distinguish its various species, must supply these defects if properly executed. The comparison of these last with each other likewise, will naturally produce a clearer and more particular notion of what is just and appropriated in each, than can be obtained by estimates formed from the writings of different authors, whose views have regarded single parts; and whose manner of treating them varies, according to their diversity of taste and disposition.

That

The faculties of the mind, whoſe offices
in the province of compoſition we propoſe
to

That the ancients in general, who have examined
the ſeveral branches of compoſition with great
accuracy, lay down the beſt rules, and exhibit the
nobleſt models for imitation in every department, will
be called in queſtion by no man who is converſant
with their works. Many modern performances both
abound with precepts, and diſplay examples that are
equally admirable. It is a conſiderable part of our
buſineſs in the following work to confirm this truth,
partly by a critical examination of ſuch obſervations,
particularly of the former, as relate moſt immediately
to the preſent ſubject, carried on with the utmoſt impartiality ; and partly by illuſtrations of the characters
by which the art is diſtinguiſhed, drawn from the moſt
eminent performances, both ancient and modern. The
author intends only from the remarks made in this
note to ſuggeſt a plea in his own vindication, to thoſe
who may cenſure him for having made choice of a
theme that hath employed the pens of ſo many illuſtrious writers; and an excuſe for his differing in opinion
ſo often from ſome of them. The relation in which
he was led to conſider one part as ſtanding to another,
makes him aſſign a narrower precinct to it, than would
probably have been the caſe, had he conſidered each of
theſe apart. This the reader will keep uniformly in
his eye.

* We propoſe here to lay before the reader ſome of

the

to confider feparately, and even if poffible to
determine with fome precifion, are the underftanding,

---

the various meanings that have been given to the word
Compofition by authors of the greateft eminence, in order to confirm an obfervation made in the preceding
note. Dionyfius of Halicarnaffus, in his excellent.
treatife ΠΕΡΙ ΣΥΝΘΕΣΕΩΣ ΟΝΟΜΑΤΩΝ, enters
upon his fubject by explaining the fenfe of this term,
which he confiders in two different lights. His firft
definition is general, relating to the common acceptation of the phrafe. Η ΣΥΝΘΕΣΙΣ εςιν, ωσπερ και
αυτο δηλοι ονομα, ΠΟΙΑ ΤΙΣ ΘΕΣΙΣ ΠΑΡ' ΑΛΛΗΛΑ
ΤΩΝ ΤΟΥ ΛΟΓΟΥ ΜΟΡΙΩΝ ΣΥΓΓΡΑΜ : Tom. 2.
p. 2. edit. Lipfic. This account of the art, in which
the whole weight lies upon a due diftribution or order
of parts, includes unqueftionably one principal province of compofition. But confidered as a definition
of the fubject taken in one comprehenfive view, it is
defective, as we receive from it no idea of the propriety and harmony of modulated language correfponding,
to the fentiment of a work, or of beauty arifing from
happy illuftration. Thefe points, however, are fully
included in his next definition, which relates to his
own fubject, and is much more particular. Εςι δε της
ΣΥΝΘΕΣΕΩΣ ΕΡΓΑ οικειως θειναι τατι Ονοματα παρ'
αλληλα, και τοις κωλοις αποδουναι την προσηκουσαν ΑΡ-
ΜΟΝΙΑΝ και ΤΑΙΣ ΠΕΡΙΟΔΟΙΣ διαλαβειν αυτον
ολον τον Λογον. ibid. Thefe definitions of the term
ΣΥΝΘΕΣΙΣ, exhibit an idea of it, only incomplete as
they

derſtanding, the imagination, or inventive
power; diſcernment, as indicating the operation

---

they regard not its connection with a certain union of
intellectual powers, an omiſſion for which our author
is no way culpable, becauſe this view of the art falls
not in with his ſubject. Another ancient Critic, who
appears to have taken a pretty full view of compoſition,
defines it very particularly. Απας τοινυν ΛΟΓΟΣ εννοιαν
την εχει, και μεθοδον περι την εννοιαν, και ΛΕΞΙΝ, εν
τυτοις ηφιρμοςαι· Της δε αυ Λεξεως εχουσης παντως
τινα, και αυτης ιδιοματα, Παλιν αυτε χηματα τε εςι
τινα και κωλα ΣΥΖΘΕΣΕΙΣ τε, και ΑΝΑΠΑΥΣΕΙΣ
και το εξ αμφοιν τυτοιν συνιςαμενον Ο ΡΥΘΜΟΣ.
ΕΡΜΟΓΕΝ: περι ΙΔΕΩΝ. βιϐ. Α. Κεφ. β'. The
critic it is true hath a regard in this account, principally to eloquence, or the art of perſuaſion. But the
definition is full, and appropriated as far as the ſubject
required it to be ſo. Its defect, as a complete view of
compoſition, is the ſame as in the former inſtance, and
for the reaſon formerly aſſigned. The great ancient
Critic has treated of ſeveral different branches of compoſition in many parts of his writings. In his firſt
book on rhetoric, particularly, he aſſigns a diſtinct chapter to each diſtinguiſhed character of this art. But his
ſentiments of the ſubject in general we muſt collect
from different parts of his works. Thus he obſerves,
that by a juſt arrangement of parts we acquire clear
ideas of objects that are at firſt obſcurely known to us,
ΦΥΣΙΚ: βιϐ. Α. κεφ. α'. and infers the neceſſity of

mentioning

ration of both; and memory, whose use
we shall endeavour particularly to specify.
                                          The

---

mentioning the members of which a subject consists
particularly and fully, in order to render it thoroughly
intelligible and useful, ibid.   He considers the rheto-
rical art under three general divisions, which comprehend different species of composition, the philosophical
in particular.   These are the ΣΥΜΒΟΥΛΕΥΤΙΚΟΝ,
ΔΙΚΑΝΙΚΟΝ, and ΕΠΙΔΕΙΚΤΙΚΟΝ. ΡΗΤΟΡΙΚ.
βιϐ. Α. κεφ. γ´.   Lastly he points out with great precision, the method of laying down an accurate disposition, id. βιϐ. Γ. κεφ. ιγ´. and ΜΕΤΑΦΥΣ. βιϐ. Γ.
κεφ. ιθ´.   But as he treats not systematically of the
subject of this essay as a general term including many
subdivisions, a definition of it regarding its origin, and
comprehending its various branches fell not in with
his designs.   Longinus, whose sphere is much more
contracted than that of our great philosopher, takes
notice of a ΣΥΓΚΛΕΙΟΥΣΑ ΣΥΝΘΕΣΙΣ, as the last
ingredient of the sublime, and necessary to connect the
other four sources which he had previously enumerated, into one body. ΠΕΡΙ ΥΨΟΣ .τμημ. η´. and αθ´.
But as this regards only a particular character of it,
which will be examined in its place, we have but just
mentioned it here. Of Roman writers who have treated of the present subject, the judicious and elegant
Quintilian is by far the most copious and particular.
In his well-known work, intitled Institutiones Orato-
riæ, (of which the reader will find much use made in
                                              the

The three firft mentioned of thefe, though
employed in fpheres that are diftinct from
each

---

the following effay, and whofe excellence is equal to
almoft any culogium) the prefent fubject is difcuffed
by itfelf. The fourth fection of his ninth book contains his obfervations on it. Here he confiders three
things as conftituting juft compofition, order, or a due
arrangement of parts; connection, (junctura) or a juft
correfpondence of the members of a fentence, as well
As of words to each other; and harmony, (numerus)
or the graceful and melodious ftructure of periods. We
fhall have occafion afterwards to examine what he hath
advanced on thefe heads. At prefent we need only
obferve, that his view of compofition, as an art, principally regards expreffion, which is the leaft part of it;
and even here likewife he hath a particular regard, as
we might naturally expect, to eloquence, which is his
fubject. It would be an endlefs tafk to felect from the
writings of the illuftrious Roman orator and philofopher, the different views that are prefented to us of
compofition. There is neither a character nor fpecies
of it which he hath omitted to examine at one time or
other in his works. It is only to be regretted that his
obfervations on this fubject lie detached, inftead of
being placed together in one view, as they thus lofe a
great part of their effect. In confequence likewife of
treating the fubject in this manner, its connection with
the faculties of the mind (which forms a firft and principal object in our eftimation, when we furvey it as a
proportioned whole) falls not particularly under obfervation.

each other, yet are required to exert united influence in every fpecies of, this art,
when properly conducted. Of this we
fhall judge with more precifion from a general confideration of their different offices.

" The underftanding is that power of
the mind which determines the relation of
parts to each other in laying down the plan
of a performance of whatever nature ;
which judgeth of its comprehenfion as
fuited to the fubject; which, following the

---

fervation. In his firft book De Oratore, and twelfth
chapter, he gives a definition of the term with confiderable extent, diftinguifheth betwixt the expreffion
and fentiment; and feparates with great propriety and
difcernment the provinces of philofophy and eloquence
from each other. Thus much for the fentiments of the
Ancients on the meaning of this term. We would
fwell out this note to too much length by confidering
the accounts of it given by modern writers, which differ in nothing materially from the preceding ones, at
leaft as far as the author can judge from his acquaintance with their works. The opinions of fome of the
moft eminent on this fubject we fhall have occafion
to adduce, and to examine likewife at large in different
fections of the following effay.

feries

series of effects to their original, investigates
a caufe; and fuperintends the conduct
of this procedure in fuch a manner as to
make the expreffion bear the fame relation
to the fentiments of any performance which
thefe laft are required to do to each other."
—"Imagination, or the inventive faculty, as
it is denominated, is that which ftrikes out
happy imitations, forms new and original
affemblages of ideas; and thus fupplies the
materials of thofe juft and beautiful illuftrations, which at the fame time improve
the expreffion of compofition, and heighten the effect of its fentiment." — "By
difcernment we underftand that faculty
which, without carrying on any regular
procefs, comprehends as it were inftantaneoufly the proper manner of treating any
fubject, by fixing upon the points that are
of principal confequence, and accomplifheth by this mean, at once, purpofes which
the underftanding alone *cannot* effectuate
in *fome cafes* by any exertion; and obtains in
thofe to which it is adapted, by a flow and
deliberate procedure." This power appears to participate of both the former, but

is

is conftituted wholly by neither. From judgment, confidered by itfelf, it differs remarkably in quicknefs of perception at all times univerfally, and even upon fome occafions, in its choice of objeɛts. From imagination it is no lefs diftinguifhed by making *a juft* inftead of a *fuperficial* or *indifcriminate feleɛtion of means*; and by going to the bottom of a fubjeɛt, inftead of fkimming lightly on its furface. Difcernment, thus including a part of the offices both of judgment and imagination, we fhall find to aɛt in different departments, according to the proportion in which either of thefe faculties is conferred on an individual. Thus when a large fhare of the inventive is united with a much greater proportion of the reafoning power, to which laft therefore it is wholly fubfervient, the intelleɛtual eye, though taking cognizance in general of all objeɛts, will be confpicuous principally, either in conduɛting, or in judging of that difquifition which is direɛted by the underftanding. It judgeth for inftance in this cafe of the force and propriety of an argument, whofe connection

nection with the ſubject might wholly eſcape the obſervation of a leſs intelligent
mind. --It brings together proofs from
every quarter, to ſupport and confirm an
hypotheſis framed originally by an act
that indicates the moſt acute perception;
and hits (to uſe the language of an eminent writer) upon that *particular point* on
which the *bent* of each argument turns, or
the force of each motive depends *." Thus
it is, that philoſophical diſcernment is peculiarly conſtituted, and becomes conſpicuous, either in the ſphere of compoſition,
when a ſubject is methodiſed and diſcuſſed,

---

* Pope's preface to Shakeſpeare. Our author aſcribes
this conduct of the great Genius whom he characteriſeth, to a talent different from that of judgment; ſomething he ſays, " *very peculiar*, and *betwixt penetration
and felicity*." I do not underſtand the meaning of theſe
laſt words very clearly. Shakeſpeare poſſeſſed in an
eminent degree the diſcernment that ariſeth from
judgment and imagination acting in vigorous concurrence, and it is one of the criteria of this power (as
we ſhall ſhow particularly in its proper place) to produce this happy but uncommon effect, which could
not eſcape the obſervation of a writer who himſelf
poſſeſſed ſo large a proportion of intellectual acumen.

or

or·in forming an eftimate of the execution
when fubmitted to critical inveftigation.

A proportion of the inventive faculty
more adequate to that of the reafoning
power, (each fuppofed to exift in an eminent degree) renders the influence of difcernment ftill more confpicuous than in
the former inftance, becaufe it appears
with *equal* advantage in this cafe, when
judging of the *arts,* as well as of the inveftigations of fcience; and will pronounce
as properly of what is *beautiful* in the one,
as of what is *juft* and decifive in the other.
The means by which both is effectuated
we fhall confider more particularly, when
we come to treat of this as a *diftinct* faculty, operating univerfally on the various
branches of compofition.

We have in the preceding obfervations
confidered the intellectual powers only as
influencing the various fpecies of the fubject of this effay.—But there are two queftions arifing from our account of thefe
which muft be anfwered before we acquire
a clear idea of *compofition as it regards the
faculties of the mind.* Is (it may be afked)
                                          the

the concurrence of thofe we have enumerated neceffary to give maftery to an author's
execution, in any department of this comprehenfive art?—We may reply without
hefitation, that though the degrees in which
this union may take place vary according
to the nature of a fubject, yet the combination in fome degree *is* neceffary for this
purpofe. But fhould it again be afked,
whether a talent for any fpecies of compofition, or a power of placing thoughts in
the happieft difpofition, and of expreffing
them in the fitteft words; whether this talent always accompanies the union of intellectual qualities abovementioned, even
when fubfifting in a high degree; we fhall
find upon enquiry, that there is no neceffary connection betwixt thefe, as the former may fubfift, when there is no peculiar
bias to the latter.

1. It is ufually thought that wherever a
vigorous imagination exerts its influence,
the mind commonly receives a propenfity
to compofition; and that the higheft walks
of this art are *always* occupied by thofe
who poffefs an eminent proportion of it.

Authors

Authors in general have not contradicted
the prevailing opinion with regard to the
connection betwixt this mental quality and
the subject of which we treat. But a little
reflection will show us that we are mistaken
in this estimation.

Upon surveying attentively the mental
powers by which man is distinguished from
the inferior creation, we shall find each of
these assuming forms so various as it operates on particular characters, that, without bestowing close attention, we may
overlook the cause from which effects
seemingly so remote from each other derive
their origin. Thus a mechanical engine,
an animated figure in history painting, a
philosophical theory, and a series of interesting and well concerted incidents, appear at first view to be objects whose connection is so distant, that it demands attention to discover that the inventive faculty, assuming different aspects, is the common parent of all. The difficulty of tracing to their original source the phænomena
that arise from imagination, is still greater,
when we consider its influence on the

actions

actions of men. Thus among the active part of mankind, who are commonly suppofed to poffefs no great fhare of this faculty, becaufe perhaps they are incapable either of difcovering, or of feeling the beauties of compofition; we are apt to overlook or not to affign to its proper caufe, the facility with which thefe men invent plans of happinefs adapted to their difpofitions, one after a former hath been difappointed; the uncommon expedients they fometimes adopt to carry thefe into execution; in fhort, their capacity of finding fuch remote and extraordinary refources as render the moft formidable dangers not only furmountable, but even familiar: yet it is unqueftionably the fame power receiving only a different direction, which produceth thefe effects in life as it is that in the fpheres of poetry and eloquence invents the fable, or fupplies the illuftrations.

It is not however only from the actions of men that we may be led to confider the bufy part of them as poffeffing in many inftances no inconfiderable fhare of imagination. A little acquaintance with life

will

will fet before us another clafs upon whofe *converfation* this faculty appears to operate in a very ftriking manner, though without extending any further. Thefe are men who inheriting from nature a certain quick-nefs and volatility of thought, which eva-porates in an inftant, are qualified to fparkle a moment in the circle of their compa-nions. But the talent of methodifing fen-timent, and that of throwing out loofe thoughts, however entertaining, are wholly different. The firft is the offspring of fancy deriving little affiftance from the rea-foning power; whereas the laft is effec-tuated by an effort indicating mature and deliberate recollection. Thus it happens that men wholly difqualified for the one of thefe employments, affume the other as a province in which nature hath fully com-penfated the defect.

As imagination itfelf is thus fufceptible of fuch different appearances, fo the un-derftanding, confiftent and uniform as its operations ufually are, participates like-wife, in confequence of its union with the former, of this variety of character. Thus

judgment

judgment united with that invention which carries a man through the busy scenes of life, derives from this power an expression so different from that which distinguisheth it in composition, as not to be marked without close attention from its effects *. Its employments are indeed so distinct from each other in these cases, that the same intellectual faculty which judgeth of the most effectual expedients in the various occurrences of life; weighing the force of an argument, or estimating the propriety of an illustration, appears in aspects seemingly incongruous, and is seldom or never

---

* Thus one of the greatest masters of reason assigns to this faculty two distinct offices, that of laying down plans of action; and that of contemplating abstracted ideas with steadiness and comprehension. Και τυτο Φανερον ομοιως εν τε τοις κατα ΤΕΧΝΗΝ, και τοις κατα ΦΥΣΙΝ. βελτιον δε το λογον εχον διηρηται τε διχη καθ' ουπερ ειωθαμεν τροπον διαιρειν. Ο μεν γαρ ΠΡΑΚΤΙΚΟΣ εςι λογος, ο δε ΘΕΩΡΗΤΙΚΟΣ. Ωσαυτως ουν αναγκη, &c. ΑΡΙΣΤΟΤ. ΠΟΛΙΤ. Η. With the same latitude another ancient philosopher considers this faculty as ΕΝΝΟΙΑ ΦΥΣΙΚΗ ΤΩΝ ΚΑΘΟΛΟΥ. ΧΡΥΣΙΠ. apud ΔΙΟΓΕΝ. ΛΑΕΡΤ. ΖΕΝ. β.6. ζ'.

able

able to act in both capacities with an equal·
degree of accuracy *.

That mental power which when·exerted
either in executing, or in judging of execution in the fields of compofition takes
the defignation of difcernment; in.com-
mon life is known by that of *fagacity*. In
the laft it is diftinguifhed by a perception of the real character, and an *infight*
(if we may thus term it) into the fecret
motives that influence conduct, no lefs
juftly than inftantaneoufly conceived, from
circumftances that efcape a common obferver. Its effect in the firft inftance we

---

* It is probably on account of this inability that we
find thofe who poffeffed the greateft fhare of reafon, fo
pathetically lamenting its weaknefs. I mention here
a paffage of Cicero preferved by St. Auftin not only on
account of its analogy to the 'prefent fubject; but as
it is expreffed with peculiar elegance and propriety.
" Homo (fays he) non ut a *Matre*, fed ut a *Noverca Natura* editus eft in vitam, corpore nudo, fragili, & in-
firmo: animo autem anxio ad moleftias, humili ad
timores, molli ad labores, prono ad libidines: in quo
tamen ineffet tanquam OBRUTUS quidam DIVINUS
IGNIS INGENII & MENTIS. Patricii Fragment. Cicer.

have

have formerly pointed out. Perhaps it
may be faid with truth, that the fame qualities which form a penetrating judge of
compofition, would form likewife the *fa-
gacious* obferver of manners and action, and
always does fo when accompanied with
experience. But whatever truth may be
in this, the reverfe furely does not hold,
that he who is acknowledged to fhow *fagacity* in the one cafe, poffeffeth always *difcernment* in the other. This is fo evident
as to ftand in need of no confirmation.

From thefe obfervations on the human
mind it will follow, that the talent above-
mentioned of placing thoughts in the happieft order, and of clothing them in the
fitteft words, accompanies not neceffarily
the poffeffion of the higheft intellectual
qualities whether acting feparately or in
union with each other. Imagination we
have feen diftinguifheth the *mechanic* as
well as the *poet*, and judgment is fhared
in common by the philofopher and the man
of bufinefs. Both faculties indeed we have
feen to be combined in this laft inftance;
and yet the perfon diftinguifhed by their

combination,

combination, not only unable to acquire
excellence in, but even to conceive ideas
of masterly compofition.—To reply to
thefe facts, that excellence in the art of
which we treat, depends not upon the poffeffion of the principal powers, but upon
the degrees in which they fubfift, will be
found upon examination to be diffatisfac-
tory. Admitting the truth of this affertion
it can anfwer no purpofe, unlefs we mean
to affirm that the fhare of reafon and imagination required to conftitute a talent for
compofition, is *neceffarily* and *effentially* fuperior to that portion of thefe which forms
an ingenious mechanic, or a man of abilities in the tranfactions of life. This, however, reflection will lead us to reject as
contrary in many inftances to the dictates
both of reafon and experience.

The firft inventor of any complicated
piece of machinery, (a clock, or a watch,
for inftance) in whofe conftruction many
inferior and regulated movements concur
to accomplifh the defign of the artift, muft
be confidered as having received from nature in an high degree not only the faculty
of

of invention, but that likewife which judgeth with acutenefs and penetration. The
extent of the former appears from his conception of fo original a work; the depth
and fubtlety of the latter, from an exqui-
fitely nice arrangement of parts; and the
mutual dependence fubfifting through the
whole. In the fame manner, the man
who is interefted in the bufinefs of life,
and is able to make various and remote expedients terminate in the accomplifhment
of fome purpofe of importance, cannot
upon many occafions be denied his claim to
a very uncommon fhare of both thefe qualities without injuftice; the one being remarkably confpicuous in the invention of
fuch expedients; the other in their application to particular purpofes. Thus, will
it be denied that a general entrufted with
fupreme authority, whofe mind is fruitful
of refources, and who by the happy means
that occur to him, extricates himfelf with
honour when placed in the moft critical and
perilous circumftances; will it be denied
that fuch a man difplays confummate genius, i, e. (fuppofing this character to de-

pend

pend principally upon imagination) great *invention* in the military art?—Admitting this to be true, muſt we not allow him like-wiſe to diſcover diſcernment in the trueſt fenſe of that word, when we obſerve that he hath foreſeen and ſuperſeded the deſigns of his rival, that his ſtratagems have not only diſplayed imagination in their contri-vance, but the greateſt addreſs in being car-ried into execution? Can we in the laſt place deny his claim to extenſive under-ſtanding, when we find that his whole con-duct hath in general been regulated by thoſe maxims that moſt commonly in-fluence the diſcreet and the prudent*?

Should

---

* The reader who would fee theſe obſervations ex-emplified, will find a variety of inſtances to his purpoſe in peruſing the hiſtory of Sertorius oppoſed alternately to the beſt Roman generals; in the detail of Hannibal's exploits while he maintained himſelf in Italy; in the conduct of Cæſar, (who wrote indeed almoſt as well as he fought) particularly after the battle of Dyrrachium. In more modern times he will meet with wonderful proofs of this military genius carried to its utmoſt ex-tent in the hiſtory of Condé and Turenne, when op-poſed to each other; in the laſt campaign of the latter

when

Should it again be replied, that however extenſive we may allow imagination
ſometimes to be in the caſes abovementioned, yet this faculty when employed at
leaſt in the higher ſpecies of compoſition,
dwelling on *ſublime* and *abſtracted* objects,
and forming as it were a new creation of
its own, muſt be originally of a *more exalted
caſt* (if we may thus expreſs it) in a mind
directed to ſuch purſuits, than when it re-

---

when he appeared as a competitor for glory with
Montecuculi; in the firſt Italian campaigns of Eugene,
and as an inſtance adequate to any of the former; in
the laſt proof exhibited by Marlborough of his conſummate abilities, when he commanded againſt Villars at
the ſiege of Bouchaine.—It will be obſerved that we
have only ſelected examples here of celebrated leaders
acting in oppoſition to each other. A man of knowledge and experience in the art of war may obtain a
ſeries of eaſy victories over a weak or inexperienced
antagoniſt. But to triumph in the midſt of danger and
difficulty by the natural reſources of a copious invention is the province of genius alone. We have likewiſe upon this occaſion conſidered only excellence in
the military profeſſion. The diſcerning reader may
apply what hath been ſaid on this ſubject to men who
act in other ſpheres of life, in which he may be aſſiſt-
ed by the preceding obſervations.

ceives

ceives any other bias of what kind foever;
we would obferve, that this objection re-
fers not to the *degree* in which invention
fubfifts, but to the particular fubjects to
which it difcovers a propenfity. Thefe
however are objects wholly diftinct from
each other. He who raifeth a mafs of iron
from the earth, poffeffeth it is evident *the
fame degree* of natural ftrength with him
who bears a quantity of gold or diamonds
precifely equal in weight to the former.
The difparity lies therefore not in the
ftrength of the two men, but in the objects to which it is directed. Swift and
Butler were neither of them geniufes of a
very exalted clafs. Yet it will not we pre-
fume be denied that the former in his Tale
of a Tub, and in the Travels of Gulliver,
the latter in his inimitable Hudibras, difcover copious, fruitful, and even original
imagination. But without eftimating the
comparative value of different objects, it
is fufficient for us to obferve at prefent,
that the mind of that perfon who prefides
over a great people and conducts the complicated machine of government with abi-
litics

lities adequate to the office*; that the intellectual powers of that commander who

---

* Quintilian, folicitous of drawing almoft every human excellence within the vortex of eloquence, will not give up the character mentioned in the text to the claim of philofophy. He contends that fuch a man ought likewife to be efteemed an orator. His words are remarkable.—"Neque enim hoc concefferim, rationem rectæ, honeftæque vitæ ad Philofophos relegandam; cum vir ille vere civilis, & *publicarum privatarumque rerum* adminiftrationi accommodatus; qui regere conciliis urbes, fundare legibus, emendare judiciis poffit; non *aliter fit profecto quam orator.* Quare tametfi me fateor ufurum quibufdam quæ Philofophorum libris continentur tamen ea jure, vereque contenderim effe operis noftri, *proprieque* ad *Artem Oratoriam* pertinere." The truth of this obfervation depends in a great meafure upon the fenfe in which we underftand the word Orator. If we underftand by this term a power of fpeaking in fuch a manner as to obtain the purpofes of convincing, pleafing and moving the paffions, it is certain that the poffeffion of the firft of thefe qualifies men principally to give laws to fociety; and that it hath diftinguifhed perfons who fhared not at leaft in any eminent degree of the laft. Such men therefore could not with propriety be denominated *eloquent*, at leaft according to Cicero's definition of the word. "Erit *Eloquens* is qui ita dicit, ut *probet*, ut *delectet*, ut flectat. Probare *neceffitatis* eft, delectare *fuavitatis*, flectere *victoriæ*."

I

lays

lays down the tranfactions of a future year, and in the profecution of his plan, accommodates himfelf to difficult, per- plexing, and unexpected obftructions; that thefe are fitted by nature to form great ideas, and whether endowed or not with a talent for compofition, poffefs an emi- nent fhare of the powers that give rife to its operating in an enlarged and compre- henfive direction.

We have now evinced from a feries of obfervation on the characters of men, that the art of which we here treat, confidered as regarding the faculties of the mind, neither accompanies neceffarily the poffef- fion of any of thefe viewed feparately; or even arifeth from the degree in which they are conferred when acting in combination. —" What then, it may be afked, *is* Compo- fition in the prefent important view of that art, and by what circumftance is it conftituted?"—We reply.—" A talent for Compofition is formed by a fhare of thofe intellectual powers we have defcribed, va- ried indeed in proportion to the value of that fpecies to which the mind hath re-

ceived

ceived a bias; but accompanied in *every*
cafe with *a propenfity* to place fuch ideas
as occur to it in lights at the fame time
happy and diverfified, to range thefe in
juft and perfpicuous difpofition; to exprefs
them in fuitable words which are felected,
with facility; and to give the whole fo
permanent a form by committing it to
writing, as that the mind may contemplate
it with pleafure upon a review." It is not
therefore from the proportion of mental
qualities conferred on any man, that we
are to judge of the degree in which he poffeffeth a talent for the art in queftion, or
even of its exiftence *. The *bias* which
thefe

---

* When we fpeak of a talent for compofition (as
that term hath been defined) we muft take care to exclude from this idea, that flight propenfity to a fuperficial kind of writing which fome men difcover, in
which the thoughts are at the fame time conceived
with quicknefs, and throw it into language with facility. This happens when trite fubjects fall to be difcuffed by minds that are either difqualified by nature
to take any comprehenfive view of things, or when
indolence, encouraged by a defective education, pre-
vents a man poffeffed of talents from putting thefe to
their

thefe receive from nature is the circumftance particularly to be attended to in
forming this eftimation. The ufual indications of this extraordinary propenfity,
and the manner of cultivating it moft fuccefsfully, whatever direction it may have
received, will be confidered, when we come
to treat of the moft proper method of
bringing the intellectual powers, when diftinguifhed by this bias, as nearly as poffible
to a juft equipoife.

2. Having thus taken a view of Compofition as connected in general with the
faculties of the mind, we are next to confider what is implied in it when viewed as
an art diftinguifhed by particular characters,
confifting of various fpecies, and contri-
buting eminently to promote the happinefs
and civilization of mankind.

---

their proper ufe. In this laft cafe, thefe, in confequence of having early received a different direction
from that in which they might have appeared to the
higheft advantage, become at laft unfit to fix in it with
fuch fteadinefs as is neceffary to the accomplifhment of
any valuable purpofe.

In

In order to acquire a juft idea of our fubject in thefe points of view, we muft here
make one general obfervation on the qualities that moft commonly go along with
this uncommon and valuable propenfity.
It is, that *deliberate* recollection, and a
gradual rather than *rapid* fucceffion of ideas
are criteria that in all cafes whatever
characterife the minds that are thus particularly diftinguifhed by nature. A little
attention to the fubject will enable us to
judge of the truth of this obfervation, (pa-
radoxical as it may at firft appear to be)
and to obviate the objections that will naturally be made to it.

Diverfified as the fubjects of Compofition certainly are, we muft yet be convinced
upon reflection, that there is no fpecies of
the art in which difpofition or a certain or-
derly arrangement of parts is not effentially
neceffary. In fome branches of it indeed
this arrangement is no doubt much more
confpicuoufly ufeful than in others; when
an Author, for example, muft defcend from
the general view of a fubject to contemplate
the particular parts of which it confifts;

or

or when fome leading fentiment is to be
fhown in different lights, and to be illuftrated by a feries of connected obfervations.   But fo indifpenfible is this requifition, that the perfection of thofe performances which are deemed the loofeft and
moft detached, lies not in the want of methodical accuracy, but in the artful con-
cealment of a regular difpofition, by which
means the entertainment arifing from certain graces thrown into a piece with apparent negligence, and the information derived from a well conducted procefs, are
happily united.

In order to render the difpofition of objects accurate, it is neceffary that the mind
fhould poffefs a power of contemplating
each of thefe fteadily by itfelf, that it may
at the fame time be fully exhibited, and
may occupy the place that moft naturally
belongs to it.   But this purpofe can at no
time be effectuated when there is a rapid
fucceffion of ideas taking place in the mind.
The underftanding (which is the parent of
this difpofition) muft curb even the moft
excentric imagination with fo ftrong a

rein, as to fix it to one place as long as
may be expedient; and to preſcribe to it
certain boundaries, within which its range
muſt at all times be limited *. Thus therefore it happens that what appears to have
been owing to a ſudden effuſion, comes
to be ſeen as ariſing from cool recollection;
and a faculty to have directed the conduct
of ſome procedure in which we might be
apt at firſt view to judge that its operation
would be in a great meaſure ſuſpended †.

---

* The Author laſt quoted, gives his ſanction to this
opinion. Thus he not only adviſeth the orator to be
cautious and deliberate in his compoſition; but to
prove that theſe ingredients conſtitute a bias for the
art in general, he adduceth the examples of Salluſt and
Virgil. " Sic ſcripſiſſe Salluſtium aecepimus, & ſane
manifeſtus eſt ex opere ipſo *labor*. Virgilium quoque
paucſſimos die compoſuiſſe verſus auctor eſt Varus.
Oratoris alia conditio eſt. Itaque hanc *moram & ſolli-*
citudinem in initiis impero." Inſtit. Orator. lib. x. cap. 3.
Deſcribing afterwards the manner in which Compoſition is carried on, he ſays, " *Paulatim* res facilius ſe
oſtendent, verba reſpondebunt, Compoſitio ſequetur,
cuncta denique ut in familia bene inſtituta, in offi-
cio erunt." Id.

† See this point more fully explained, Section II.

Theſe

Thefe obfervations when followed properly out, will enable us to comprehend
the caufe of a phænomenon formerly taken
notice of;—that in many inftances imagination exerts remarkable influence on the
converfation of men, who are difqualified
to exercife it in any branch of Compofition *. The *fallies* of wit, the *quicknefs*
of repartee, the power of comprehending
a *diftant* hint; and of expreffing with facility ideas that arife inftantaneoufly in the
mind, indicate (as we formerly obferved) a
certain *volatility* of thought that is loft in
an inftant *; but which conftitutes the character of an agreeable companion, and fits
the perfon, whom it diftinguifheth, peculiarly for focial life. But, in the art of
which we treat, we have endeavoured to
fhow that qualities wholly different from
thefe muft be exerted in order to characterife a good writer. When the man therefore in whom they are acknowledged to fubfift, attempts to range his thoughts at leifure, and to combine a feries of objects fo

* Page 13.

juftly

juftly as that each may throw fome light upon another, in a comprehenfive detail; the *heat and freedom* with which he thinks upon other occafions, renders him then unfit to form *an adequate eftimate*; and the *rapid fucceffion of his ideas to exprefs with perfpicuity* that which may occur to him. He on the other hand, who with an animated and vigorous imagination, is qualified to felect at leifure from the variety of objects fuch as are moft appofite, and calculated from the *order* in which they are placed to promote his general purpofe, muft it is obvious, in order to excel equally in both characters, be able to think at one time with promptitude, and even precipitance; and at another with deliberate recollection; or his excellence confined to this laft fphere, will ceafe to be confpicuous in the other.

It will, we are here aware, be immediately faid, that however neceffary this gradual fucceffion of ideas may be to excellence in fome fpecies of Compofition, it muft be limited to the two branches of philofophy and hiftory. But with regard

to

to others, (particularly the poetic art) rapid tranfitions, and apoftrophes feemingly
unconnected, not only produce the ftrongeft effect, but even the appearance of thefe
is neceffary to perfect the execution. Thus
where it will be afked would be the beauty
of the ODE, (that high and inchanting
fpecies of poetic compofition) if we fhould
deprive it of thofe animated fallies, thofe
abrupt and daring flights of genius, which
arife from an imagination intenfely agitated, and ftarting with little apparent connection from one object to another *? The
                                    fame

---

* From fuch views as thefe it probably was that fome
of the ancients were led to confider poetry in general
as a kind of enthufiaftic effufion arifing from a divine
and irrefiftible impulfe; and the POET infpired by his
MUSE, like the fibyl on her tripod, throwing out dark
myfterious, and prophetic exhibitions. Thus even in
later ages among the Romans, the word VATES fig-
nified equally a *poet*, and a *prophet*. Strabo confiders
poetic enthufiafm as a kind of divine infpiration re-
fembling the prophetic. Ενθυσιασμος επινευσιν τινα
Θειαν εχειν δοκει, και ΤΩ ΜΑΝΤΙΚΩ γενει πλησιαζειν.
β.6. I. Plato in the fame manner fets out in his beautiful dialogue on this fubject by calling poetry ΕΝΘΕΙΑ
                                    ΔΥΝΑΜΙΣ,

ſame queſtion may be applied with ſome variation to every other ſpecies of the art, the didactic alone excepted.

But before we pronounce a deciſion on this ſubject, let us endeavour to diſtin-

---

ΔΥΝΑΜΙΣ, an inſpired energy, and goes ſo far as to affirm οτι Ο ΘΕΟΣ ΑΥΤΟΣ εςιν ὁ λεγων, that God himſelf is the ſpeaker in their compoſitions. ΠΛΑΤ. ΙΩ. Again he tells us, as the reſult of his obſervations on this ſubject, Εγνω ουν αυ και περι ποιητων εν ολιγω τουτο, οτι ου ΣΟΦΙΑ ποιοιεν ἁ ποιοιεν, αλλα Φυσει τινι και ΕΝΟΘΥΣΙΑΖΟΝΤΕΣ ωσπερ οι ΘΕΟΜΑΝΤΕΣ και ΧΡΗΣΜΩΔΟΙ. ΑΠΟΛΟΓ. ΣΟΚΡ. κεφ. Ζ. Ariſtotle and the elegant writers of the Auguſtan age ſpeak much more rationally and philoſophically on this ſubject. The reader who chooſeth to enquire into their ſentiments, may conſult particularly the firſt and tenth chapter of the Poetics of the former, and the writings of Cicero throughout. Admiting however the definition of Plato to be juſt and appropriated, it will no more follow, that a man whoſe powers are ab-ſorbed in the contemplation of abſtracted objects, ſhould on *that account* be diſqualified to ſurvey theſe ſeparately with attention, and to diſpoſe of each in the beſt manner, than that his eye when beholding an agreeable and diverſified landſcape, ſhould be always diſqualified to take cognizance of particular beauties or defects.

guiſh,

guifh, on every occafion, betwixt the
ftrength of that impreffion which one object makes upon a great imagination, and
a feries of thefe paffing before it perhaps
in quick but fuperficial review. Keeping
this neceffary diftinction in our eye, we
fhall find that even in thofe poetic productions in which we meet with the boldeft
turns, and the moft unexpected tranfitions, the genius of the POET appears in
the fignificance that he gives to particular
lineaments of his portrait; in the colour
that he throws upon the moft ftriking and
diftinguifhed features; in the felection of
appropriated images; and in the attitude
and difpofition of every feparate figure of
the piece, a work that requires him to
dwell with attention on the ideas that pafs
fucceffively in review before his mind to
whatever degree of fervid contemplation it
may be wrought up *.

In

---

* This affertion may require to be exemplified —
Let us take an example from one of the moft feemingly irregular productions of the bard, whom *im-*
                                              petuous

- In the moft perfect productions of genius, both ancient and modern, the *difcern-*
[illegible] *ing*

---

petuous imagination moft eminently diftinguifheth. It
is his third Olympic addreffed to Theron of Agrigen-
tum. Upon a fuperficial view of this ode, nothing is
confpicuous to the reader, but an enthufiaftic bard addreffing Caftor, Pollux, and Helena (deities who have
no concern in the games of Greece) inftead of invoking Jupiter, Minerva, or Apollo; or beginning with
the praifes of the hero whom he profeffed to celebrate.
With no apparent connection he drags Hercules into
the ode a little after; and tranfports his reader in an
inftant from the plain of Olympus to the Utopian clime
of Hyperborea. Having informed us that Hercules
tranfplanted an olive from this country to Greece,
that the Olympic victors might be crowned with it,
he takes occafion to pay a compliment to Theron with
which the ode concludes.—Such is the firft appearance
of this piece in which a number of heterogeneous ideas
feem to have poured upon the mind of the poet, and
to have been jumbled together without coherence.
But when we come to obferve, that by reprefenting as
facred every circumftance relating to thefe games, the
higheft honour was reflected upon the conqueror, who
was thus fuppofed to be the peculiar favourite of the
gods; when we are informed that Caftor and Pollux
were fuppofed to have been appointed by Hercules the
guardians and patrons of the *confecrated olive*; when
we advert likewife that being tranfplanted from a

country

ing reader will find this capacity of cool recollection, thofe criteria that indicate a gradual fucceffion of ideas in the thoughts of the writer diftinguifhing his performance upon every occafion.   Thus we ob-

---

country whofe inhabitants were thought to enjoy *perfect felicity*, the happinefs of Theron is more ftrongly fet before us, by having this fymbol of pleafure wreathed around his head, than by the moft ftudied defcription :—when we attend to thefe circumftances, we are led to admire the addrefs of the poet in the conduct of his fubject ; the artful and even judicious felection of his topics, and the *arrangement* obvious in the *whole piece.* It were eafy to fhow likewife that the imagination of Pindar, impetuous as it is, yet dwells with fteadinefs upon particular objects; and that he difcovers at the fame time vivacity and precifion in the conception, the colouring, and the difpofition of his figures. In the very ode that we have felected on this occafion ; obferve the beautiful and finifhed picture which he fets before the reader, of the moon fhining on the altar of Jupiter, at the time when this olive was conferred on the conqueror.

$$\eta\delta\epsilon \; \gamma\alpha\rho \; \alpha\upsilon\tau\omega$$
$$\pi\alpha\tau\rho\iota \; \mu\epsilon\nu \; \beta\epsilon\mu\omega\nu \; \alpha\gamma\iota\sigma\theta\epsilon\nu-$$
$$\tau\omega\nu \; \delta\iota\chi\omega\mu\eta\nu\eta\varsigma \; \omega\lambda\omega\nu \; \chi\rho\upsilon\sigma\alpha\rho\mu\alpha\tau\omega\varsigma$$
$$\epsilon\sigma\pi\epsilon\rho\alpha\varsigma \; \omicron\phi\theta\alpha\lambda\mu\omega\iota \; \alpha\upsilon\tau\epsilon\phi\lambda\epsilon\xi\epsilon \; \mu\eta\nu\alpha.$$

ΠΙΝΔ. ΟΛΥΜΠ. Γ.

ferve

ferve Homer, like a confummate general
overlooking the battle from an eminence,
maintaining a majeftic and uniform com-
pofure in the midft of tumult and univerfal
commotion. He defcribes particularly the
ground upon which the armies engaged;
carries the reader's eye fucceffively from
one fcene to another, as they may be fuppofed to have changed their fituation:
he drops one hero fometimes in the moft
interefting part of the action, that he may
introduce another, whofe different manners give an entertaining variety to the
poem, and to the difplay of whofe peculiar
character the circumftances are happily
adapted. In fhort, when a *crifis* is brought
on in the action, we find this great genius
paufing in the midft of his career to render
by fublime and appropriated imagery every
circumftance relating to the combatants,
a fucceffive object of admiration. Thus
the helmet, the plumage, the fhield, the
buckler, and the very point of the fpear
of Achilles are called in to heighten the
defcription of that exalted fphere in which
this hero conftantly moves. This conduct

duct is wholly different from that which
a man would have purfued, whofe ideas
poured in with hafte and rapidity. Such
a man, had he attended to *all* the circumftances which Homer hath difplayed to
fuch advantage, would have paffed each
of thefe over as quickly as poffible, in
order to arrive at the principal event.
Embarraffed with the variety of his materials, his work would confift rather of
brilliant ftrokes fcattered profufely throughout, than of proportioned figures completely exhibited. In fhort, whatever fpecies of Compofition we may fuppofe a
man of this character to attempt, his ideas
muft be loofe and disjointed, his expreffion obfcure and inaccurate, though felected with much difficulty; and unable
to fupport either the majefty of defcription, or the feries of argument, every part
of his performance would be left uncom-
pleted.

From the whole therefore it is we pre-
fume obvious, that imagination, however
naturally irregular, muft be able to *contemplate with attention* the figures that
                                    compofe

compofe a whole piece; and an Author of whatever denomination, to adjuft the members of his work with coolnefs and recollection, otherwife he will be unequal to the tafk of exhibiting each (at leaft in Compofition) with grace, proportion, and energy.

We have, in the courfe of our obfervations on this fubject, taken our examples principally from one of the higheft fpecies of poetry, becaufe it is, *here,* that the qualities we have mentioned as accompanying a propenfity to the art of which we treat in this work, are judged to be unneceffary, if they can be fo in any cafe whatever. Having thus therefore. fhown their influence and importance in this fphere, we have much eafier work with the others; in which an ultimate end is *obvioufly* kept in view, while we follow the writer through a methodifed enquiry; and attend to the operation of each intellectual power, as well as to the effect arifing from their general combination. Philofophy, hiftory, eloquence, and criticifm, confidered in this point of view, will amply confirm the pre-

8

ceding

ceding obfervations; from which at prefent we may define Compofition, when
viewed as confifting of diverfified characters, and diftinguifhed into various fpecies; to be " that ART by which the feveral parts of a fubject are fo juftly fitted
to each other, as to form a *proportioned*
and *beautiful whole*."—Of the manner in
which this end is accomplifhed, of the
office affigned to each faculty, as well as
of the *united* power of all in bringing it
about, we now proceed to treat more particularly.

SECTION II.

Of the Province of the Underftanding in
Compofition.

AMONG the faculties of the mind,
that by which man is chiefly diftinguifhed from all inferior creatures, forms
in the prefent, as in every fimilar inveftigation, the great and primary object of
attention. The offices therefore of the underftanding, as thefe have already been
explained

explained in general, we fhall now confider particularly as far as the prefent fubject is concerned, according to the method
formerly laid down *.

The criteria from which the judgment
of a writer is rendered principally confpicuous, are the difcovery of a theory or
hypothefis; the difpofition of parts in the
plan of a work in fuch order as moft effectually promotes an ultimate purpofe;
the comprehenfion of this plan as adapted
fully to the fubject of whatever kind; and
finally a certain propriety of fentiments
and of illuftration, which univerfally indicates the prevalence of this faculty, and
may therefore be regarded as a perpetual
defignation of it.—On each of thefe heads,
confidered by itfelf, we fhall throw together fome obfervations.

1. Upon a firft view it may appear fomewhat extraordinary to aver that any eminent fhare of *reafon* is indicated by the
difcovery of an hypothefis, as invention of
every kind is ufually afcribed to imagina-

---

* Section I. page 7.

tion,

tion, which is on that account denominated, by way of eminence, the inventive
faculty. The propriety with which this
term is applied to it we shall have occasion
to examine in the subsequent section. It
is of importance to the present subject to
observe, that two distinct kinds of invention will be found to take place in the different branches of Composition, and to
characterise the persons who excel in it.
The first of these is distinguished by an af-
semblage of original ideas brought together without much recollection; by the
peculiar and happy lights that are thrown
upon truths already known, either in consequence of a well adapted expression, or
the application of new and uncommon illustrations; by the unbeaten paths into
which an Author falls; and by the sudden
flashes of light (if we may thus express it)
which he casts around him. In these offices it is obvious that imagination is *principally* employed, which never fails to excite when obviously predominant, a desire
of deviating upon *every occasion* from the
received opinions of mankind.

The

The other kind of invention is conftituted by the intenfe and fteady effort of
underftanding, which eftimating the comparative ftrength of arguments, and advancing from fimpler to more compounded
exhibitions in its refearch, deduceth at laft
fome conclufion from principles formerly
known, which may at the fame time be
new, and eftablifhed upon the jufteft foundation. A procefs of this nature is directed principally, if not wholly by the judgment of the writer: it is completed by
patience and affiduity; qualities that are
particularly characteriftical of the prevalence of this faculty, whofe exertion either enables a man to ftrike out fome truth
that had been formerly undifcovered, or
to build a new fyftem from the light in
which he placeth received maxims.

When we mention the placing common
fentiments in a new point of view as a
fpecies of invention fometimes arifing from
judgment, and fometimes principally from
imagination, we are not to fuppofe that it
will be a matter of much difficulty to diftinguifh the caufe from which this effect

is

is derived in particular inftances. We have already afforded a criterion fufficient to determine this matter when it was obferved, that when a work is chara&terifed by the prevalence of imagination, even where no *original* fentiment is difplayed, yet fome peculiar energy will diftinguifh the expreffion; or fome ftriking and uncommon illuftrations will give ftrength and energy to the thoughts *. Reafon on the contrary never aims at merit of this kind. Confidered by itfelf, what Addifon fays of the foul when viewed abftra&edly from its paffions, may be applied with great propriety to this faculty of it. "It is flow in its refolves, and equally delibe-

---

* A modern critic fets this matter in fo juft a light by the ufe of a beautiful and appropriated image, that the reader of tafte will perufe it with pleafure. Speaking of the difficulty of entering into chara&ters he fays—"Quare fapienter Plato ut lævaret hoc onere philofophos præcepit, ut in *fumma* rerum confifterent, ad *fingula* ne defcendent. Nempe *fuprema* & *propinqua* *coelo aeris pars* a turbis libera eft: non cogitur illa in nubem, non in tempeftatem propellitur, non verfatur in turbinem. *Inferior* tonat ac fulminat." Prolus: prima."

rate

rate in its. execution. It requires therefore often to be awakened by the paffions,
that the man may be vigorous and attentive in the profecution of his defigns *."

To this cautious procedure it is owing,
that a difcovery effectuated by the underftanding is always confirmed by clearer as
well as more fatisfying evidence, than that
in which another power of the mind propofeth the end, and reafon is compelled to
fupply the moft probable means of bringing it about †. In this laft cafe the power
above mentioned is ftraitened in every exertion; and we difcover with very little attention, that circumftances are brought together to fupport an untenable propofition,
which neceffarily fail in the accomplifhment of their purpofe. But in, the other
inftance, when judgment at the fame time
propofeth a certain end, and conducts the
feries of obfervation or of argument that

---

* Spectator, Vol. iv. No. 255.

† " Cum fit pofita (ratio) in inventione nec elocu-
tionis ornamenta magnopere defideret, aut circa memoriam & pronunciationem laboret." Quintil. lib. vi.
cap. 5.

leads to its attainment, the tendency of each of thefe to promote this purpofe is at once confpicuous; and all, when taken together, naturally coalefce in that point in which they ought to concentrate. Thus the whimfical theory of Malebranche *, and that of our ingenious countryman Burnet †, though relating to fubjects wholly diftinct from each other, yet equally embarrafs their authors, though far from being deficient in clearnefs of intellectual perception; and lead them either into the higheft refinements of metaphyfical inveftigation ‡, as in the firft inftance, or into

---

* De la Recherche de la Verité.

† See his celebrated work entitled Sacra Theoria Telluris.

‡ The great doctrine inculcated in this extraordinary work is, that fpirits living in the divine mind, in the fame manner as bodies occupy fpace, all things are feen by thefe as exifting originally in the deity. Recherche liv. iii. part 1. This ftrange hypothefis has led our author into many abfurd, though ingenious difquifitions, which it is not our bufinefs to examine here. The principal of thefe (particularly his idea of an *infinite Reafon*) the judicious Locke hath expofed and refuted with great precifion and ftrength of argument. See the Examination of Malebranche, in his Works.

forced

forced conſtructions of paſſages tortured from their obvious ſignification, as in the laſt *. The reaſon of this embarraſſment in both is, that the ultimate purpoſe of each work is that which imagination, not reaſon, originally ſuggeſted. But having been once adopted, this faculty is called in as an aſſiſtant to ſupport poſitions which it would perhaps have rejected. Still however we obſerve its ſtrength; but it is ſtrength miſapplied. Like Samſon when deprived of ſight, it retains its vigour, but employs it not to rear a fabric but to put ſuch materials together as may be thrown down.—Let the reader of diſcernment compare either of theſe with the excellent work entitled the Analogy betwixt Natural and Revealed Religion, in which the underſtanding purſues a certain purpoſe thro'

---

* It is not our preſent buſineſs to enter into the proof of this obſervation. The reader who conſiders the manner in which this moſt ingenious writer hath managed the proofs of his theory that are drawn from Scripture, will obſerve the plauſible appearance which he gives to an interpretation of paſſages that will not bear to be cloſely examined.

a ſe-

a feries of rational and fatisfactory evidences; and he will perceive the eafy procefs by which this faculty obtaineth its
end when permitted to operate *univerfally*
as a principal, inftead of the *conftraint*
and *obfcurity* that mark its progrefs, when
employed to fupport hypothefes which it
did not form.

It ought likewife to be obferved on this
head, that when it is an author's purpofe
either to difcover or to elucidate truth by
an accurate enumeration of principles and
inferences, the mind muft advance in its
work with the utmoft circumfpection, as
in the fcale of arguments corroborating
each other, the defect or weaknefs of *one*
ftep is fufficient to marr the effect of all.
Difproportion of parts is indeed much more
confpicuous in fuch a work, than in compofition embellifhed with metaphor and
imagery. In this laft cafe we are willing
to fuppofe that an author hath protracted
his examination of a favourite topic, and
hath ftrained a particular branch of his
work beyond its due dimenfions, from the
natural and irrefiftible impulfe of a warm
imagination.

imagination. But in the other, as the reader receives lefs entertainment from the external decorations, he is at leifure to examine attentively the proportions of the figure, and is ftruck with a defect in this circumftance that might have other-wife efcaped the moft accurate obferver. An underftanding adequate to its fubject, and unimpelled by other powers that marr its operations, by keeping one ultimate aim clofely in fight; and by fetting in a clear light every ftep by which we ap-proach to it, feldom permits this fault to become fo obvious as to give offence even to thofe, whofe powers of difcernment en-able them to decide on this point with the greateft precifion.

Upon the whole, the requifition princi-pally neceffary to carry on the difcovery of unknown truth, is an underftanding unembarraffed in its purfuit by another power, and adopting the idioms of imagin-ation only to elucidate its principles *,
inftead

---

* Two celebrated ancients, Ariftotle and Quinti-lian, feem to think very differently of the propriety

instead of being admitted to evince the genius of the writer, while they throw an air of obscurity over his performance.

---

with which metaphors ought to be introduced, and of their use in Composition. The former (perhaps somewhat too hastily) condemns these altogether as productive universally of obscurity, and will not allow even images, which he distinguisheth from the other, to be introduced, when these have a tincture of poetry. The latter points out their use and expedience with great accuracy. Αλλος ει (says the Greek philosopher) και Μεταφοραν ειρηκεν, οιον ει την επιςημεν αμεταπτω-τον, &c. ΠΑΝΤΑ γαρ ΑΣΑΦΕΣ το καΊα ΜΕΤΑ-ΦΟΡΑΝ ΛΕΓΟΜΕΝΟΝ. ΤΟΠΙΚ. βιϐ. ζ. In another place he says, Εςι δε και η ΕΙΚΩΝ Μεταφορα· Διαφερει γαρ μικρον· Οταν γαρ ειπη του Αχιλλεα— Ως δε Λεων επορυσεν.—ΕΙΚΩΝ εςιν. Οταν δε Λεων επορυσε, ΜΕΤΑΦΟΡΑ. Δια γαρ το αμφω ανδρειους ειναι, προσηγορευσε μετενεγκας Λεοντα τον Αχιλλεα· Χρησιμον δε ΕΙΚΩΝ και εν λογῳ. ΟΛΙΓΑΚΙΣ δε, ΠΟΙ-ΗΤΙΚΟΝ γαρ. Οιςεαι δε ωσπερ αι μεταφοραι. ΡΗ-ΤΟΡ. βιϐ. Γ. κεφ. δ.

"Indocti quoque (says the Roman critic) non sentientes, metaphora frequenter utuntur. Eas facimus, aut quia necesse est, aut quia significantius, aut quia decentius. Ubi nihil horum praestabit, quod transfertur improprium est." Quintil. Institut. lib. viii. c. 6.

II. From

II. From confidering the difcovery of truth, as regulated by the underftanding, we come now to take a view of this power as employed particularly in regulating the difpofition of parts, in fuch a manner as contributes moft effectually to promote the defign of the whole. In this important province of its work, reafon may be viewed both as laying down the *general* plan or method in which a fubject is to be treated; and as ranging the ideas that occur upon entering into an examination of *particular* parts in a juft and natural order.

1. That it is the underftanding alone which regulates the general difpofition of fentiments and illuftrations in all cafes whatever, will be acknowledged immediately, when we attend to its conftant manner of procedure. From that flow recollection by which this faculty is diftinguifhed, it is qualified to difcover the beft method of treating any fubject, whether fimple or copious; and after having thoroughly inveftigated its nature, to take cognizance of the propriety, as well as

com–

comprehenfion of a general defign *.—We
obferved formerly, that there is no fpecies
of

---

* Pliny fpeaks of juft difpofition, in the art of which
we treat here, as the effect of an extenfive acquaintance
with the writings of the learned. " Utinam Ordo, fal-
tem & tranfitus .& figuræ fimul fpectarentur. Nam
invenire præclare, & enunciare magnifice, interdum
etiam *Barbari* folent ; *difponere apte*, &c. nifi ERUDI-
TIS negatum eft." Epiftol. lib. iii. Epift. 13. This
obfervation is no doubt thus far true, that by being
converfant with works in which an exact method is
laid down and followed out, we acquire a habit of
ranging our ideas on every fubject in a certain regulated fucceffion, which is the effect in a great meafure
of art and attention. This is probably what our author means by that APT difpofition which he appropriates peculiarly to the learned. Otherwife, as the
reafon of every man who is capable of inventing, prefcribes to him likewife fome method of ranging together the means of obtaining a certain end, nothing
but a total deprivation of this faculty could make him
jumble crude conceptions together in fo difcordant a
manner, as to afford no glimmering of light by which
we may trace his defign. For (to adopt the language
of a confummate judge) " Ut opera extruentibus, fatis
non eft faxa, atque materiam, & cætera ædificanti uti-
lia congerere ; nifi iis collocandis Artificum manus
adhibeatur : fic in dicendo, quamlibet abundans rerum copia, cumulum tantum habeat atque congeftum,
nifi illas eafdem in ordinem digeftas, atque inter fe
com-

of Composition in which a certain harmonious arrangement of parts is not essentially neceffary. This order, as was likewife obferved, is no doubt much more confpicuous in the conduct of a philofophical theory *, or in treating of any complex fubject, than in loofer and more negligent compofition, as it may be termed. But the perfection of this laft, however feemingly irregular, lies not in the

---

commiffas *Difpofitio* devinxerit. Oratio carens *hac virtute*, tumultuetur neceffe eft, & fine rectore fluitet; nec cohæreat fibi : multa repetat, multa tranfeat, velut nocte in ignotis locis errans; nec initio, nec fine propofito Cafum potius quam Concilium fequatur." Quintil. Inflit. lib. vii. c. i.

* The rules of philofophical difpofition are comprehenfively laid down in few words by one of the firft and beft of critics. Αναγκη του τροπου τυτου προαγειν εκ των ασαφεστερων μεν τη φυσει, ημιν δε σαφεστερων επι τα σαφεστερα τη φυσει και γνωριμωτερα. Εστι δ' ημιν το πρωτον δηλα και σαφη τα συγκεχυμενα μαλλον· Υστερον δε εκ τυτων γινεται γνωριμα τα στοιχεια και αι αρχαι, διαιρουσι ταυτα, &c. Τα παιδια το μεν πρωτον προσαγορευει παντας τυς ανδρας, πατηρας, και μητερας τας γυναικας· Υστερον δε διοριζει τυτων εκατερον· ΑΡΙΣΤΟΤ. ΦΥΣΙΚ. βιβ. κεφ. Α.

want

want of difpofition, which would include
that of every other excellence; but in a
certain accurate, though apparently negligent diftribution of parts, in which the
mind perceives fymmetry, upon a clofe
examination, and beauty, conftituted as
much by the happy pofition of elegant
decorations, as by their original invention *.

---

* To the examples of this already adduced from
the writings of the ancients, we need only to add at
prefent, that the firft of Roman philofophers appears to
have been fo fenfible of the advantages that refult from
an accurate difpofition in his own art, that he wrote a
treatife purpofely on this very fubject, entitled De
Partitione Oratoria, which is now unhappily loft. In
his work however entitled De Oratore he treats this
point at great length, and lays down the rules of exact arrangement with his ufual precifion. "Ut aliquid
ante rem dicamus, deinde ut rem exponamus ; poft ut
eam probemus, noftris præfidiis confirmandis, contra-
riis refutandis ; deinde ut concludamus, atque ita per-
oremus. Hoc dicendi genus natura ipfa præfcribit."
Lib. ii. c. 76. Again he fays, " Neque difputemus
quibus affequi poffimus ut ea quæ dicamus intelligan-
tur. Latine fcilicet dicendo verbis ufitatis, &c. non
difcerptis fententiis, non præpofteris temporibus, non
confufis perfonis, non perturbato ordine." Lib. iii.
c. 13.

Eloquence,

Eloquence, in whofe compofition an exact and perfpicuous order ought invariably
to be obferved, is here altogether out of
the queftion. But what fhall we fay of
certain gay effufions of wit and humour,
in which thoughts appear to be carelefsly
thrown out juft as they occur, and of thofe
animated fallies that derive their origin
from a glowing and plaftic imagination?
—When thefe laft confift only of a fingle
thought, the end is effectuated as foon as
this thought is placed before the mind in
fuitable colours; and the only difpofition
requifite for this purpofe is that of language and imagery, of whofe propriety
the underftanding decides with a precifion
proportioned to its ftrength and perfpicacity. But when the defign in both cafes
is fomewhat more complex, as demanding
a various affemblage of ideas, we may obferve that a *climax* is either carried on as
in the laft inftance, when it is from the
difpofition of inferior objects that the principal derives its importance; or in the
firft, that objects are put together fo as
to reflect light on each other, and to accomplifh

complifh an end that is kept clofely in
fight. · It is, as we may foon perceive,
the judgment of an author that brings
about both the purpofes that are here
taken notice of. When the circumftances
in the conduct of an action or defcription
are made to rife in their fignificance, fo as
to arreft the attention, as well as gradually
exalt the reader's imagination as he proceeds; this procefs, though not perhaps
confidered in a proper view, juft when the
mind is intenfely animated by the fubject,
yet upon recollection will difcover an arrangement carried on by that faculty which
is the parent of order ; and which hath affigned to each member that place in con-
tributing to produce this effect, which it
ought moft naturally and juftly to occupy.

With regard in the fame manner to the
loofeft effufions of humorous pleafantry,
is it from unconnected fallies that we receive entertainment * ? The defcription
that

* In conducting pieces of this kind, men of genius
are fometimes apt to adopt from negligence a faulty
expreffion,

that is replete with ridicule, pleafes as
much by being judicioufly introduced, as
when obferved to be wrought up with
pointed and particular ftrokes ; and the tale
that excites the moft agreeable fenfations,
even though feemingly abruptly introduced, yet pleafes in confequence of an
appofite difpofition, by which it is brought
to coalefce with the defign of the whole.
Not only therefore does this governing
power of the mind place ideas in a cer-

---

expreffion, (efpecially when a figured diction is attempted) which the malignity of an adverfary will
make him impute to defign. It has ever been a common cafe, as an excellent modern critic obferves, " Viros eruditos fæpe improprium ex negligentia ftylum
quafi tropicum aut figuratum habere, ex quo errore
fit, ut quod per *incuriam* effufum eft, id de *induftria*
dictum exiftiment, adeoque urgeant quod urgeri non
debet." Clerici Ars Crit. vol. I. part. ii. fect. 1. c. 11.
This fault is commonly occafioned by having fixed
attention too clofely upon fome one part, in endeavouring to obtain which the author unwarily lays himfelf
open in another. That apparent negligence which
gives fome pieces fo inchanting an air of elegance, is
the effect of defign, not of accident ; and in order to
be gained in perfection, *correctnefs* of language is as
neceffary to be attended to as mufical arrangement.

tain

tain methodifed order, when thofe fubjects
are treated in which its operation is at firſt
view *leaſt perceptible*; but an extenſive
ſhare of it may likewife be frequently difcovered by a penetrating judge to have
been exerted in a province, in which a fuperficial reader might deem its exercife to
be *leaſt requiſite*. The underſtanding in all
the inſtances we have here adduced, brings
into one point of view the principal members or outlines of a figure; and though
not perhaps exerting the fame ſteady recollection that renders inferior means fubfervient through the whole courfe of a
work to fome purpofe of importance, is
yet equally confpicuous in the conduct of
both.

2. Having thus taken a view of the
ſphere of underſtanding in the prefent art,
as far as the general plan or method of a
work is regulated by it; we now proceed
to confider its influence on the difpofition
of fubordinate parts, ranged together in
fuch clofe and natural order as gives confiſtence and regularity to the whole.

As

As in the former obfervations we viewed reafon as the parent of difpofition in the general fenfe of that word; we are here to trace its operation more particularly in maintaining that fecret connection throughout; without which, a performance muft ceafe immediately not only to be edifying, but intelligible.

In the various fpecies of Compofition, the connection fubfifting betwixt the parts of a difcourfe, is fometimes fuch as an ordinary fhare of underftanding will enable a man to trace without difficulty; and fometimes fo fubtle and delicate as to be perceptible only to the reader of difcernment. A connection of the firft kind takes place in any performance, when we follow the author from one point to another in his procedure; and obferve him attending firft to the general parts of his plan, and next to the objects that fall fucceffively under particular branches of it, until the work is completed by the union of all. When this is the cafe, it is a matter of no great difficulty to judge of the fteps by which a procefs of any kind is

8   carried

carried on; and even though we do not
thoroughly comprehend intermediate fentiments, to pronounce upon the coherence
and ftability of the whole.

A conne&tion however equally clofe,
though of a much lefs obvious kind, takes
place upon many occafions, chiefly in the
higher kinds of the art of which we here
treat; and fuch as it is the province. of
difcernment (in the proper fenfe of that
term) to trace out particularly. This happens either when the thread of fentiment
is wrought out fo finely as to be perceptible, like the film of a fpider, only to the
eye that can *minutely* examine it; or when
ftrokes by which it is propofed to penetrate the heart are thrown out with little
apparent regularity, and may be confidered
as bold deviations from the fubject. With
regard to the firft, it often happens that
thoughts are fpun out in fuch a manner
by paffing through a metaphyfical alem-
bic, as to efcape the cognizance both of
the author or the critic. It is no doubt
one of the fureft proofs of underftanding
to be able to determine the boundary, beyond

yond which this power cannot afcertain
the reality of objects ; and thofe who have
rafhly attempted to pafs it, have involved
themfelves unavoidably in ambiguity and
error. We find it often difficult to trace
the connection of ideas in fuch difquifitions, even when thefe are fufficiently diftinct from the abftracted nature of the fubject that fuggefts them. The tafk appropriated here particularly to the reafoning
power, is that of adhering fteadily to a
general purpofe, and of connecting a feries
of intermediate ideas, by whofe interven-
tion it is to be gained both with that end,
and with each other.

The fecond clafs of objects in which we
obferved that it is a matter of difficulty
many times to trace a clofe connection,
confifts of ftrokes that exalt the imagination, or penetrate the heart. Here the underftanding of the writer is deemed by the
fuperficial to exert no confpicuous degree
of influence. Our judgment, however,
when we decide thus at random, is much
too haftily formed in this matter. Attention will fhow thofe who are qualified to

judge of it properly, that in order to have any juft admiration of thefe beauties, it is neceffary that we fhould enter into the train of *concealed ideas* which eftablifh a connection *not lefs real,* becaufe it may be at firft imperceptible betwixt thefe ftrong apoftrophes and the circumftances immediately preceding, though the mind glances over fuch intermediate points of arrangement fo fuddenly at the time as not to feel their immediate impreffion *.

In

---

* We may add here to the remark in the text, that though when the mind is powerfully influenced by any reprefentation, it confiders not particularly the connection of this with the circumftances that preceded in every point of view, while the impreffion is yet ftrong; it is ftill in proportion as this correfpondence is really perceived to take place in a greater or lefs extent, that a more or lefs powerful effect is produced by it upon the mind.—The celebrated adjuration of Demofthenes by the heroes who fell at Marathon and Salamis, to convince the Athenians that they had not done wrong in facrificing their lives at Chæronea, muft have affected but weakly thofe (if there were any fuch among his auditors) who knew only in general that the battles he referred to had been fought with the enemies of Greece, but were unacquainted with

the

In order to fet in a clearer light the truth of this remark, let it be farther obferved, that though where a fecret connection is perceived invariably to take place, we are not always ready to trace it out particularly; yet when it is either really wanting, or even when at any time we are at a lofs to difcover it, the defect

---

the peculiar honour reflected by thefe victories on the people of Athens, as well as with the glorious caufe in which they fought. Thofe among them whofe anceftors had fallen in thefe engagements, and who had been accuftomed to revere them as the martyrs of liberty, would be ftrongly influenced by a circumftance that placed before them illuftrious perfonages in fo confpicuous and honourable a light. They would enter with ardour into the intention of the orator, and would compare together the caufes thus forcibly illuftrated. But a man qualified by this circumftance to compare the actions; interefted in a manner perfonally in both; juft arrived from the field of Chæronea, and obferving that Demofthenes feems " to put that defeat (as an ingenious critic explains it, Effay on Original Genius, p. 212.) on a level with the glorious victories obtained at Marathon, &c." by conceiving inftantly the full meaning of the fpeaker; and lofing no part of the connection, would be ftruck with this oath in a manner different from the others; and would feel all the emotion which it was intended to excite.

becomes

becomes then at once conspicuous, and is
compensated by no excellence whatever,
either of sentiment, or expression.   Thus
upon perusing the allegorical portrait of
Cebes, he who receives the highest entertainment from observing the just and beautiful manner in which the various incidents of human life are pourtrayed, the
errors of mankind detected, and the causes
personified from which these last are derived ; will yet, it is obvious, find disgust
and satiety take place, even when he is
contemplating perhaps the most exquisite
part of the fable, as soon as he becomes
unable either to observe that peculiar propriety with which the characters are delineated ; or to mark that correspondence
of his allegorical personages with the originals existing in his own mind, which
they are brought to set before him.   As
we have, therefore already seen coolness
of recollection and exact proportion cha-
racterising in general the most perfect
productions of poetry and eloquence ; we
shall find likewise a disposition equally
harmonious taking place uniformly in the
                                        subor-

fubordinate members. The real value of a performance in either art can only be eftimated by that perfon who following the author in his wildeft excurfions, can trace the manner in which he hath been led to affociate apparently diffimilar ideas; and thus beholds proportion and harmony fubfifting through the whole piece; while he whofe perceptions are lefs exquifite, or who is difqualified to judge of the fubject, either cenfures particular parts as grofsly defective, or condemns the whole as the disjointed reveries of a heated imagination.

Thefe obfervations on the fubject of connection will enable us to account very naturally for an opinion entertained by the lefs intelligent part of mankind, that judgment and imagination are feldom or never united in the fame mind in any confiderable meafure. When a work is impreffed principally by the latter of thefe powers, they cannot trace the operations of the former in the fame manner as when it is confpicuous in an unornamented feries of remarks and inferences; and thus

F 3

becaufe

becaufe reafon doth not affume the only
form in which they are accuftomed to difcern it, every man choofeth rather to fuppofe that fome defect takes place in the
mind of another, than to acknowledge it
in his own. Thus it happens that as that
internal and delicate perception by which
the mind entering into the fpirit of an Author, fupplies certain concealed circumftances, is rarely to be met with; works in
which there is the clofeft and moft exquifite correfpondence of parts are cenfured
as deficient in this important character;
and that faculty which arrangeth ideas is
deemed to have been conferred in a very
inconfiderable meafure, where its energy
is really exerted in an eminent degree*.

It

---

* It muft no doubt be acknowledged, that when we
confider arrangement in Compofition as taking in many
diverfified objects, particularly in works of length,
and where it is neceffary to infufe a large proportion of
the idioms of imagination; a man of genius will find
confiderable difficulty in preferving it uniformly through
his whole performance. "Nam & conjuncta quæremus,
& genera, & partes generibus fubjectas; & fimilitu-
dincs,

. It muſt no doubt be acknowledged, (as we ſhall endeavour more fully to evince afterwards) that it is the province of the *diſcerning*, rather than of the *judicious* critic, to fill up thoſe chaſms by which the productions of genius are often marked, ſo as to connect parts in a performance

---

dines, & diſſimilitudines, & contraria, & conſequentia, & conſentanea, & quaſi præcurrentia, & repugnantia, & cauſas rerum veſtigabimus; & ea quæ ex cauſis arta ſunt & majora, paria, minora quærimus." Cicer. de Orat. lib. ii. c. 39. Here the reader of diſcernment will be at no loſs to make an allowance for the defect of a writer, and to diſtinguiſh ſuch faults as ariſe from exuberance of imagination, from blemiſhes perhaps leſs in themſelves, but compenſated by no peculiar excellence either of ſentiment or expreſſion. Μενω δε ουκ ολιγα και αυτας αμαρτηματα (ſays the ſpirited and diſcerning Longinus) και Ο μηρου, και των αλλων οσοι μεγιςοι, και ηκιςα ταις πταισμασιν αρεσκομενος, ομως δε ουκ αμαρτηματα, μαλλον αυτα εκυσια, καλων η παροραματα δι' αμελειαν, ειχη πυ και ως ετυχεν, υπο μεγαλοφυιας ανεπιςατως παρενηνεγεμενα. Επειτοι γε απτωτος ο Απολλωνιος ο των Αργοναυτικων Ποιητης, και τοις βουκολικοις πλην ολιγα των εξοθεν ο Θεοριτος επιτυχεςατος. Αρουν ΟΜΗΡΟΣ αν μαλλον η Απολλωνιος εθελοις γενεσθαι, &c. ΠΕΡΙ ΥΨΟΥΣ, τμημ. ΛΙ.

that

that may be deemed to have little relation
to each other. As high colouring commonly renders its objects obfcure, at leaft
to thofe who cannot view the image and
its original apart from each other; fo the
breaks and daring fallies of an enraptured
imagination are apt to render the whole
unintelligible. Even when this power
operates not in fo confpicuous a manner,
it happens as often that obfcurity becomes
characteriftical of a work in which *too
much* is left to be fupplied by the reader,
as that difguft is excited in him when too
little appears for this purpofe. In order
therefore to preferve the juft medium betwixt thefe extremes, as the difcerning faculty which judgeth of the excurfions of
genius, ought to regulate thofe fo as eafily
to comprehend their connection, fo the
underftanding in other branches of Compofition fhould difcover its thorough knowledge of a fubject, by placing every idea
clearly before the mind of a reader, and
by leaving only fuch thoughts to be fuggefted by him as the objects laid open to
him naturally and unavoidably introduce.

Thus

Thus it is that a writer of good fenfe moft clearly evinceth the folidity and compafs of his judgment. A reader is flattered when he finds it in his power to complete as it were the intention of the author upon every topic by fome obvious additions of his own; and whether confcious or not that thefe were defignedly left to him, is fenfible of no deficiency from fuch an omiffion in point of connection.

III. As in the preceding obfervations we have endeavoured to fhow the procefs by which reafon either effectuates the difcovery of truth, or eftablifheth order and connection in every branch of Compofition; we are next to confider it as confpicuous in that comprehenfive view of a fubject which fhows that no material part hath efcaped attention. This power of comprehending and of adjufting a variety of parts to each other, is peculiarly characteriftical of the judgment of a writer; and ferves to diftinguifh it from imagination (properly fo called) which ftarts from one object to another without ever taking in or regulating a great and diverfified feries.

ries. This indication of an enlarged underftanding, in order to be complete, demands attention to be extended to a much
greater diverfity of objects than we may
at firft view fuppofe.   It requires not only
that every part of any confequence fhould
be included in the general eftimate of a
fubject, which though difficult, it is leaft
uneafy to perform; but that the manner
of treating every point of whatever kind,
fhould be that which is beft adapted to its
nature; and the illuftrations made ufe of,
fuch as convey the moft adequate idea of
their original objects that can poffibly be
prefented.   It often happens that a mind
equal to the firft of thefe requifitions is deficient in the laft.—To the full exhibition
even of a complicated theme when viewed
in general, nothing more is in fact neceffary, than that obfervation which regulates the draught and the outlines of a
figure; of whofe fitnefs for *this purpofe* we
may pronounce without hefitation; while
we fufpend our judgment of it as adequate
to the fulleft difplay of fubordinate parts,

until

until theſe fall ſeparately under examination. -

When we mention as an evidence of
comprehenſion, the treating every point in
the manner that is beſt adapted to its nature, we are aware that a certain verſatility
as well as compaſs of thought is neceſſary
to this purpoſe which is rarely to be met
with. The knowledge of the beſt method
of treating any ſubject, and the power of
carrying this with adequate energy into
execution, are circumſtances altogether different from each other. Many perſons
ſufficiently underſtand the importance and
utility of means which they are yet unable
to employ properly in the purſuit of a certain end. The mind is ſeldom equal to
every part of a theme that requires its faculties to act in various, and ſometimes in
oppoſite directions. In ſome it acts as in
its native element. But in others, the faculty required to predominate appears to
have been forcibly wreſted (if we may thus
expreſs it) from its natural bias. Its exertions are therefore unequal, its expreſſion
ſtrained, and its conduct in general of that
kind,

kind, which befpeaks a man who is better able to judge, than qualified to execute. Comprehenfion of intellect however, though it may be confidered in fome fenfe as independent of adequate execution, is then powerfully evidenced, when an author though not difcovering equal maftery in the management of every inferior part of his fubject, efpecially when confifting of many divifions; yet adopts and follows out a method that is upon the whole agreeable; and fuch as fhows the juft degree of energy in fome cafes, and a decent aptitude in all. We may obferve indeed as a criterion univerfally characteriftical of this faculty that in proportion as the judgment of a writer is extenfive, he will more obvioufly perceive what weight ought to be laid, either upon points which an ordinary reader might overlook, but which introduced and explained with propriety imprefs a fentiment forcibly on the mind; or upon the general ftrain of a character, as it may thus be rendered appropriated and interefting.

1. Examples

1. Examples to confirm the truth of theſe remarks will occur upon examining the moſt approved ſtandards either of philoſophy or of the fine arts. The Socratic method of reaſoning, beyond all others, appears to have ariſen from this knowledge of all the circumſtances that carry conviction to the underſtanding. Thus we find in the Dialogues of Plato, the philoſopher not merely ſuiting his arguments as nearly as poſſible to the character of the ſpeakers; but introducing his ſubjects from the ſimpleſt occurrences, and drawing his illuſtrations from ſuch remote, and yet natural reſources, as moſt ſtrongly evinced his addreſs and comprehenſion *. In this manner

---

* The reader who contemplates the Socratic manner in the preſent point of light, will be entertained as well as inſtructed by attending to the various methods that are ſucceſſively employed to promote the ends of this philoſophy. He will find Socrates ſometimes (as in the Euthyphron) obtaining the confidence of a ſuperſtitious bigot by a ſeries of compliments artfully addreſſed to his ruling paſſion, and by touching his weakneſs with ſo delicate a hand as to make him pleaſed and ſatisfied with reaſoning that expoſeth it. At others, (as

manner truths of the greateſt importance
are gradually laid open to perſons whoſe

(as in the Protagoras) after having ſoothed the pride of
the imperious ſophiſt, and diſpoſed him to liſten with
patience to a few ſimple queſtions apparently directed
only to obtain information, he lays open the falſity of
his maxims; and thus inculcates the ſublime doctrines
of philoſophy with irreſiſtible energy, while he appears
to be converſing familiarly on the plaineſt topics, and
even about the ſimpleſt utenſils of life. Varying at
other times his method of addreſs to the character of
more modeſt and diſpaſſionate hearers, we may obſerve
this great man in the Meno, Theagis, Crito, Lyſis,
and the two Alcibiades, diſcourſing of virtue, wiſdom,
propriety of conduct, friendſhip, rectitude, prayer, &c.
and in a manner at the ſame time ſo ſimple and com‑
prehenſive, happily uniting the dignity of the philoſo‑
pher with the affability of the friend, that we ceaſe to
wonder at the ſublime panygeric made upon him in his
own ſtyle likewiſe, by the young Acibiades, who com‑
pared him to thoſe ſtatues of ſylvan deities whoſe out‑
ſide appeared rough and unpoliſhed, but when opened
were found only to be *caſes* containing images of ALL
THE GODS! The Protagoras and Crito of Plato con‑
tain in particular ſtriking evidences of the philoſopher's
comprehenſive view of things. In the former the ſo‑
phiſt's arguments are refuted by reaſoning drawn as it
ſhould ſeem from very diſtant reſources. In the latter,
Socrates takes a moſt extenſive ſurvey of an im‑
portant ſubject, in anſwering the reaſons by which his
friend would have perſuaded him to make his eſcape.

curioſity

curiofity is deeply interefted in the procefs. Nor is the full defign of the philofopher perceived by his antagonift, until the conclufion, which he aims to eftablifh, ftrikes at laft with irrefiftible evidence upon the mind.

It is fcarce poffible to conceive any method more expreffive of a comprehenfive underftanding than that which is here prefented to us, when properly carried on. In order to bring it fuccefsfully into practice, it was neceffary that the philofopher, after being fully fatisfied of that truth which he intended to prove to his adverfary, fhould be able to conduct in fuch a manner intermediate means apparently foreign to his purpofe, but tending in reality directly to it; as that every obftruction being removed, the mind fhould yield that affent which convincing argumentation finally commands.

2. It was remarked likewife that as an enlarged underftanding becomes thus confpicuous in the conduct of an argumentative detail, it is not lefs fo in maintaining upon fome occafions confiftency of character.

racter. Comprehenfion of intellect is undoubtedly evinced when a character in
which various excellencies, imperfections,
and foibles are blended, is maintained with
fo much propriety through an extenfive
work, as to be known and approved at all
times by thofe ftriking fignatures that diftinguifh it from others. We muft care-
fully feparate here the province of imagination in accomplifhing this purpofe from
that of underftanding. It is undoubtedly
by an effort of the firft of thefe, that thofe
incidents are invented which call into confpicuous exercife the qualities that are here
combined in various affemblage. But it
is by the laft that an affinity is eftablifhed
univerfally betwixt the event and the quality difplayed by it, and the incidents in
general are difpofed in fuch a manner as to
fhow the whole to the higheft poffible advantage. Of this compafs of thought by
which a writer may evince the clearnefs as
well as extent of his underftanding, we
fhall have occafion to treat more particularly, when we come to examine the fpecies

cies of Compofition in which it is moft completely difplayed.

IV. We have now confidered the province of the reafoning faculty in the art of Compofition as conftituted by the invention of a theory, the arrangement and difpofition of parts, and the comprehenfive eftimate which it forms of a fubject. From our remarks on the general operations of this power in the departments abovementioned, it will appear, that a very large proportion of it may take place, and in fact does fo upon many occafions without being difcovered. An ordinary obferver therefore, when effects arifing from judgment are blended with fuch as are derived from imagination; without fome general criterion by which the influence of reafon may be always determined, will be apt to form unjuft and fuperficial eftimates. In order therefore to fet this matter in a proper light, and to complete our view of the operations of the underftanding as far as the prefent fubject is concerned; we may in general obferve, that wherever judgment exerts any confiderable degree of in-

fluence, fomething juft and appofite, fomething particularly appropriated to the fubject or occafion, will appear in *the fentiment*
of a performance. Other marks by which
its prevalence may be difcovered, as ftrength
of argument, juftnefs of defign, fymmetry
of parts, or progreffion of evidence, either
relate to particular arts, or to thofe branches
of Compofition which require this faculty
moft eminently to predominate. But in
all productions whatever, *propriety of fentiment* is invariably characteriftical of an
author's underftanding; and points indeed
fo naturally to this original, as never, when
difcovered, to be afcribed to another. But
what, it will be faid, is meant by this term
propriety when applied to the fentiment of
Compofition in the various fpecies of the
art? It is a vague and general defignation
that admits of different views, according
to that branch of the prefent fubject to
which it is applied; and its fenfe ought
therefore to be determined and exemplified
in each of thefe departments confidered by
itfelf. This requifition is undoubtedly juft,
and in order to anfwer it, we muft enter

fome-

fomewhat more particularly into the fubject.

Propriety characterifing the different
fpecies of Compofition, fuggefts different
ideas, according to the nature and tendency
of each. Thus in philofophy, where it is
expected that every pofition will be confirmed by the beft adapted evidence, propriety of fentiment is faid to obtain when
the author, though fometimes drawn into
little digreffions, yet keeps clofe in general
to the principal object of his refearch; and
felects from the various arguments or illuftrations that occur to him, thofe whofe
immediate tendency is to prove or explain
the point which he hath ultimately in
view *. In hiftory, where the narrative
manner

---

* No ancient writer appears to have ftudied this philofophical propriety more than the elegant philofopher
mentioned in the preceding note. It is true indeed, that
he freely indulges himfelf in digreffive circumftances;
and his fublime imagination even catcheth at fometimes the figures and diction of poetry. See his
ΦΑΙΔΡΟΣ, ab init. See likewife vol. ii. of this work,
fect. iii. But when any point of real impor-

tance

manner takes place of the didactic, sentiments have propriety, when thefe grow
as it were naturally out of the detail, and
feem to be neceffary parts of the work itfelf, rather than fuperfluities that may be
lopped off from it *. In eloquence, propriety

---

tance is canvaffed, the reafoning is ufually conducted
with great accuracy and attention. Thus Socrates fays
to his friend in the true fpirit of a philofopher : Σκο-
πεισθαι ουν χρη ημας ειτε ταυτα πρακτεον ειτε μη. Ως
εγω, ᾱ μονος νυν, αλλα και αει τοιαυτος, ως των
ετων μηδενι αλλῳ πειθεσθαι η τω λογω ος αν μοι λογι-
ζομενῳ βελτιϛος φαινηται. τας δε Λογας ᾱς εν τω εμπρο-
σθεν ελεγον ου δυναμαι νου εκβαλειν επειδε μοι η τυχη
γεγονεν. Αλλα σχεδου τι ομοιϛε φαινουται μοι, και
τοιαυτος ωρεσβευω και τιμω ως και προτερου, &c.
ΠΛΑΤ. ΚΡΙΤ.

* There is no occafion here for methodifed obfervations, and protracted periods. The former give a ftiff
air to the hiftorian's compofition. The latter fatigue
inftead of entertaining the reader. Comprehenfion
and concife expreffion are the two criteria by which
thoughts that grow out of hiftorial narration ought always to be characterifed. When Livy has related at
large a decree of the Athenian people againft Philip,
from whofe refentment they hoped to be protected by
the Romans, he gives his own fenfe of their conduct
by

priety of fentiment requires, that the orator
fhould fix upon fuch motives and arguments

---

by faying,—" Athenienfes quidem *literis, verbifque qui-*
bus folis valent, bellum adverfus Philippum gerebant."
Dec. iv. lib. i. Thefe few words contain as much
fenfe as might be made to fill out a volume. They reprefent the low ftate to which the powerful republic of
Athens was reduced; and the term *bellum* particularly
in the prefent connection, throws the ftrongeft ridicule
on their procedure. Of a different kind from this
is the following obfervation of one of the moft judicious of Roman hiftorians, on the funeral of Auguftus.
Yet it is interwoven in fuch a manner into the body of
his work, that this laft would have feemed to be incomplete without it. " Die funeris, milites velut
præfidio ftetere, multum irridentibus qui ipfi vi-
derint, quique a parentibus acceperant, diem illum
crudi adhuc fervitii & libertatis improfpere repetitæ,
cum occifus Dictator Cæfar, aliis peffimum, aliis pul-
cherrimum facinus videretur: nunc fenem principem
longa potentia, provifis etiam hæredum in rempubli-
cam opibus, auxilio fcilicet militari tuendum, ut fepul-
tura quieta foret." Annal. lib. i. This manner of laying circumftances together hath an excellent effect in
hiftory. It carries back the reader upon the winding
up of a fcene, to the recollection of events that might
have efcaped his memory; and placeth thefe in fuch a
light as is at the fame time agreeable and inftructive.
Let us take one other example of this propriety of fen-

timent

ments as he knows will make the moft lafting impreffion upon the audience to whom
his difcourfe is addreffed; and that the
whole fhould be enforced ·by obfervations
judicioufly adapted to the nature of the
fubjeƐt, and to the circumftances of the
hearers *.—With regard to the poetic art
indeed,

---

timent from a modern hiftorian. Voltaire fpeaking of
the adminiftration of France under the duke of Or-
leans, obferves, that the celebrated Syftem of Law
which feemed to threaten the ftate with ruin, contributed in the event to fupport and even enrich it. It
gave an aƐtive fpirit to the nation, occafioned the re-
vival of commerce, and gave birth to the India company, which had been ruined in the wars.

- This fenfible obfervation hath great propriety in this
conneƐtion. It is indeed fuggefted naturaliy by the
preceding account of things. But the effeƐt of a civil
war, and that of this *great game*, (as he juftly calls it)
upon the human mind, when viewed philofophically as
improving certain fatulties of it, feems at the fame time
a new and inftruƐtive method of treating the fubjeƐt,
as fuch confiderations tend to enlarge our knowledge
of human nature.

* It hath been often obferved with truth, that the
chriftian religion affords a wider field to the orator, and
propofeth nobler and more animating motives to influence the conduƐt of mankind, than any other fyftem
of principles whatever. Yet it muft at the fame time
be

indeed, as it admits of much greater variety of Compofition than any of the

---

be acknowledged, that in *propriety of fentiment*, confidered as arifing from an attention to the *peculiar circumftances of the hearers*, the fubjects on which ancient orators were led to expatiate fuggefted arguments more perfuafive as being drawn from immediate exigencies, than could have arifen from a plan of duty whofe moral fanctions were not inftantly to take place. Thus Demofthenes calling up to the Athenians the ghofts of thofe who fell at Marathon and Salamis, as formerly referred to; Tully invoking the Alban groves and altars polluted by the debauchery of Claudius; Manlius, when accufed of treafon before the Roman people, pointing to the Capitol, which in their own memory had been faved from deftruction by his intrepidity; and Gracchus fignificantly directing the eyes of his audience to the very fpot that had been ftained with the blood of his brother;—thefe it is obvious laid before their hearers motives of powerful and irrefiftible energy. Vide Demofthen. de Coron. Cicer. pro Milon. Liv. lib. vi. c. 20. and Cicer. de Orat. lib. iii. c. 56. On the other hand however, it ought to be obferved at the fame time, that if we confider the motives of chriftianity as operating indeed more univerfally, but lefs inftantaneoufly than the former; it will follow that the chriftian orator may evince a very fuperior degree of judgment, by felecting from fuch as occur to him thofe that are beft adapted to his purpofe; and by applying them in that manner which he knows will have the ftrongeft and moft permanent effect.

G 4

others

others it is more eafy in moft cafes to perceive the effects of this propriety of fentiment, than to fay particularly by what it
it is conftituted. Without however having
recourfe to the various fpecies of this art,
it may be obferved, that we always ap-
plaud the judgment of the writer, when
we find moral and inftructive fentiments
wrought into his performance, . without
either leading the reader from the fubject,
or breaking the unity of defign *. In defcriptive

---

* In the Georgics of Virgil (a theme indeed naturally productive of moral obfervation) the reader whofe
mind is fufceptible of impreffion from fentiments that
rife out of a paftoral fubject, will find many of thefe
introduced with the ftricteft propriety. To a man who
had been difappointed in purfuing the plans of ambition, how juft muft the following obfervation have appeared which the fubject of the poet fo obvioufly introduceth

Fortunatus et ille, Deos qui novit agreftes,
Pana, Sylvanumque finem, Nymphafque forores!
Illum non populi fafces, non purpura regum
Flexit,——
Non res Romanæ perituraque regna ; neque ille
Aut doluit miferans inopem, aut invidit habenti.

GEOR. lib. ii.

This

ſcriptive pieces particularly we view theſe as buſtoes diſpoſed artfully in variegated ſcenery, where they form agreeable and attractive decorations.

This propriety of ſentiment likewiſe conſtitutes one of the principal beauties of Thomſon's Seaſons; a work ſo univerſally read, that the ſelection of any particular example is rendered unneceſſary. One of the moſt ſtriking inſtances of this kind the author remembers to have met with, is in a little ode by Mr. Gray, beginning " Lo where the roſy-boſomed hours, &c." After having painted in rich and glowing imagery the inſect youth as on the wing,

Eager to taſte the honied ſpring,
And float amid the liquid noon, &c.

theſe images are applied with exquiſite propriety in the following moral reflection ariſing likewiſe immediately from the ſubject.

To contemplation's ſober eye
Such is the race of man ;
And they that *creep*, and they that *fly*,
Shall end where they began.
Alike the *buſy* and the *gay*
But *flutter* thro' life's *little day*,
In Fortune's *varying colours* dreſs'd ;
Bruſh'd by the hand of *rough miſchance*,
Or *chill'd* by age, their *airy dance*,
They leave in duſt to reſt.   GRAY's Odes.

To a reader poſſeſſed of poetic feeling, this painting will need no illuſtration. To one who wants this ſenſibility, no illuſtration would be of uſe.

The

The underftanding claims as a province peculiarly its own, the power of diftin-guifhing any performance by this charac-teriftic of propriety. It effectuates this purpofe by giving clofe attention as well to the nature of objects, as to the juftnefs of their difpofition; and by taking into its eftimate whatever is neceffary to render the exhibition adequate and complete. Thus it is that the fentiment in hiftorical narra-tion rifes fo naturally out of the detail, as if it made a part of, and was neceffary to fum it up. Thus a clear relation is per-ceived to take place in the difquifitions of philofophy, betwixt the obfervations or arguments, and the end, whether an ulti-mate or fubordinate one, which thefe are adduced to bring about. In the firft cafe, a judicious and of confequence compre-henfive furvey of events includes thofe fen-timents that either render the narration in-ftructive, or ferve to connect one part of the fubject with another; in both which cafes their propriety is obvious. In the laft inftance where narration takes no place, it is the power of underftanding likewife

that

that by permiting nothing to pafs that is either frivolous or unappropriated, renders the whole an object of rational approbation.

With regard to the arts of eloquence and poetry, where an ampler range is opened to imagination; can any reafon be affigned why effects of *the fame kind* fhould not likewife be confidered as derived from the fame original? And does it not indicate a defect of this faculty, when thefe are wholly overlooked as *fignatures of it*, merely perhaps becaufe they appear in a fpecies of richer and more diverfified Compofition? At many times indeed we may venture to affirm, that a fingle thought thrown out at once, and feeming to rife out of the fubject by a kind of new creation, will difcover to a mind *capable of taking in its whole force*, greater extent of judgment and deeper infight into the fprings by which the mind is moft powerfully actuated, than thofe elaborate refearches by which truth is elucidated, after carrying on a progreffive and complicated detail.

This

This attention to propriety of sentiment as the test of understanding, will show us that the opinion, however universally prevalent, is fallacious, that the distinguishing criterion of this power is *strength* and *justness* of argument. In order to judge properly of this point, we must make allowances for the various subjects of speculation, each requiring to be treated in a manner peculiar to itself. As florid epithets therefore, and pompous declamation, would be justly looked upon in a discourse professedly philosophical to be evidences of a defective understanding; so a series of reasoning uniformly supported in a piece (which as far as any subject can be treated in this manner) ought to be purely pathetic or descriptive, indicates in fact a deficiency of judgment as much as the former. The difference only is, that in the one case an author discovers that defect in the execution of his subject, which in the other is conspicuous from his choice of it.

To the criteria abovementioned as characteristical universally of the mental power, whose office we are here considering, we may

add

add as the laft indication, that it is this faculty which makes the expreffion bear a
juft relation to the fentiment in any fpecies
of Compofition; and that gives accuracy
in the application of images to thofe objects which they are brought to illuftrate.
The original invention of thefe laft is unqueftionably owing to imagination. We
cannot however have a furer proof in any
particular inftance of the fuperiority of
this faculty above that of reafon, than
when we obferve images to be indifcriminately fcattered through a work without
regard to the thoughts as not requiring to
be thus illuftrated; or when we find thefe
difcordant to their objects, and, like fhreds
of tapeftry before the piece is completed,
exhibiting only a fingle limb, or fragment
of the figure, inftead of fetting the whole
before the eye in its natural proportion.
From that invariable attention to arrangement and fymmetry, which we have obferved to characterife reafon, we may lay
it down as a principle, that whatever errors a heated imagination may give occafion to in the application of images as confifting

fifting of foreign and unappropriated circumftances, yet we fhall feldom or never
find a *judicious* author employing thefe
when they are obvioufly inadequate, or
when by recurring too frequently they
pall upon the mind, and throw an air of
obfcurity on the piece.

It is by the concurrence of the circumftances thus enumerated and explained
that Compofition is rendered *correct*. This
important character therefore obtains perfection in confequence of a fteady and affiduous exertion of judgment. The degree in which it ought to obtain, the attention it fhould exercife, and its effect in
general on the art of which we treat here,
will be confidered in a fubfequent branch
of the work.

Thus we have endeavoured to lay before the reader fome account of the extenfive province affigned to the great faculty
by which man is diftinguifhed from inferior creatures, in the various departments
of Compofition. The reader will obferve
that in our remarks on this fubject, we
have kept in fight the operations of this
faculty

faculty confidered apart from the others; that effects derived from *reafon alone*, may be clearly difcriminated from thofe that owe their origin either to fome other mental quality, or to a combination of all. By purfuing this courfe, we propofe to accomplifh a beneficial purpofe both to an author and his critic. The firft, when he is meditating a defign, may judge from the criteria that are here laid down as fhowing the prevalence of underftanding, how far his own is adequate to it, and in what points it may be deficient. The laft, when by having viewed the faculties of the mind in this light, he knows how to put every thing to its *proper account*, will be unembarraffed in the whole of his procedure; and fhould the obfervations on this branch of the prefent fubject be found to have propriety, may found his decifion on furer evidences, than he who takes a general and indifcriminate furvey.

SECTION

SECTION III.

Of the influence of Imagination in Compo-
sition.

IMAGINATION, or the inventive faculty as it is denominated, we have already defined as employed in Compofition,
to be that " which ftrikes out happy imitations, forms original affemblages of ideas;
and thus fupplies the materials of thofe
juft and beautiful illuftrations, which at
the fame time improve the *expreffion* in this
art, and heighten the effect of fentiment *."
It is proper to obferve before we enter particularly into this fubject, that this intellectual power cannot be viewed precifely in
the fame light as the former; which we
contemplated as fingle and independent of
every other. The loofe and unconnected
effufions of fancy wrought into no form
by the controul of reafon, can only be
viewed as the extravagant ravings of a
madman. We propofe therefore here to
follow as clofely as poffible the track of

---

* Sect. I.

this

this excentric faculty; and to point out effects of which it is ultimately the caufe:— but, as we fhall not always take notice of the influence exerted by the underftanding in rendering thefe effects the objects of *rational* entertainment, the reader himfelf muft feparate the operations of thefe powers from each other, in which he may receive direction from the preceding obfervations.

We have in the courfe of this work frequently diftinguifhed imagination by the defignation of the *inventive power* *, that
its

---

* A critic of the prefent age endeavours to make a diftinction betwixt *invention* and *imagination,* which he fays, " though nearly allied *in their fignification,* yet are " fomewhat different from each other." Invention he defines to be " the *faculty* of difcovering *certain relations* " among various objects, from whence we form a new " and beautiful affociation of ideas. Imagination is " the faculty of illuftrating and embellifhing thofe " ideas by new, apt, and ftriking images and figures." —I am entirely of this gentleman's mind with regard to the neceffity of giving clear definitions of the terms we employ; without which it is true that we may " cavil " without end, and create confufion inftead of *begetting*

its operations may be easily and clearly
known from thefe of any other intellectual
endowment.

_____

"conviction." See Ruffhead's Life of Pope, p. 447,
448. But by a want of precifion in the prefent cafe, I
am afraid that his own definitions give rife to fome part
of thofe effects which he fo freely and juftly cenfures.
" Invention he fays is the *faculty* of difcovering certain
" relations, &c." The term *faculty* employed here,
naturally fuggefts the idea of fome intellectual power
different from thofe with which we are acquainted, as
neceffarily productive of certain confequences. It
ought therefore to have been analifed ; i. e. the author
fhould have fhown, either in what refpects it is diftinct
from the others, or in what manner it is conftituted by
their union. Neither of thefe however has this writer
attempted, further than by telling us, that we difcover
by it *certain* relations, &c. *Certain* relations! What
relations? Thofe that enable us " to form a *new* and
" *beautiful* affociation of ideas." In an affociation of
ideas recommended by *novelty*, we have fhown in the
preceding fection, that the underftanding or judgment
may upon fome occafions be *folely* employed. See p.
28, &c. With regard to the *beauty* of fuch affociation,
I would afk in what manner is this character conftituted? Does it lie in the juft combination, and methodical arrangement of ideas ? To confer according to
our author's own decifion the province of judgment.
See p. 449. From thefe obfervations it would feem,
that by the faculty here termed invention, our author
means that of reafon, or underftanding. But this he
                                        will

endowment. As this term muſt occur ſo
frequently when we treat of imagination,
it

---

will not permit us to ſuppoſe. For enumerating in the
very next page the qualities that conſtitute genius, he
mentions invention and judgment as faculties perfectly
diſtinct from each other. Again,—is this beauty
conſtituted by the novelty, *aptitude,* and vivacity of the
colours with which ideas are decorated?—No.—Theſe
characters are ſtamped on Compoſition by imagination
which it is his buſineſs to diſtinguiſh from invention.—
Since then this extraordinary faculty is diſtinct both
from judgment and imagination ſeparately viewed,
does it ariſe from the union of both powers?—Neither
is this the caſe according to this gentleman's idea of
the term, for in the enumeration above referred to, he
takes notice of invention as a faculty by which the poet
is enabled to perceive the relations of objects, and to
form a ſtriking and intereſting union of theſe, p. 449,
before he aſſigns the provinces either of imagination or
of reaſon in forming his character.—Yet in the ſame
page, after having aſcribed to invention a power of
placing objects in a certain " ſtriking union," he mentions this " ſtriking union" as the effect not of invention, but of " ſolid and correct judgment." This ingenious gentleman (in whoſe work, notwithſtanding
theſe inadvertencies, there is much juſt and valuable
criticiſm) has embarraſſed himſelf in his account of
this characteriſtic of genius, by giving the deſignation
of a *faculty* of the mind to ſomething that is only to be
conſidered as indicating its exiſtence. Invention is not

itſelf

it will throw light on its various modes of exertion, if we endeavour to determine particularly the meaning of the phrafe.

Invention

itfelf an intellectual power. It is an effect fometimes derived from reafon, when principles already known are laid together in fuch a manner, as to give rife to fome conclufion in which there is at the fame time both novelty and truth: fometimes it proceeds from a warm imagination, as when unufual and ftriking affemblages of ideas are prefented to the mind; or even when known truths are placed in a light remarkably attractive by new and peculiarly happy illuftrations. It is an effect of difcernment conftituted by the union of both thefe powers, when judgment is confpicuous at the fame time in the methodifed arrangement of ideas, and imagination in their originality, and manner of being fet off to advantage. This laft however is denominated with peculiar propriety the *inventive faculty*, becaufe its combinations being more uncommon than thofe of the underftanding, and *feeming* often to have been effectuated by a glance of thought, we afcribe to imagination a kind of creative energy of which the former when left to itfelf appears not to participate. It is to this power of the mind likewife as we fhall fhow afterwards, that difcernment owes its quicknefs of perception, as well as its choice of extraordinary means. That its province in Compofition is much more extenfive than that which we have feen prefcribed to it by this author of embellifhing ideas by new, and ftriking figures,

Invention as a general defignation is applied to every thing in which there is novelty. Fancy therefore viewed as the parent of invention, is confidered as the original fource of thofe new and ftriking affemblages or imitations which a mind endowed with any large proportion of it is
faid to *create*. But what are we to underftand by this laft epithet? The explanation
of it will include that of the other, and is
indeed the more neceffary, as terms of this
kind not properly underftood when applied
to the human mind, are apt to fuggeft to
an unintelligent reader a fenfe which the
authors never meant to convey by them.—
In the moft abftracted fenfe of this word
as relating to difcoveries purely *original*, of
which the fenfes receive no patterns, we
muft be convinced at once, that with regard to man, it can have no fignificance
or propriety whatever. The ideas infinitely diverfified that are conveyed to us
by the fenfes; or that arife from the vari-

---

figures, we fhall endeavour to evince at large when
we confider the various manners in which its energy
is difplayed.

H 3

ous lights in which the mind contemplates
its own operations,—thefe are indeed by
what we term a plaftic imagination affociated, compounded, and diverfified at pleafure. Difcernment, in the proper acceptation of that term, is difcovered in feizing
remote points of refemblance betwixt objects that have no apparent fimiliarity; and
in the elucidation of truth from topics
which the man of mere fancy, or of mere
reafon might wholly overlook. But in the
whole of this procefs, the originality obvioufly refults from the manner in which
objects are felected and put together, fo as
to form upon the whole an unufual combination; though thefe when feparately
viewed may each of them be fuch as the
mind hath formerly been habituated to
contemplate.

From this power of placing known truths
in fuch points of view as make a forcible
and permanent impreffion, thofe difcoveries arife in which philofophical inveftigation is made ufe of. Here the mind having confidered the moft probable means of
obtaining a certain purpofe, lays down a

few ſimple and obvious truths from which
it forms more compounded exhibitions in
a proceſs cloſely ſuperintended by the faculty that eſtabliſheth methodical arrangement. Ideas that are familiar to the mind
when ſeparated from each other, impreſs
ſome truth that is new to it, in conſequence
of a certain peculiar diſpoſition; and impart in ſuch aſſociation truths that arreſt
not attention more ſtrongly by their originality, (if that term may here be applied with juſtice) than they may be ſubſervient to edification in conſequence of their
comprehenſive nature and importance. By
varying a little a ſimilar train of familiar
perceptions we ſhall eaſily comprehend the
preciſe meaning of the term Invention when
applied to the various branches of ſcienti-
fical enquiry; and the different ſenſe in
which it is taken from the epithet *creative*
which diſtinguiſheth other ſpecies of Compoſition. Thus in every kind of analo-
gical reaſoning, experience ſupplies the
materials upon which the theory proceeds.
We are indeed ſtruck in the proſecution of
reaſoning conducted on this plan, when

H 4   an

an obvious relation is difcovered to take place betwixt things that appeared to be wholly different. But the fatisfaction derived from fuch an enquiry arifeth as we find upon reviewing the procefs, not from any originality of the objects themfelves, but merely from the novelty of that fituation in which thefe are expofed to view.

Thus far, having followed out the firft idea of invention as conftituted by any exhibition in which there is *novelty*, we may afcribe it with propriety to the philofopher who conducts to fome unexpected conclufion a feries of arguments or to the orator, who fixeth on the moft appofite topics of perfuafion*, Thefe however, though

standing

* There appears to be a remarkable difference of opinion betwixt one of the firft of ancient and of modern writers with regard to the meaning of the term Invention. Cicero in his work entitled De Inventione, of which only one half remains at prefent, confiders this as the principal character of an orator. Bacon, on the contrary, will not admit that he who fixeth on the beft arguments hath any title to the defignation of an inventor. " Inventio argumentorum (fays he) Inventio *proprie* non eft. *Invenire* enim eft *ignota* detegere;

ſtanding high in their diſtinct profeſſions, and juſtly eſteemed as men of genius, yet occupy only a ſecondary rank as inventors, when compared with him who preſents every moment new aſſemblages of objects to the mind, illuminated with the richeſt colouring; and to whoſe genius we apply the deſignation of *creative* in conſequence of ideas riſing as it would ſeem ſpontane-

---

non ante cognita recipere aut revocare." De Augment. Scient. lib. v. c. 3. But the ſentiments of theſe upon the preſent ſubject may be eaſily reconciled. Should it be allowed that the choice and application of argu-ments may diſcover no eminent ſhare of invention, yet it is undoubtedly ſhown when theſe arguments are brought to enforce ſome new propoſition. This is ob-viouſly the " ignota detegere" which he ſpeaks of, and its author is unqueſtionably poſſeſſed of invention. The ſelection and application of topics of perſuaſion in elo-quence denominate the ſame character, and it is this which Cicero calls the principal part of eloquence. Another ancient writer conſiders not only invention in general, but various degrees of it as diſcovered here. Αλλ' επει των πρωβλημάτων ειδη ποικιλα, και τω πραγματων αι ζητησεις διαφοροι, ποικιλας, και τας ΕΥΡΕΣΕΙΣ παραδωσομεν ωσε τεθεισης υποθεσεως, αυτικα ειδεναι εφ' ο τρεπτεον εσιν εις ευρεσιν της προκαταςασεως τεχνικην. ΕΡΜΟΓΕΝ. περι ΕΥΡΕΣ. βιϐ. β. τμημ. Α.

ouſly

oufly from the thought of the writer, and falling like the rude materials of the univerfe into beautiful arrangement. It is in this procefs that we are to look for the great principle of *poetic imitation*. In the ftrict fenfe of that word, the poet is no more a creator or maker than the hiftorian or philofopher. But his imagination is ftruck with expreffions in the various objects contemplated by it, which it poffeffeth likewife the power of painting in the moft vivid colours. When many of thefe are brought together, the fame faculty that perceived them at firft, affociates them in a manner altogether unufual. To thefe affociations we give the defignation ORIGINAL; and to the power which produced them, that of INVENTIVE or CREATIVE *.

From

---

* As this curious and important branch of the fubject may appear to require a fuller difcuffion than we have here had occafion to afford it in the text, we fhall here throw together a few additional obfervations on it. Ariftotle not only confiders every fpecies of poetry as derived from imitation, but he points out the moft diftinguifhing branches of the art, as taking their rife from that bias of the character. Σεμνοτεροι τας καλας εμιμεουντο

From the whole reflection will point out
to us two diftinct caufes in the mind, from
· · which

εμιμουντο πραξεις, &c. οι δε Ευτελεσεροι τα των
Φαυλων, πρωτου ψωγυς ποιουντες, &c. περι ΠΟΙΗΤ.
χεφ. Δ. Purfuing this train of thought a little further,
we may obferve, that in the fcale of genius, thofe who
are denominated makers or inventors are fuch as copy
immediately from nature, as their great and perfect original. Thofe who poffefs a very confiderable fhare of
this character without ever rifing to a level with the
firft, are fuch as fometimes ftrike out new figures in
the contemplation of this confummate pattern, and
fometimes content themfelves with beautifying and improving upon the inventions of others. The laft clafs,
wholly confined to the latter fpecies of imitation are
difqualified by any art to reach the former; and are
therefore never fuppofed to be diftinguifhed by *original
merit*. To the two firft of thefe the term inventive may
be applied with propriety, if we confider it as a criterion by which the higheft degree of genius may be diftinguifhed from an inferior, or very moderate proportion of it; in which cafe he who ftands in the loweft
rank appears only as a fervile and fecondary imitator.
It is however in ftrict truth improper to apply the word
imitation merely to a few of the arts; when upon
taking a more enlarged view of things, we fhall find
fome particular fpecies of imitation characterifing every
branch of Compofition. Thus the philofopher in his
moft abftracted refearches evidently difcovers this principle,

which every fpecies of originality is ultimately to be traced. The one is, its power
of forming fuch various, new, and ftriking

---

ciple, when he delineates the forms either of external
or of internal beauty, from that perfect model which is
the object of his fenfes, or from that image which he
perceives to be imprinted on the mind. In copying
likewife the expreffion of any intellectual power, we
fall naturally into fome mode of imitation. This becomes immediately perceptible when the effects of any
paffion are to be reprefented, as the expreffion is then
tinctured (if we may adopt that epithet) with the colour
required to predominate; and the images are rendered
as fignificant as poffible of the object to be defcribed.
A kind of fecondary imitation we may obferve to prevail among the feveral arts, whofe idioms being mu-
tually transfufed give peculiar beauty and energy to
each other. Thus an eminent ancient hiftorian fhows
the origin of rhetoric upon this principle, and explains
in a very ingenious manner the fteps by which it was
carried forward. Πρωτιϛα γαρ η ποιητικη κατασκευη
παρηλθεν εις το μεσον και ευδοκιμησεν. Ειτα εκεινον
ΜΙΜΟΥΜΕΝΟΙ λυσαντες το μετρον, τ'αλλα δε φυλαξ-
αντες τα ποιητικα συνεγραψαν οι περι Καδμον, περι
Φερεκυδην, και Εκαταιον. Ειτοι οι υϛερον αφαιρουντες
αει τι των τοιητων εις το νυν ειδος κατηγαγον ως αν' απο
Υψους τινος, ΣΤΡΑΒ. βιϛ. Α. We fhall have occafion to fhow afterwards that this beautiful fpecies of
imitation prevailed much more among the ancients
than it is permitted to do in modern times.

combinations

combinations of truths univerfally acknowledged as open at laft unexpected a-
venues of knowledge. The other is its
propenfity to imitate upon all occafions
the different characters and appearances of
nature; whether viewed as exhibiting the
moft beautiful external fcenery; or throwing expreffions infinitely diverfified into
the characters of men. In proportion as
its perception of thefe laft extends to remote circumftances and connections; and
fuch as are leaft perceptible, the marks of
originality are rendered ftill more confpicuous; and in confequence of the *novelty*
which thefe give to a performance the imitative powers of the author acquire the denomination of invention.

That this power of imitation is fomething diftinct from that which we denominate the reafoning faculty, it will require
little attention to evince. The difference
muft indeed be rendered obvious from this
fingle confideration; that an eminent fhare
of the firft of thefe often diftinguifheth
men, who are void of the laft, at leaft with
regard to its higheft fcene of operation.
Thus

Thus we can eafily conceive that a man may be capable of tracing with great accuracy effects from a caufe, or, vice verfa, a caufe from effects, who is yet wholly difqualified, upon viewing the external beauties of nature, to paint thefe by certain happy and exquifite ftrokes of imitations. It does not indeed follow that he who poffeffeth this imitative talent may not likewife be qualified to exercife that of reafoning juftly. But an inftance in which it appears that one of thefe is disjoined from the other, clearly fhows that they are effentially different. Now if this is the cafe, as argumentation carried on properly to accomplifh a certain purpofe indicates the exercife of reafon; fo an imitation happily executed can arife only from that power to which we give the name of imagination. But it hath been already fhown that to certain imitative beauties we affign the appellation of *original* expreffions. It follows therefore that the faculty from which thefe are derived may be characterifed peculiarly by the epithet *inventive*.

Applying

Applying therefore this defignation to it, let us enquire what fpheres are appropriated to it in the province of Compofition. We propofe to confider its operations as regarding the images, the incidents, the fentiments, or the characters that occur in the various fpecies of this art. In one or other of the views opened to us by thefe, it will appear that we contemplate imagination; and we fuppofe it then only to be predominant in the higheft degree, when the feparate teftimonies of its exiftence act in vigorous combination.

I. Under the general defignation of images, we mean here to comprehend not only thofe fignificant allufions by which a particular thought is placed vividly before the mind, but every fpecies of *illuftration* by which fentiments either acquire the advantage of being clearly difplayed, or of making a forcible and lafting impreffion. Of thefe there are two kinds, each of which hath its peculiar importance. The firft takes place when an event or action of effential confequence is completely difplayed by fome fignificant and appropriated

image,

image, drawn from external objects, and purfued through a detail of circumftances. The fecond kind is conftituted when maxims or fentiments of importance are explained by appofite metaphors, or are impreffed on the mind by fuitable examples. It is principally in the higher branches of poetry that we are to look for the firft of thefe. In epic particularly where *admiration* is almoft conftantly to be excited by holding up fome ftandard of confummate excellence, it is at the fame time neceffary, that the principal character fhould be expofed in a variety of lights; and that every circumftance relating to it fhould add ftrength to the paffion which ought to rife higher as the author proceeds. This great effect is wholly to be afcribed to the grandeur of thofe fublime images by which every object is fucceffively exalted. The folemnity with which thefe are introduced, the circumftantial manner in which they are difplayed, and our own propenfity to extend our idea of the object until it is equalled with the illuftration; thefe united circumftances operate fo powerfully on the mind,

as

as to ſuſpend as it were the influence of reaſon. Tranſactions thus deſcribed become in fact ſo deeply intereſting as to awaken in us the ſame paſſions that would have ſeized immediate ſpectators of the ſcene *.

In

---

*. " On ne peut reüſſir dans le ſtyle elevé du genre ſublime qu'on ne ſoit entierement perſuadé que ce ſtyle ce forme de choſes qu'on a dire des grandes images qu'on s'en fait ; & de l'elevation du genie, plus que de celle de l'expreſſion, de l'eclat de paroles & de cette attirail de periphraſes recherchées." Rap. Reflex. ſur l'Eloq. tom. ii. p. 37. This ſentiment a reader of taſte will conſider as much more juſt and noble than that of another critic of the ſame nation, who ſeems to conſider an exact conformity in every point betwixt the image and the object to be illuſtrated, as indiſpenſibly neceſſary at all times to conſtitute juſt compoſition. Boſſu du Poeme Epique, liv. vi. chap. 3. Here our critic takes a very frigid and defective view of his ſubject. A great genius, when his mind is filled with ſublime conceptions, will not even think of keeping up this rigid conformity, by which he might obtain the praiſe of correctneſs, at the expence of being charged with coldneſs and inſipidity. When an illuſtration at ſuch times correſponds to the object in ſome remarkable circumſtance, we not only allow the writer to throw in others which have no ſuch immediate connection with it, but we conſider theſe as

I the

In every fpecies of didactic compofition
it is obvious that this ftyle of exalted imagery would be wholly improper, and indeed unnatural. A judicious writer will

---

the exuberance of an imagination inexhauftible in materials; and fhewing that it poffeffeth a larger proportion of thefe than neceffity requires. Of this kind
the reader will meet with many ftriking examples in
the Iliad, the Paradife Loft, and the Gierufalemme
Liberata. We may however, obferve, that though
this free ufe of the prefent figure obtains among the
moft eminent poets, yet it is not meant to affirm that
an image *exactly* correfponding to its original will fail,
even in this fpecies of compofition, of making a forcible and adequate impreffion. This conformity ought
particularly to be ftudied when feveral different figures
are collected into one group, and the illuftration is
applied fucceffively to each. When Æneas is defcribed as afcending to the top of his father's houfe to
learn whence arofe the tumult in the city, how ftrongly does the following image fet before our eyes the
man, the place, and the fcene that broke out upon
him !

In fegetem veluti cum flamma furentibus auftris
Incidit, aut rapidus montano flumine torrens
Sternit agros, fternit fata læta, boumque labores,
Precipitefque trahit fylvas :—ftupet infcius alto,
Accipiens fonitum, faxi de vertice paftor.

Æneid. lib. ii.

therefore

therefore have recourfe here to the other kind of illuftration which confifts of employing metaphor or example. It ought to be obferved that though the mind willingly fubmits upon fome occafions to the illufion of fancy; yet this only happens when it is thoroughly captivated by a feries of interefting events; and rather than lofe the pleafure of perufal, we are willing to look upon thefe (if we may thus exprefs it) as *momentary* realities. This impofition is rendered more or lefs effectual, as the illuftrations participate in a greater or lefs degree of ftrength, beauty, and variety. By thefe means attention is very forcibly arrefted by an event otherwife too inconfiderable to have at all attracted it; as obfervations in the fame manner which might have been otherwife overlooked, by being thus powerfully inculcated, become fubfervient to the purpofe of enlarging our knowledge of mankind.

In the province of fcience, where criticifm exercifeth more rigid feverity, the inventive power is principally beneficial, when, under the direction of underftand-

ing,

ing, it fuggefts a mode of expreffion fo happily and juftly metaphorical, as conveys peculiar energy to philofophical difquifition, and placeth hiftorical tranfactions in the moft ftriking points of view. We muft diftinguifh here betwixt *examples* which refer to a whole feries of obfervation taken together, and metaphors which relate wholly to one part or object in this feries. This will be beft underftood from particular inftances. It is the purpofe of Cicero in the dialogue entitled the Dream of Scipio, to imprefs the belief of the immortality of the foul. In order to effectuate this purpofe, the great Africanus is introduced as addreffing one of his greateft defcendents, and at the fame time that he mentions the evidence of this truth, as powerfully exemplifying the happinefs of the bleffed by comparifon with the higheft enjoyment of mortals. With this view he points to Carthage * the fcene of future

---

* " Oftendebat autem Carthaginem de excelfo et pleno ftellarum, illuftri et claro quodam loco." Somn. Scipion.

triumph

triumph to the perſon whom he addreſſed, and acquaints him of happineſs incomparably higher than that which may ariſe from this conqueſt, to be enjoyed in a future ſtate *. He proceeds to convey an higher idea of this happineſs by making it to ariſe from the contemplation of the .UNIVERSE, that *magnificent temple* † (as he nobly calls it) of the Deity; in compariſon of which the world itſelf is a point, and the Roman empire altogether, an almoſt imperceptible atom!—Every reader muſt be ſenſible of the advantage which the philoſophical ſentiments of this dialogue acquire from being exemplified in ſo exalted a ſtyle of imagery.

Metaphors, or ſhort compariſons as theſe may be denominated, are applied indeed

---

* " Sic habeto : omnibus qui patriam conſervaverint, adjuverint, auxerint, certum eſſe in cælo ac definitum locum, ubi beati ævo ſempiterno fruantur. Imo ii vivunt qui ex corporis vinculis tanquam ex carcere evolaverunt: veſtra vero quæ dicitur vita, mors eſt." Id. ibid.

† " DEUS IS, cujus templum eſt *omne hoc quod conſpicis.*"

to

to particular objects, inftead of thus illuftrating fentiments that ftand in connection
with each other. Yet their effect when
properly applied, is fuch as every reader
poffeffed of fenfibility muft feel as highly
interefting.—When Socrates, in his laft difcourfe, is laying open the myfteries of his
philofophy, he informs his difciples that
above the heaven in which the ftars are
placed, there is another region denominated
the æther. The earth we inhabit he re-
prefents as a kind of fediment drawn from
the other, like thofe grofs particles that
fall to the bottom when duft is fprinkled
on a fine fluid. We, he obferves, who inhabit this grofs region are fo little fenfible
of it, that we fancy ourfelves to live in the
pureft one; " in the fame manner as per-
" fons fuppofed to inhabit the bottom of
" the fea might judge that furface through
" which they fee the fun and ftars, to be
" the heavens; and having never been
" able to raife themfelves above it, are ig-
" norant that we inhabit a purer and
" higher region than theirs, and meet
                                    " with

" with none to give them information *."
Here the sentiment of the philosopher is
strikingly and aptly conveyed by an image
corresponding to one object in every circumstance.

A temperate use of this figure produceth
likewise an happy effect in historical narration, where an author of genius is naturally led into it by the recital of some momentous transaction. His imagination
catcheth fire from the incident he relates;
and while he is studying to clothe it in
suitable language, suggests to him an adequate image. Thus describing a mob pre-

---

* Ημας ουν οικευτας εν τοις κοιλοις αυτης λεληθεναι
και οιεσθαι ανω επι της γης οικειν. Ωσπερ ει τις εν
μεσω τω πυθμενι τε πελαγες οικων, οιοιτο τε επι της
θαλαττης οικειν, και δια τε υδατος ορων τον ηλιον και
τα αλλα ασρα, την θαλατταν ηγοιτο ουρανον ειναι·
Δια δε βραδυτητα τε, και ασθενειαν, μηδεπωποτε επι τα
ακρα της θαλαττης αφιγμενος, μηδε εωρακως ειη εκδυς
και ανακυψας εκ της θαλαττης εις τον ευθαδε τοπον οσα
καθαρωτερος και καλλιων τυγχανει ων τε παρα σφισιν,
μηδε αλλε ακηκοως ειη τε εωρακοτος. ΠΛΑΤΩΝ.
ΦΑΙΔ. κεφ. νη.

cipitate

cipitate and furious in all its motions, he seizeth the idea of a torrent swelled with the storms of winter*. The array of an army on march somewhat disordered by inequality of motion is with great elegance and propriety compared to the swelling of a billow of the sea†. A prince naturally of good dispositions, but easily thrown into passion, to the ocean serene at times, but apt to be agitated by every breath of wind ‡. A historian may even

---

* Ο θεει τε εμπεσων τα πραγματα ανευ νου, χειμαρρω ποταμω ικελος.   ΗΡΟΔΟΤ. Θαλ.

† ΞΕΝΟΦ. περι Κυρ. p. 77.

‡ ΗΡΟΔΟΤ. Ευτερ. To the metaphors here mentioned we may subjoin, as one of the happiest and most beautiful illustrations that is to be met with, one that is made use of by the celebrated Lucretia Gonzaga to a learned man who complained of his poverty.—
" Essendo voi (says she) persona dotta, mi maraviglio che di sì strana maniera vi attristiate par la povertà:— quasi non sappiate la vita dei povere esser simile ad una navagatione presso il lito; & quella de ricchi non esser differente da coloro, che si ritrovano in mare. A gli uni è facile gittar la fune in terra, & condur la nave a sicuro liogo, & a gli altri e summamente difficile." Lettres di L. Gonzaga, p. 215.

sometimes

ſometimes uſe the ſublime images of poetry,
as we ſhall ſhow afterwards, either when
his mind is exalted by the greatneſs of an
event; when he is drawing an illuſtrious
character; or when certain remarkable
tranſactions require to be exhibited with
ſtrength and vivacity of colouring. In
all theſe caſes it would be uſeleſs to attempt
proving that it is the faculty of imagination which ſeizeth the illuſtration, as it is
judgment that applies it. Both theſe facts
are admitted on all ſides.

II. From contemplating the inventive
power as the fountain of beautiful illuſtration, we are next to conſider it as exerting
eminent influence in the *invention of incidents.* This laſt effect we may view as indicating immediately the prevalence of
fancy, without whoſe continued operation
we cannot ſuppoſe it at any time to take
place. It is conſtituted by no very difficult, but by a very ſtriking effort of this
faculty of the mind, calling up either fic-
titious perſonages, or ſuch as receive conſiderable heightening from its *creative* pencil; and adapting to each a ſeries of events,
from

from whofe novelty, variety, and importance we commonly judge of the degree in
which, imagination is conferred. This
amufing, ingenious, and inchanting exercife of fancy, forms, though not perhaps
the moft fublime, yet by far the moft various and agreeable lights in which we find
it difplayed. In following out thefe, the
mind is loft in a kind of ideal labyrinth;
in which the fame power that fuggefted the
incidents to the author, takes cognizance
of thefe principally, and excites the moft
pleafing fenfations to the perfon who pe-
rufeth his performance.

We fhall not, therefore, form an inadequate idea of the invention of incidents,
if we confider thefe as indications of an
imagination various, flexible, excurfive;
capable of confiderable extent of comprehenfion, and poffeffing a power of work-
ing up into the moft attractive fhapes,
materials fupplied by experience, and of
forming unufual combinations. But we
fhall be miftaken if we confider this criterion of genius (unlefs perhaps in fome
very rare inftances) as indicating the greatnefs,

nefs, fublimity, or even exuberance of that
power from which it takes its rife. This
laft obfervation will appear perhaps extraordinary to many readers at firft view;
becaufe as there is no characteriftic of imagination more obvious to every man than
that of contriving a complicated feries of
events; fo, with the bulk of mankind,
whatever implies excellence in the only
fphere of exertion which they have been
accuftomed to appropriate to this quality,
is naturally fuppofed to difcover its predominance not only in the greateft extent,
but in the higheft degree. Reflection
however will lead us to make a wide dif-
'tinction between thefe objects. But in
order to render this thoroughly compre-
henfible it will be neceffary to enter into
the fubject more particularly.

The incidents of any work confidered as
the immediate offspring of imagination,
may be viewed either as means of arreft-
ing attention by their variety, novelty,
and agreeable arrangement; or as circumftances that upon fome occafions aftonifh
and exalt the mind by that grandeur and
fublimity

fublimity of which they are viewed as indications. In the firft of thefe views it is
obvious, that if we judge a *great* imagination to be characterifed by the complicated incidents that it works into a fable,
we fhall then be led to admire the authors
of the *old romance* much more than thefe
of the Iliad, the Æneid, or Odyffey. For
the former have varied their narration
with a detail of imminent dangers, for-
tunate efcapes, unexpected interviews, fur-
prizing revolutions, fuccefsful temerity,
and refolute enterprize; to which in the
writings of the others (the Odyffey itfelf
not excepted) we meet with nothing of
this kind in all refpects adequate. Upon
the fame principle the Orlando Furiofo
might be preferred equally both to the
one and other, diftinguifhed as it is by fo
amazing a feries of ftupendous events, that
the mind is loft among them as in a labyrinth, and cannot difentangle the parts
of fo complicated a plan.

It will ferve however to convince us
that no very eminent fhare of imagination
is required to effectuate this purpofe if

we

we reflect that a comparifon of the works formerly mentioned with the Iliad, &c. will induce us to judge either that their authors posseffed but an inferior proportion of imagination, or that the irregularity with which it appears to have operated, is wholly unaccountable and extraordinary. For if we lay it down as a principle, that the invention of incidents is always the criterion of a vigorous imagination, it will then follow, that a faculty which is deemed equal at one time to the accomplifhment of a noble and interefting purpofe, ought likewife to be equal to another arifing from the fame caufe; and demanding it is fuppofed an exertion no higher than the former. Should we judge therefore the invention of characters to demand no greater effort of the faculty above-mentioned than is difplayed in the prefent cafe; we may naturally afk by what means it happens, that authors who have attained fo high a degree of excellence in one of thefe fpheres, are yet fo deficient in the other? for amidft all that variety of events by which the works that exhibit marks of

this

this invention are feparately characterifed, the reader, who may expect to meet with a correfponding variety of qualities in the minds and deportment of the principal perfonages, will be furprifed to find evidences in this point of view of barren invention, defective arrangement, and upon the whole of an infipid and difgufting uniformity. The numerous inftances which we meet with in thefe works, becaufe they indicate always the exiftence of imagination, are upon a fuperficial view fuppofed to determine its extent. But however beautiful in themfelves, yet the illufion fubfides when they are contemplated in this laft light, and we perceive the weight that ought to be laid upon them.

In the fame manner it muft be obvious that if the variety of events that may take place in a work, are no indications of a great, they are as little to be regarded as the marks of an exuberant imagination. The laft mentioned quality is faid to characterife this power of the mind when it is obferved to throw out a profufion of images; to clothe its objects in the moft

luxuriant

luxuriant drapery; when in fhort, not fatisfied with what is merely proper and expedient, it adds likewife whatever is fuppofed to be beautiful and ornamental.

However, very little attention will ferve to convince us that the talent of colouring Compofition is wholly diftinct from that of inventing incidents; and that though few men poffefs the former, who are not likewife capable of exercifing the latter of thefe, yet the exertion of this laft by no means implies a power in the perfon whom it diftinguifheth, of difplaying the other to equal advantage. Thus will it be faid that, in the works formerly mentioned where we meet with a feries of ftupendous and aftonifhing events; thofe picturefque images are introduced which place the various fcenes in fucceffion before the very eye of the fpectator * ? Are the

events

---

* It is not meant that thefe remarks fhould be applied either to the Orlando Furiofo, or to Spencer's noble allegorical poem, in both of which the defcription is almoft as diverfified as the events :—it is only intended to evince, from taking a view of works diftinguifhed

events even when fuppofed to be fuch as
might arreft the attention of a judicious
reader, as thefe defcribed, or does the author who invents, appear able to paint
them with that rich, vivid, and expreffive
colouring, which confers importance on
the moft trivial circumftances, and excites
admiration by fomething wholly independent of any tranfaction, as the mind is
taught to feel this paffion when a fenfation
entirely oppofite muft have been raifed
even by correct and chaftifed compofitions * ? Do we obferve, in fhort, that
the power of multiplying and diverfifying
events is naturally characteriftical of that
which throws out a blaze of imagery, and

---

guifhed only by numerous incidents, that the degree
of imagination required to effectuate this purpofe is
not fo eminent as is ufually fuppofed; and to affign
an author in whom this excellence is principally confpicuous, his proper rank in the fcale of genius.

* " Tum eft Hyperbole virtus, cum res ipfa de qua
loquendum eft, naturalem modum exceffit. Conce-
ditur enim amplius dicere, quia dici quantum eft non
poteft: meliufque ultra quam citra ftat oratio." Quintil.
lib. viii. cap. 6.

riots

riots in luxurious ornament; or do we affociate with this idea, that likewife of a
perfon,

Qui irritat, mulcet, falfis terroribus implet
Ut Magus, & modo me Thebis, modo ponit Athenis?

After all however it is not our defign
to infinuate that the fpecies of invention
laft mentioned is never to be regarded as
the criterion of fertile and copious imagination *. Our obfervations on this fubject regard rather the nature of thofe objects which this faculty delights to contemplate, than the degree in which (ex-
cluding this laft confideration) it may be
acknowledged to fubfift. The truth is,
our judgment of the genius of a writer
depends wholly upon the principle we lay
down as the moft effential teft of this uncommon character. If a difplay of various

---

* Εςι δε ου το οπωςυν (fays Longinus fpeaking of
the adjurations of Demofthenes) τι ομοσαι μεγα, το
δε πυ και πως, και εφ' ων καιρων, και τινος ενεκα. Αλλ'
εκει μεν ουδεν ες' ει μη ορκυς, και προς ευτυχυντας ετι,
και υ δεομενυς παρηγοριας τυς Αθηναιυς. ΤΜΗΜ. 15.

and complicated events is viewed as the
evidence of original invention, a judgment
will be formed of the imagination from
which thefe were derived, either as a
reader may be directed by the nature of
the incidents, or from their diverfified
combinations perceived to take place. If
on the other hand we confider the greatnefs and luxuriance of this faculty as indicated by the novelty and grandeur of
thofe illuftrations, fentiments, or characters which may pafs before the mind as a
fubject may require any one of thefe alternately to prevail :—in that cafe, the former
fpecies of invention will fuggeft the idea
of verfatility rather than elevation of
fancy ; and even an incident comparatively
great and interefting will rarely be confidered without the concurring circumftance
of exalted imagery, as the certain characteriftic of a fublime imagination.

In order to render this remark more
thoroughly comprehended,—let it be obferved,—that in eftimating the greatnefs
of any event whatever (contemplated in
the prefent point of view) we muft overlook

look the natural advantages or difadvantages of the perfons by whofe miniftration
it is fuppofed to be effectuated. By *natural*
advantages, &c. I underftand thofe qualities which we are apt invariably to affociate with a certain order of beings, as
fuperior ftrength, magnitude, velocity, perfeverance, whofe exiftence and combination being wholly independent of the
author, cannot reafonably be fuppofed to
give him additional merit. Thus Milton
arming his celeftial combatants with the
mountains; and Homer placing in the
hands of his human heroes broken rocks,
ftones of enormous fize, fhields and fpears
proportioned to their prowefs; and even
clothing them from the armoury of Vul-
can;—thofe two great geniufes are with
regard to thefe circumftances on a level
with each other. The comparative extent
and fertility of their invention muft be eftimated from proofs more immediately expreffive of an imagination able to explore
the latent fources of wonder, and to aftonifh the mind with great and unexpected
combinations.—Taking this truth there-

fore

fore for granted, it will follow that as an
author can juftly, lay claim to no great
merit as an inventor from the fuperior
ability of his perfons, fo the events that
arife from this circumftance, confidered as
adapted to it with juftnefs and propriety,
are proofs indeed of accuracy and clear
underftanding, but not of exuberance or
fublimity of imagination. In this laft
point of view there is indeed a kind of
prefumptive evidence that he who at the
fame time felects the moft dignified perfonages, and employs thefe in tranfactions
proportioned to their greatnefs, poffeffeth
himfelf an imagination fitted to take in
exalted and fublime ideas. But this very
prefumption is a decifive proof that the
events themfelves, however extraordinary,
carry no conviction along with them as to
this matter; fince after having heard thefe
recited, our judgment is ftill fufpended,
until we obferve the manner in which a
work is executed. Thus let us fuppofe
that we had been informed of the combat
of Michael and Satan, in the Paradife Loft,
without knowing at the fame time that

ftyle

ftyle of exalted imagery, and thofe circumftances expreffive of divine genius that are
wrought into the defcription. Was a
ftranger told more particularly that the
author of this work defcribed an engage-
ment betwixt beings of a fuperior order;
carried on fometimes by the conflux of
hofts encountering in the air, fometimes
by the combat of their leaders oppofed to
each other which fufpended the action;
let us judge him to be informed that the
prize for whofe poffeffion thefe combatants
fought, was as far beyond the reach of
man's ambition, as the perfons themfelves
exceeded him in ftrength and capacity;
and finally, that the action terminated by
the defcent of the Almighty, and by a
punifhment inflicted on his enemies befit-
ting omnipotence; it is obvious that the
evidence of the author's genius arifing
from this account would be at moft prefumptive and conjectural.—In order to be
thoroughly convinced whether he poffeffed
an imagination adequate to fo great a fubject, we would immediately have recourfe
to the work itfelf, and take in the circum-

ftances

stances formerly suggested.   When we
come to examine it in this point of view,
our attention is called off from the incidents to the characters, the sentiments, and
the splendor of the imagery.   In these
lights, when before the commencement of
the battle we meet with such a stroke as
the following :

> High in the midst, exalted as a God
> Th' apostate in his sun-bright chariot sat;
> Idol of majesty divine ; inclosed
> With flaming cherubim and golden shields;
> Then lighted from his gorgeous throne; for now
> 'Twixt host and host but narrow space was left
> A dreadful interval !

or when we behold this great arch-angel
recoiling from the stroke of Abdiel

> ——   ——   —— as if on earth
> Winds under ground, or waters forcing way,
> Sidelong had push'd a mountain from his seat,
> Half sunk with all his pines !

perhaps these, and a few other strokes of
the same kind would convey to a real judge
of poetic Composition a truer idea of the
genius of Milton, than a simple narration
of all the incidents (various and noble as
these are) of this divine performance.

From

From the whole then we may conclude, that a numerous and diverfified feries of incidents is always an evidence of a flexible and excurfive, commonly of a copious and comprehenfive imagination; and that in fome inftances it affords the higheft prefumption that this faculty is at the fame time fublime and exuberant. It forms likewife by far the moft various and agreeable exercife of this faculty; fo agreeable indeed, that even its wildeft and moft irregular excurfions afford an entertainment from which we never rife difgufted or fatiated. When the rules of credibility are once wholly violated, an author muft either give the utmoft difguft to his readers, or he ought to fet no bounds to the excurfions of fancy. This laft circumftance it is which gives fuch high merit of one kind to thofe delightful tales which go under the name of Arabian Night's Entertainments. The mind in perufing thefe is inchanted with the wild and variegated fucceffion of objects ever new, and dwells upon thefe with that kind of pleafure which it receives from a dream where many pleaf-

ing

ing illusions are floating perpetually before the imagination.   In this cafe we
permit ourfelves willingly to be impofed
upon, and rather than lofe the pleafure of
viewing fuch beautiful machinery as the
fylphs in the Rape of the Lock, or fuch
fublime beings as the Mohammedan Ge-
nii, we are contented to affign both a momentary exiftence.——But when actions
wholly beyond the power of man are afcribed to a merely human agent (as in
thofe monftrous collections of abfurdities
entitled, Clelia, Cleopatra, Caffandra, &c.)
and that in fo ferious a manner as if thefe
were real, we reject the impofture with
indignation, and confider the attempt as
an infult on the underftanding.

III. Having thus taken a view of imagination as the fource of beautiful imagery
and of diverfified incidents in the various
fpecies of Compofition, this power falls
next under our confideration as throwing
out new and ingenious fentiment.—Sentiment! (will fome reader exclaim) of what
fentiment is imagination the parent?—
This important province is confidered as
occupied

occupied wholly by the underſtanding. We have already obſerved that the power here contemplated ought always to be viewed either as acting in direct ſubſerviency to that of reaſon, or at leaſt as united with ſome ſhare of it. That ſentiments in order to have either propriety or connection with each other, muſt be ſuch as the underſtanding hath approved, is a truth which no man will call in queſtion. Of thoſe however, there are ſome which in conſequence of indicating a certain wildneſs which we conſider as a criterion of imagination; of being thrown out with promptitude rather than with accuracy; of being placed in looſe arrangement; of preſenting in ſhort, upon the whole, ideas which the mind rather contemplates as brilliant, with a tranſient ſatisfaction, than dwells on as juſt with fixed attention;— we aſcribe originally to that power whoſe various offices we here enumerate.

As thoughts that have a kind of wild originality derived from fancy, a man of reflection will conſider many of thoſe ingenious conjectures in philoſophy which
will

will not stand the test of a close examination. Sentiments of the other kinds are
such as we meet with most commonly either in superficial sketches of a subject not
brought to perfection ; or in those loose
pieces in which ideas are carelessly express-
ed as they occur, and methodised arrangement is professedly set aside. When we
consider Plato's account of the origin of
rivers, fountains, &c. from a capacious
reservoir in the bowels of the earth, we
admire the sublime genius of the philosopher, but are sensible that this notion
had its origin in his imagination. We
have already shewn that a close attention
to method often takes place even in those
sallies of wit and humour in which it is at
first view least perceptible. When this is
the case, we acknowledge the whole conduct to have mastery. There are, however,
pieces that please upon the whole as imitations of nature, in which a lively fancy
appears to have delineated objects just as
they occurred, and to have coloured so
highly thoughts that indicate quickness
rather than depth of conception, as to
merit

merit the appellation of having originally fuggefted them.

Thefe we muft obferve with very little attention to be the peculiar and immediate provinces of imagination; which, inftead of proceeding by flow and deliberate gradations in its procefs, making every ftep in the fcale of evidence lead naturally to another, is characterifed by its combination of diffimilar ideas, affociated from points of refemblance extremely remote, but whofe union, when once formed, is by this very circumftance rendered ftriking and uncommon. In the feries of thoughts, however, arifing in this manner from various exertions of the inventive faculty, fome will no doubt appear to have been immediately derived from the different external forms of nature. Others on the contrary, wholly fubordinate to, and incidentally rifing as it were from the former, will grow out from the principal fubject, which like a vigorous plant will thus appear furrounded with fhoots, which fhew the native ftrength and fertility of the root from which they fprung. Of thefe, the former

former conftitute a vein of fentiment purely original, and require a very large proportion of what is denominated plaftic or creative imagination :—the latter are only to be confidered as the confequences of being thrown into a certain track, in which when a man of no uncommon genius is once fet out, he may either improve upon, or add to the difcovery of the original inventor.

In whatever light, however, we view imagination as the parent of new and ingenious fentiment, it muft be acknowledged extremely hazardous to fubmit to its guidance in this delicate exertion. The province of imagery and that of incidents is indeed naturally occupied by this power, becaufe we know no other adequate to invention in either.—But in the fphere of fentiment, the qualities which formerly rendered fancy an agreeable and entertaining companion, become the immediate caufes of our diftruft and fufpicion. Thus its vivacity will lead us to be diffident of the clearnefs and comprehenfion of its theory ; its verfatility, of the juftnefs and

fymmetry

fymmetry of its proportions; its power
of feizing remote points of refemblance
will induce us to call in queftion the accuracy of imitation; and the unufual combinations which it prefents to the mind
will very naturally infufe a fufpicion of
their folidity and truth. Coherence and
proportion are never to be regarded as the
native offspring of imagination. This faculty will indeed invent in any branch of
fcience whatever; but without the fuper-
intendence of the former, its difcoveries
will confift of loofe and unfupported affertions, uncommon perhaps, and ftriking at
firft view; but which being placed in no
juft connection, and forming no links in
the chain of progreffive evidence, afford
not any folid improvement to the mind,
and are recollected only for their brilliance
and novelty. The mind likewife under
this direction is wholly inadequate to the
tafk of examining its decifions with coolnefs and leifure; and miftaking fome diftant refemblance of truth for the object of
which it is in purfuit, it is fatisfied with a
curfory

curfory view, and is called off immediately by fome newer profpect.

Upon the whole, therefore, in this fphere of imagination it will appear necef-fary beyond any other, that this power be kept within the clofeft limitations; as a foundation wrong-laid, or formed of im-proper materials, will render a ftructure however beautiful to the eye, yet defective in ftrength, folidity, and duration. Thus even where the judgment of an author is comprehenfive and penetrating, it may yet be employed by the former to fupport a whimfical and extravagant hypothefis. In this cafe indeed it will be no difficult mat-ter to diftinguifh the fpheres of each; and at the fame time that we admire the ro-mantic theory of fancy, we may contemp-late with wonder the acutenefs and fub-tility of that judgment which can fupport it by fubtle diftinctions and the moft plau-fible arguments. A work of this kind will however be viewed by the difcerning judge only as a fplendid monument of hu-man weaknefs; and as a proof of the many

errors

errors into which a man will be led by
endeavouring to render that convincing to
the reafon of others, which had its origin
from a different faculty in himfelf. No
work therefore will ever be valuable in
point of fentiment, unlefs when the imagination of the writer acts in immediate
fubferviency to his underftanding, which
reviews its various objects, and felects fuch
as have fitnefs for a certain end from the
promifcuous affemblage. Thus it will
happen that the tendency of thefe when
duly eftimated will be, to extend the reader's knowledge of his fubject, rather than
amufe him by ftriking on his fancy; and
that the whole will evince that fagacity
and good fenfe which is the parent of accuracy, perfpicuity, and proportion.

IV. From the preceding remarks on the
fpheres and operations of fancy in the prefent fubject, its importance in Compofition
will, we prefume, be fufficiently confpicuous, and its modes of exertion will become in fome degree familiar to the mind.
Of thefe however (various as they are) the
higheft and moft difficult remains to be
                                    confidered

confidered as difcovered in the higher fpe=
cies of Compofition in the invention of
characters. As we have already feen in
the courfe of our obfervations, that the
other indications of this faculty may appear in a confiderable meafure, where this
laft is either wholly wanting, or extremely
deficient; and as experience muft convince
us that the introduction of characters diftinguifhed by ftrokes of originality, and
fupported with dignity through a complicated feries of events; that this is one
of the rareft efforts of genius, and fuch as
requires the greateft proportion of intellectual qualities *; it will be no incurious
                                    refearch

---

* The truth of thefe remarks will be fully evinced,
if we confider only the various circumftances to which
an author muft attend in order to render his characters
fuch as may acquire approbation from the more judicious or difcerning. Thefe are fo juftly ranged, in
the following paffage, by an author who was well acquainted with human nature, that nothing farther
needs to be added on this part of the fubject.

"Natio: (primo exfequenda eft) nam & gentibus pro-
prii mores funt; nec idem in Barbaro, Romano, Græco
probabile eft. Patria: quia fimiliter etiam civitatum
                                              leges,

reſearch to examine the cauſe which renders this invention particularly difficult,
and which leads a reader of diſcernment
to value it ſo highly where it is found upon
examination to take place.

In that ſpecies of invention which ariſeth as we have already ſeen from known
objects placed in ſtriking and unuſual combinations, it will be acknowledged, that
the eaſieſt taſk is performed by that perſon whoſe excellence lies in having ſelected
from the variety of external ones thoſe
which have perhaps eſcaped the attention
of former imitators. The moſt arduous is
aſſigned to him, who ſurveying ideas purely
intellectual, and to whoſe diſcovery or
arrangement the ſenſes cannot be ſuppoſed

---

leges, inſtituta, opiniones habent differentiam. Sexus:
ut latrocinium facilius in viro, veneficium in fæmina
credas. Ætas: quia aliud aliis annis magis convenit.
Educatio & diſciplina: quoniam refert a quibus &
quo quiſque modo inſtitutus. Habitus corporis: du-
citur enim frequenter in argumentum ſpecies libidinis,
robur petulantiæ, his contraria in diverſum. For-
tuna: nec enim idem credibile eſt in divite aut pau-
pere propinquis, amicis, clientibus abundant & his
omnibus deſtituto, &c." Inſtitut. lib. v. cap. 10.

at all to contribute, is yet able to form
such various, juft, and animated expreffions; to accomplifh fuch new and happy
exhibitions of nature as refult from the
union of experience and difcernment. In
the firft cafe, an author has indeed the merit
of rendering a profpect peculiarly pleafing
by placing at proper intervals objects calculated to excite at the fame time pleafure
by their beauty, and wonder by their novelty. This merit, however, is confiderably leffened, when we reflect that the
materials of which the whole is compounded lie open to the fenfes. Imagination therefore, when employed to cull out
amidft an exhauftlefs variety, fuch forms
as have been paffed over without obfervation, acts the fame part as he who by a
peculiar quicknefs of external perception,
even without the aid of experience, fhould
obferve in a collection of diamonds a few
of the pureft water, and felect thefe for his
own ufe; after the whole had undergone
the fevereft fcrutiny, and every jewel of
real value was deemed to have become a
fucceffive object of admiration. Here
therefore

therefore we afcribe to the inventive faculty quicknefs and energy; we are ftruck
with the acutenefs and novelty of its perceptions. But employed as we ftill fuppofe it to be in the felection of objects
which have an independent original; or
in the imitation of beauties which it cannot improve; we confider it upon the
whole as poffeffing only a kind of fecondary originality; and its work as the fuccefsful difplay of an elegant landfcape.

When from this view of imagination in
the former cafe, where it works upon materials laid before it, we pafs to the latter,
where thefe in confequence of their nature
and diftance are collected at leaft with
greater difficulty, and the mind is agreeably flattered with the thought of raifing
in fome fenfe a new creation;—when we
contemplate this exertion of fancy, the
profpect affumes a very different appearance. The mind inftead of taking cognizance only of external objects, is employed to combine remote and abftracted
ideas, independent of it indeed with regard
to their original exiftence, but which are

placed

placed in a point of view wholly extraordinary, and whofe union forms altogether
an object never formerly perceived. While
the one therefore only imitates beauties
prefented to him by fenfation, the other
by a ftrenuous effort of reflection placing
the radical qualities by which man is diftinguifhed in an uncommon light, becomes
properly the inventor or maker of a new
character. He exceeds therefore the other
in the fame proportion as the painter, who
by throwing innumerable animated and
diverfified expreffions into the faces of an
audience, fuggefts the full meaning, action,
and vehemence of the orator; would be
admitted to excell him whofe merit lay in
difcerning and copying a caricatura *.

It

---

* That we may not be judged from the comparifon
ftated here, to have magnified one effort of imagination
at the expence of detracting from another in which
the energy and extent of that faculty are extremely
confpicuous; it may be proper to obferve, that, by
copying a caricatura, it is not meant to reprefent the
objects of defcriptive Compofition as in general either
mean in themfelves, or as indicating when pourtrayed
with accuracy and elegance, a fcanty proportion of the
inventive

It will be faid perhaps, in anfwer to
thefe obfervations on the invention of characters,

---

inventive faculty. It is only intended to fhow this in
its proper light, when fet in oppofition to that fpecies
of invention by which genius appears to be principally
characterifed. That authors of the firft clafs occupy
however, a very high rank in the ftyle of genius is
by no means denied, and will indeed be obvious to
any perfon who has tafte to difcern the refined and
exquifite beauties of defcription, and a fufficient fhare
of imagination himfelf to judge of the exertion by
which thefe in moft inftances are felected and pourtrayed. The ingenious author of the Effay on the
Writings and Genius of Pope, has pointed out fome
ftrokes of this kind in Thomfon's Seafons which are
in themfelves truly original, and have efcaped the
notice of former critics. Sect. ii. p. 42, &c. I know
no writer indeed who in a work profeffedly defcriptive
has equalled in all refpects this amiable poet. Theocritus indeed, at firft view, may appear to ftand in
competition with him, but the merit of the Greek
upon nearer infpection will appear to be inferior to
that of the Britifh poet. In the Idylliums of the former
it will be obferved that there is little defcriptive beauty
of the kind here referred to. The principal merit of
thefe inchanting poems confifts in their peculiar tendernefs of fentiment, and of an exquifite and inimitable fimplicity of expreffion. This fimplicity as it
feems to be incompatible with ftrength or variety of
epithet, excludes indeed naturally picturefque and in-

L 3   tenfely

racters, that we have not only in a preceding part of this work attempted to
prove

---

tenſely animated Compoſition. Accordingly we rarely
find Theocritus adopting the epithetical ſtyle; and
when he does ſo his epithets are the ſimpleſt imaginable. He generally gives every rural object its common deſignation, and hence ariſeth that unaffected eaſe
which as the genuine language of nature is ſo univerſally intereſting.

Ω Λυκοι, ω Θωες, ω αν ορεα φωλαδες αρκτοι
Χαιρεθ᾽, ω βωκολος υμμιν εγω Δαφνις ᴋᴋ᾽ ετ᾽ αν υλαν
Ουκετ᾽ αν αδρυμως, ᴋᴋ αλσεα· Χαιρ᾽ Αρεθοισα,
Και ποταμοι τοι χειτε καλον κατα Θυμβριδος υδωρ.

ΘΕΟΚ. ΘΥΡ.

In the Seaſons of Thomſon we meet with examples
of both ſpecies of the beauty here referred to, along
with others which the Sicilian bard appears not to have
been capable of rivaling. That union of ſimplicity
and tenderneſs, which forms ſo inchanting a combination, the reader will diſcover in the pathetic tale of
Amelia and Celadon, as inſtances of rich and exquiſite
painting are univerſally to be met with. This amiable and judicious poet is diſtinguiſhed likewiſe eminently by one excellence which I have not obſerved to
be aſcribed to him in the high degree he ſeems to deſerve. I mean that of improving the moſt trivial circumſtance by inſtructive and appropriated illuſtrations.
To adduce but one example :—how juſt and expreſſive
is the following image, when after having deſcribed
the

prove that imitation in ſome ſenſe extends to the whole compaſs of human inveſtigation; but this repreſentation of character proceeds in moſt caſes obviouſly from the principle above-mentioned, as it implies only the power in an author of copying ſuccefsfully thoſe characters with which experience and obſervation have rendered him converſant.

Admitting the truth of both theſe remarks, it ought ſtill however to be remembered, that in the firſt caſe where a character is marked with ſtrokes of originality, and ſtrikes us, upon the whole, rather in

---

the birds as conveying " the moſt delicious morſel to their young," the poet immediately ſays

——— Even ſo a gentle pair,
By fortune ſunk, but form'd of generous mould,
In ſome lone cott amidſt the diſtant woods,
Suſtain'd alone by providential Heaven,
Oft' as they weeping eye their infant train,
·Check their own appetites and give them all.
We ſhall conclude this long note by obſerving that deſcriptive poetry in ſuch inſtances as theſe, aſſumes indeed a dignified aſpect, and indicates in the writer an high ſhare of the moſt valuable qualities both intellectual and moral, that are conferred on mankind.

the

the light of what may be suppofed to take place, than of what we have had occafion to witnefs as actually exifting; in this cafe we have already feen the term invention to be applied with particular propriety. In the other, where the imitation is more perceptible, we muft yet acknowledge it from the refined and abftracted nature of the objects imitated, to demand an exertion of which an imagination able to ftrike off exact refemblances in the field of external beauties, might be deemed incapable.

Great, however, and comprehenfive as we muft fuppofe an imagination to be, that is adequate in moft inftances to the invention of characters, reflection will yet lead us to diftinguifh the degrees in which this faculty takes place, as indicated by the following circumftances: by the various qualities that enter into a character; by the difcriminating ftrokes that ferve to give it ftrength and peculiarity; and by its grandeur as arifing from native greatnefs and fublimity of genius.

Thefe indications we fhall here confider feparately, in order to have a full view

of

of the province of this power in Compofition.

1, With regard to the firſt mentioned,
the qualities that enter into a chara&er, it
will be acknowledged that the Ulyſſes of
Homer, diſtinguiſhed by ſo various an
aſſemblage of ſtriking qualifications, ſets
the inventive powers of this writer in a
much ſtronger light than either his Neſtor
or Diomed, whoſe chara&ers are more
uniform. Theſe laſt, however, taken in
with the former, fill us with the higheſt
admiration of a mind capable of varying this
aſſemblage ſo much, and of comprehending
the parts of ſo complicated a detail. It is
indeed a taſk incomparably more difficult
to exhibit a variety of diſtin& qualifications as combined to form one chara&er,
than to parcel theſe out as it were among
many perſons, and to aſſign each a ſeparate virtue or vice which along with a few
common and ſubordinate acquirements
complete the exhibition.

When a very various aſſemblage of
qualities meet in one chara&er, each muſt
receive different expreſſions according to
thoſe

thofe with which it is united, while at the fame time the diftinguifhing marks muft be uniformly maintained by which it ought on all occafions to be known. When, on the other hand, only a few are brought together, many of thefe expref- fions are neceffarily loft, fuch of them in particular as arife from the union of one qualification with others that are diffimilar to it. The office therefore that is affigned to imagination, when a prevailing quality is exhibited only in few lights, even though ftrong and picturefque, is deemed with great juftice inferior to that which it exercifeth when the fame quality, whether moral or intellectual, is placed before the mind in many different views, as it re- ceives a caft from intricate, ftriking, and unufual combinations.

In the portrait of Ulyffes that wifdom which forms his diftinguifhing character- iftic, is happily expofed in fo many points of view arifing from other virtues, or even imperfections which it calls out to obferv- ation, as will ferve to illuftrate fully the preceding remarks.—Thus when joined with

with juft and glowing indignation it prompts, him to chaftife vice or infolence (as in the punifhment of Therfites in the Iliad, or of the fuitors in the Odyffey) with a feverity unexpected perhaps, and fuddenly exerted, but which appears upon examination to have been the effect of thought, and adapted properly to the occafion *. When co-operating with heroic fortitude and the love of his country, it becomes in the laft exigence a principle by which he is induced to place himfelf in the breach againft a victorious enemy †, all other expedients having proved ineffectual ‡. Animated by zeal in a critical moment, it produceth the moft active and vigorous meafures §. In dangerous circumftances, on the contrary, it is cool, confiderate, and fruitful of refources ¶. When joined with ambition, it is eloquent and infinuating ‖, intrepid and refolute; the fame

---

* ΙΛΙΑΔ β. ΟΔΥΣ. χ.   † Id.

‡ ΙΛΙΑΔ. λ. 401, &c.   § Id. β. 265.

¶ See his night-adventure with Diomed ΙΛΙΑΔ. κ. 240, & feq.

‖ See his fpeech to Achilles. ΙΛΙΑΔ. Γ. 225, &c.

power

power which fuggefts at one time the moft
prudent councils *, permitting at another
the nobleft emulation †.—In fine, amidft
all this variety of paffions, temptations,
and dangerous enterprizes, inftead of being
fometimes dropt as might naturally be expected, or of acting frequently by interrupted exertions, it is a confiftent and operating principle, affuming the direction
upon every occafion, and appearing moft
confpicuous in thofe fituations where from
the paffions of human nature it was moft
difficult to be preferved.—In the two characters of Neftor and Diomed, diftinguifhed
as both are by the fame predominant
quality, it is placed, however, in lights extremely different both from that of Ulyffes,
and from each other.   The wifdom of the
former is principally the refult of experience in an old man, endowed naturally
with fagacity and penetration; as that of
the latter is the refult of early reflection in
a young warrior, who, unaided himfelf by
experience, has ftill docility enough to re-

* ΙΛΙΑΔ. λ. 312. τ. 154. 215.
† Id. η. 168. ψ. 755, &c.

ceive

ceive inftruction from a fage with whom, notwithftanding the difparity of years, a general fimilarity of difpofition eftablifheth an intercourfe of good offices *.

---

* The friendfhip that is obferved on every occafion to take place betwixt Neftor and Diomed, difcovers at the fame time the judgment of Homer, and his exten- five knowledge of the human heart. The laft men- tioned might be fuppofed at firft view rather to have made choice of Ulyffes, whom he appears indeed to treat upon all occafions with particular refpect. But befides that thefe laft might be confidered as rivals, a character which neceffarily excludes any great degree of intimacy, the general fimilarity which takes place betwixt Neftor and Diomed renders their mutual friendfhip perfectly natural. Neftor poffeffeth that calm and confiderate valour which appears always to have been regulated by prudence, and which is now moderated by a very confiderable fhare of experience. Diomed with both the former of thofe qualities, is from his early youth deficient in the latter; and ap- plies to the fage whom he reverenceth as a father, to have this defect compenfated. This affection will likewife appear to be ftill more natural, if we confider it as beftowed on a perfon who poffeffed great benig- nity and fweetnefs of difpofition. Thus the eloquence of Neftor is particularly characterifed as diftinguifhed by the milder and more infinuating graces.

—————— τοισε δε Νεϛωρ
Ηδυεπης ανορουσε, λιγυς Πυλιων αγορητης
Τοῦ και απο γλωσσης μελιτος γλυκιων ρεεν αυδη.

ΙΛΙΑΔ. α.

It

It may indeed be obferved, with the ftricteft truth, that in the whole conduct of this perplexing detail an eminent fhare of judgment is indifpenfibly requifite, as well as a vigorous and extenfive imagination. That the laft of thefe however is principally confpicuous in it will be acknowledged when we reflect that its peculiar province, as hath been already evinced, is to give that air of originality to any performance which refults from a new and various affemblage of objects; and in proportion as thefe are fingular in their kind, or diverfified in their fituation, are we naturally induced to confider that genius as creative and exuberant which gave birth to fo many agreeable and interefting circumftances.—In this procefs the power of invention is particularly diftinguifhed as taking an enlarged and extenfive range in the field of fpeculation; as affociating ideas drawn from the moft remote refources; and as aftonifhing the mind by the variety, beauty, and perpetual novelty of its materials. To reafon the difficult tafk is affigned of preferving coherence and fymmetry

metry betwixt the feparate members of the piece amidft a diverfity of objects con- ftantly fluctuating, and therefore demand- ing the united efforts of difcernment, ex- perience, and attention.

2. Thefe remarks on imagination as difcovered in the invention and conduct of a complicated character, will enable us to form fome idea of that degree of it which is neceffary to give the perfons lively, pe- culiar, and difcriminating features. As therefore, in the province already pointed out, the inventive power is required to poffefs extent and comprehenfion, fo in the prefent we confider as difplayed to the greateft advantage its vigour and energy. A ftrong and vivid imagination is known as certainly by this criterion, as a fight uncommonly piercing and vigorous is dif- tinguifhed by its clear, and accurate per- ception of external objects, either delicate in their ftructure, or requiring from their pofition an organization peculiarly excel- lent. In characters, as in every other fpe- cies of inventive exertion, there are certain marks, by whofe aid, even when thefe are

recommended by novelty and supported with judgment, we may yet discover the radical strength or imbecility of the power from which they derived their origin. Thus in the other spheres of this faculty its coldness and debility are supposed to be indicated by a certain languor of expression much more easy to be felt than described, by sparing and feeble illustrations; by faint and inadequate colouring; and, finally, by so obvious a defect in the picturesque and animated as leaves us at no loss to distinguish the cause from which these proceed. This debility likewise becomes always most conspicuous when the author attempts to excel in the higher species of Composition. Some degree of discernment may perhaps be deemed necessary to discover it in the more simple branches of this art; because where strength and energy are not considered as indispensibly requisite, it is sometimes difficult to distinguish that execution which a subject naturally demands from that which is the consequence of a defective imagination. But when some strenuous effort is required, and when the mind

sinks

ſinks under the greatneſs of its ſubject, even a common obſerver becomes ſenſible of the defect, and can judge of the inequality betwixt the theme and the ability of the writer. A number of characters therefore, in the ſame manner as images, in which we find no great variety of qualities, and the greater number common, or but little diſcriminated from each other, may be contemplated as marks of an imagination inadequate to this high ſtrain of invention, even when in other reſpects it is capable at once of enlarged comprehenſion, and of vigorous exertion*.

As

* It would, no doubt, be deemed temerity to apply this obſervation to one of the greateſt geniuſes of antiquity, who has otherwiſe ſo nobly occupied the higheſt ſphere of human excellence; I mean the divine author of the Æneid; did not the teſtimony of ſome excellent critics concur with proofs that ariſe from the poem itſelf compared with the Iliad, to ſhow its juſtice and propriety. Thoſe have with great truth remarked, that in his *fidus Achates,* his *fortis Gias, fortiſque Cloanthus,* his *Niſus* and *Euryalus,* whoſe adventure is ſo obviouſly copied from Homer, and whoſe characters are ſo little diſtinguiſhed by ſtrokes of originality: and finally, that his Æneas himſelf, a calm and moderate

As a ftrong imagination therefore will give to its characters fignificance and pe- culiarity, fo we may eftimate in a great meafure, the degree of its ftrength from the nature of that theme, or action, which it is employed to celebrate. Thus we have feldom reafon to expect that a man of cool and temperate fancy will make choice of a fubject demanding not merely the temporary, but almoft invariable pre- valence of qualities, in which he muft feel himfelf (comparatively at leaft) to be deficient. Even fuppofing him from the partiality of mankind in circumftances of this nature, not to be fenfible of this de- fect, yet the choice of fuch a man will fall much more naturally upon a general fub- ject (fuch as that of the Æneid or Phar-

---

hero, brave indeed, pious and intrepid; but indi- cating from thofe very qualities an imagination more chafte and temperate, than the fierce, the impetuous, the implacable Achilles; our critics have remarked, that thefe are all indications of an invention unequal to this high rank of excellence, and defective in that vigour with regard to peculiarity of character, which however is difplayed fo eminently in the narration, ex- preffion, and colouring of his work.

falia),

ſalia), great perhaps, and comprehenſive, with whoſe magnificence the mind is elevated and dilated, than merely upon the effects of one particular paſſion, and that too the moſt impetuous and ungovernable of all that actuate the human mind. In this laſt caſe it muſt be obvious that the firſt propoſal of ſuch a theme would ſuggeſt to us the idea of an imagination rapid, glowing, and intenſely ſpirited from the conſideration of thoſe ſallies abrupt and animated to which this paſſion muſt neceſſarily give riſe, and of that dark but expreſſive colour, which muſt naturally tincture and predominate in the character.

Contemplated in the preſent point of view, the author of the Iliad will be found to excel all other uninſpired writers as much in the ſtrength of thoſe ſignatures which diſtinguiſh his perſons, as in the ſplendor, richneſs, and beauty of his illuſtrations. His ſubject is preciſely of that kind which a daring imagination could alone have adopted. He breaks into it likewiſe with an abruptneſs ſuited to the theme, and with one ſtroke of his creative

M 2 pencil

pencil gives the outlines of an hero un-
bridled, furious, implacable, refentful, in
whom thofe diftinguifhing qualities are
afterwards called out, and are fo ftrongly
marked in the detail of his conduct.

MHNIN αειδε Θεα Πηληιαδεω Αχιληος

" Sing (fays he) O goddefs, the wrath
" of Achilles the fon of Peleus."—The
Roman poet, whofe imagination in confequence of its equability was more fitted
to take a comprehenfive furvey of various
objects, but lefs to difcriminate thefe from
each other by vigour and energy, opens
his fubject with a detail of circumftances,
which, however noble and interefting in
themfelves, yet ftrike not the mind fo
forcibly when taken together, as the fingle
ftroke of his inimitable rival *.

Arma

---

* The remark made in the text on the invention of
Homer, as difplayed in the ftrength of his ideas, and
in the mafterly ftroke by which his perfonages are
marked and introduced, will imprefs the mind more
ftrongly when we compare the introduction of the
Odyffey with that of the Iliad, as exprefive of his own
character in the various periods of life. As in the
latter, when his genius was in its full maturity and
vigour,

Arma virumque cano. Trojæ qui primus ab oris
Italiam fato profugus, Lavinaque venit.
Littora, &c.

It were eafy to evince by a variety of
examples drawn from the higheft ftandards
of poetic Compofition, both ancient and
modern *, the manner in which a genius
diftinguifhed by the characteriftic above-
mentioned will difplay it in the various
pourtrait of manners. The reader, however, by carrying the preceding obfervations along with him will be able to judge
for himfelf in this matter, a fuller difcuffion of which belongs more properly to
a fubfequent fection.

3. From the confideration of an extenfive and vigorous invention as difplayed
in the various ingredients, and in the dif-

---

vigour, we find him breaking abruptly into his fubject,
and choofing the moft various and difficult imaginable; fo in the former when the fire of his imagination
muft have fubfided with age, we find his hero defcribed as recollected and moderate, and the bard entering coolly into the detail of circumftances when he
propofes his theme.

* Ανδρα μοι εννιπε Μουσα πολυτροπον, ός μαλα πολλα
Πλαγθη.

criminating

criminating ſtrokes of a character, we are led naturally to view it in this enlarged ſphere of its operation as exhibiting evidences of greatneſs and ſublimity. Theſe we ſuppoſe always to be indicated when ſome perſonage of ſuperior merit is introduced either as a principal or ſubordinate actor in the piece, and when amidſt many critical, important, and unexpected incidents, we find the native dignity ſo invariably ſupported, as that without difficulty we can from the circumſtances in which the perſon is placed, form an idea of the manner in which his actions will be regulated. We muſt here, however, make a diſtinction betwixt comprehenſion and ſublimity of genius as diſcovered in this conduct, ſince the former of theſe is principally conſpicuous in the nature of the ſubject *,

whereas

---

* It is neceſſary to obſerve here, that this view of a comprehenſive ſubject as indicating in ſome branches of Compoſition a great imagination, ought by no means to be confounded with what hath been advanced in a former part of this ſection on the invention of incidents. It was obſerved that theſe laſt however great

or

whereas the latter wholly relates to ſome
individual as the perſon to whom all is
referred. Thus in the Paradiſe Loſt it is
obvious that the firſt propoſal of a ſubject
comprehending heaven, hell, the chaos,
and origin of all things; a ſtate of nature
altogether different from the preſent, and
objects in the ſame manner diſtinguiſhed
from thoſe with which we are converſant,
that the propoſal of this ſubject muſt fill
our minds with the idea of a genius capable of taking in an uncommon compaſs of
thought, and great in proportion to the
abſtracted nature of thoſe objects it was

---

or extraordinary afford no certain characteriſtic of a
ſublime imagination, unleſs when ſomething exalted
appears likewiſe either in the ſentiment or imagery.
When we obſerve a ſeries of theſe extremely complicated to be diſpoſed in exact order, and to follow each
other ſo naturally as to give uniformity and conſiſtency
to a fable, we judge with propriety the underſtanding
of the author to be accurate, and his imagination
comprehenſive.—But to conſtitute a *great* diſplay of
genius, each of theſe taken ſeparately muſt have ſome
proportion of grandeur in order to form one noble and
magnificent whole. In this caſe, the comprehenſive
nature of the ſubject may be ſaid to denominate not
only an extenſive, but a great imagination.

M 4   employed

employed to contemplate. The character
of fublimity, on the other hand, arifeth
principally from the deportment and conduct of certain diftinguifhed perfonages.

In general it may be obferved on this
branch of the fubject, that nothing contributes more to fix the denomination of
fublimity upon a work, than when a great
mind is reprefented as rifing fuperior to
the fhocks of adverfity. In circumftances
invariably profperous, or even chequered
fometimes with the fhade of affliction, it
is difficult to fupport this defignation with
propriety, which feems to require conftantly that the fympathetic feelings of human nature fhould be awakened, and that
the mind fhould be able to form fome
comparifon betwixt the paft and the prefent, and dwell on both with a folemn and
melancholy pleafure. This circumftance it
is which confers fuch peculiar dignity on
the Satan of Milton, who is therefore reprefented by a rival poet as the hero of
his work. When we contemplate this
auguft perfonage as maintaining a fteady
and unfhaken fortitude in a fituation of

all

all others the moſt ruinous, where even
——— ——— Hope never comes,
　That comes to all :.
when we behold him coaſting the regions
of darkneſs in his arduous journey to earth,
encountering alone the ſhock of elements;
daring his tremendous foe to the combat;
deceiving Uzziel, oppoſing Gabriel; and,
finally, perſiſting amidſt dangers of every
kind until he had effectuated his purpoſe;
when in all theſe ſituations we keep in
our eye the glory of his former ſtate, and
yet ſee him coping with the higheſt cre-
ated beings, even when he ſtood
——— With faded ſplendor wan:
the pernicious nature of his enterprize, the
malevolence of his diſpoſition, and even
the deſtruction which he is repreſented to
have brought upon the human race, cannot prevent us from ſurveying him with
an admiration and pity, which though it
ſhould be culpable, cannot be ſuppreſſed.

　In fact, however, the admiration excited by qualities of this kind upon being
traced to its ſource, will be diſcovered to
exiſt without dependence, not only on moral character of what kind ſoever, but even
on

on the more ftriking light in which a perfon muft appear when contemplated by an individual as a friend or an enemy. In this laft cafe, it may indeed happen, that the medium of prejudice will either obfcure the luftre of thofe qualities where they are acknowledged to fubfift, and by that means confiderably leffen our admiration; or by concealing thefe from us altogether, will remove the caufe from which this paffion proceeds. But both the inftances above-mentioned are proofs that the theory we have here laid down proceeds upon juft principles, as it is obvious that a mind diftinguifhed by the virtues of fortitude, intrepidity, and a certain daring ambition, is contemplated in general with an admiration which can have no other foundation but thofe excellencies, fince we find this always correfponding to the degree in which the former are fuppofed to take place.

From this train of obfervation we will readily comprehend the reafon for which true fublimity of character requires moft frequently to be difplayed in adverfity.

The

The virtues of which we have ſeen it principally to conſiſt, are all of them either
of that kind (as thoſe of fortitude, patience,
intrepidity, &c.) which can only be exerted in actual and reſolute oppoſition to
evils, or of that, (as hardy enterprize, or
aſpiring ambition) which leads us immediately to foreſee that theſe muſt be en-
countered. In the laſt mentioned caſes the
ſublime of character appears perhaps greater
than in the firſt. Imagination in this inſtance is left at liberty to form an idea of
perils to be met with when the perſon ſets
out on ſome daring and arduous attempt,
whereas in the other, it is fixed down to
the contemplation of ſuch events as the
author has already invented. So much
does our pleaſure in all caſes whatever ariſe
rather from the expectation of what is to
happen, than from the enjoyment of what
is actually poſſeſſed.

Thus we have endeavoured by following the track of imagination along the
various ſcenes in which its influence is diſplayed, to ſhow its real value and importance in the art of Compoſition; to diſtinguiſh

tinguifh its genuine exertions when guided
by found judgment from fuch as are the
confequences of its intemperance, or which
it fhares in common with other intellectual
faculties, to fhow the degree of its ftrength
or comprehenfion as determined by the objects to which it is directed; and, finally,
to afcertain its merit as the power of invention by marking its effects in the fimpleft as well as the moft diverfified fields
of its exercife.   We might, indeed, have
further contemplated this power as the
parent of allegorical perfonages, and as
productive of that machinery with which
fable is decorated.   But in both thefe refpects (as far as they have not fallen within
the preceding obfervations) we will naturally be led to confider imagination in the
fubfequent fections of this effay.

SECTION IV.

Of Penetration, or Diſcernment, as it re-
gards Compoſition.

THE offices of the two principal intellectual powers we have conſidered
particularly in the preceding ſections, as
far as the preſent ſubject is concerned.
Before we proceed any farther, it may be
proper to pauſe a little here, and take a
general view of what each of theſe topics
hath ſuggeſted. The faculty of reaſon,
and that of imagination we have ſeen to
be eſſentially different from each other;
not only in their original choice of objects,
but in their method of procedure, in order
to obtain an ultimate purpoſe. The underſtanding we have obſerved, when employed either in methodiſing the parts of a
comprehenſive plan ſo as to give the whole
proportion, or in carrying on a proceſs of
regular argumentation to a period, accompliſheth its purpoſe univerſally by means
that indicate caution and circumſpection.
On

On the contrary, the aſſemblages that are formed by imagination conſiſt of ideas inſtantaneouſly combined, in which the mind expects to meet rather with animated expreſſions than juſt diſpoſition; and with ſtrokes that excite momentary ſenſations, inſtead of ſuch as terminate in permanent conviction. When therefore, it was obſerved in another part of this work, that deliberate recollection and a *gradual* rather than a *rapid* ſucceſſion of ideas, are criteria that accompany a talent for Compoſition*; the remark is to be underſtood of minds, in which this faculty, though loſing no part of its natural quickneſs and energy, is fixed by that of judgment ſo ſteadily upon each particular object as to contemplate and diſplay it with preciſion. The inventions (if we may thus term them) of fancy when viewed apart, as far as ſuch a view can be taken of it, bear no marks of this preciſion. Its flights are ſudden and irregular; its tranſitions frequent and unconnected; and its procedure

---

* Sect. i. p. 31.

ſuch

fuch as difpaffionate reafon rather negleds than cenfures.

When we examine with clofe attention that combination of qualities greatly diver-fified, by which the charaders of men are diftinguifhed, refledion will point out to us the marks of an intelledual power dif-ferent from both the former in its manner of operation; whofe effeds we fhall en-deavour to unfold more particularly, as it has not as far as we know been formerly diftinguifhed from others. The reader will judge from what has been already ad-vanced, that the power here referred to is that denominated the faculty of *Difcern-ment*, of which we formerly endeavoured to give fome general idea. We fhall here enforce thofe obfervations, 1. by making fome remarks on the charaders or fignatures by which this power of the mind is parti-cularly diftinguifhed from the others, and on the union by which it is conftituted. 2. We fhall confider its peculiar province, and manner of operation in the various de-partments of Compofition.

1. The

1. The word Difcernment we have formerly obferved, points out " that mental
" faculty which, without carrying on any
" regular procefs, comprehends as it were
" inftantaneoufly the proper manner of
" treating any fubject, by fixing upon the
" points that are of primary importance;
" and accomplifheth, at once, by thefe
" means purpofes which the underftand-
" ing *alone* cannot effectuate in fome cafes
" by any exertion; and abftains in thofe
" to which it is adapted by a flow and de-
" liberate procedure *." The term in this
acceptation correfponds to a fight clear,
piercing, and qualified to take immediate
as well as ample cognizance of the objects
that are prefented to it.   That there is a
quality of the mind diftinguifhed by thefe
characters, no man (whether poffeffed of
it himfelf or not) will call in queftion, who
reflects upon the ideas which the decifions
and fentiments of thofe in whom it is
judged to predominate, call naturally up
to his thought.   When we attempt to ex-

---

* Sect. i. p. 11.

plain

plain any point in which there is confiderable difficulty, as many, perhaps the far
greater number of men, muft be gradually
led to comprehend it by having every part
of the procefs clearly laid open, and every
objection regularly fuperfeded; there are a
few with whom this method of proceeding
is unneceffary. As foon as the fubject is
laid down, and a few principal evidences
laid before them, thefe take in the whole
by a kind of intuitive perception; fupplying the intermediate means fo quickly, as
to render particular reprefentation inex-
pedient. Such perfons we commonly denominate men of *quick parts,* or of *acute
intellect.* When engaged in the fame manner in the bufinefs of life, the fame qualities by whofe exertion they are *acute critics*
in the former inftance, render them *penetrating obfervers* in the other. In this laft
cafe indeed, fome part of that knowledge
of mankind which experience confers, muft
be acquired, without whofe influence the
greateft abilities muft fail of judging with
adequate comprehenfion. But when there
is a concurrence of this laft with certain

qualities which we fhall explain afterwards, the man becomes capable of entering deeply into the characters of thofe with
whom he is converfant. He gains a facility of reading in the countenance thofe
fenfations, however clofely concealed, that
actuate the heart*; and of collecting from
cafual, loofe, and unfupported affertions
thrown out apparently at random, as hints
of what might have been advanced, fuch
fignificant and diftinguifhing criteria as
are decifive of their juftnefs, propriety, and
importance.

When we confider with the fame object
in view, the finer arts as they are called,
particularly thofe of poetry and eloquence,
effects fimilar to fuch as have been already
mentioned, naturally point to the fame
original caufe. The tranfitions particularly
in purely poetic compofition, are often

---

* " Eft in primis *acuti* (fays a penetrating judge of
human nature) videre, quo judex dicto moveatur,
quid refpuat : quod ex *vultu fæpiffime*, & aliquando etiam
dicto, factove ejus deprehenditur. Et inftare profici-
entibus, & ab iis quæ non adjuvant, quam molliffime
pedem oportet referre." Quintil. Inftit. lib. vi. c. 5.

abrupt,

abrupt, and at firft view appear to be unconnected. The thoughts likewife feem
to ftand detached from each other; and by
the high colouring of imagination are frequently rendered obfcure. Eloquence we
have feen in the fame manner to be often
moft confpicuous, when abrupt interroga-
tions, and ftrokes of nature and paffion are
thrown into a difcourfe, whofe connection
with the preceding circumftances is apparently remote, and to be fully comprehended only by thofe who have a thorough
knowledge of the heart *. As the perfon
who works by thefe means upon the moft
powerful principles of human nature, muft
know every method of calling them into
ftrenuous exercife; he likewife who is
fenfible of the full force of every motive
that is applied for fuch purpofes, muft, it

---

* " In iis caufis (quæ funt frequentiffimæ) quæ vel
folis extra artem probationibus, vel miftis continentur,
afperrima in hac parte dimicatio eft, nec alibi
dixeris magis *mucrone pugnari.* Nam & firmiffima
quæque memoriæ judicis inculcanda funt, & præftan-
dum quicquid in actione promifimus, & refellanda
mendacia." Id. ibid.

is obvious, poffefs a confiderable proportion of the fame intelligence; and of the
faculty that lays open to him the heart
and affections.

That this mental power, by whatever
defignation it may be made known, ought
to be confidered in a diftinct point of view
from either of thofe whofe offices we have
yet mentioned, will be obvious from the
following account of its nature and effects.

1. We have already taken notice of one
ftriking difference betwixt the faculty of
difcernment, and the underftanding or
reafoning power ftrictly fo called, as the
former is diftinguifhed by a quicknefs of
perception, which ftands in oppofition to
the flow and cautious procedure of the
latter *. This is one of thofe obfervations
which

---

* It is from having viewed the underftanding in
this light that an eminent writer is enabled to lay
down fo particularly the different methods by which its
influence may be counteracted. Thefe he reduces to
three heads, which he confiders as extending to the
principal fubjects in which it is exercifed.—" Vel per
illaqueationem fophifmatum quod ad *Dialecticam*
pertinet; vel per præftigias verborum, quod ad
Rhetoricam;

which it is neither necessary nor indeed practicable to confirm by regular argumentation. Every man's feeling and experience must decide on the truth of it. It is only requisite that we observe, in order to know how far the powers here compared together, really differ in their method of operation; whether there are not many persons possessed of unquestioned judgment as discovered either in carrying on, or in examining a regular procefs of argument, who far from taking in the whole the view of capital strokes when exposed separately, find even the images that illustrate sentiment to some minds, so many obstructions to a perfect knowledge of the subject; and enter into it thoroughly only when objects pass succeffively in re-

---

Rhetoricam; vel per affectuum violentiam quod ad *Ethicam.* Quemadmodum enim in negotiis quæ cum aliis contrahimus, vinci quis & perduci solet, vel astu, vel importunitate, vel vehementia, ita etiam in illa negotiatione interna, &c. Neque vero tam infeliciter agitur cum humana natura, ut illæ artes & facultates ad rationem deturbandam valeant; neutiquam vero ad eandem roborandam & stabiliendam." Bac. de Augment. Scient. lib. vi. p. 366. edit. Ravesten.

view,

view, defcribed in the fimpleft words, and
placed in arrangement fo nearly perfect,
as not to be deficient in any point of the
fmalleft confequence. Should this be granted, we are naturally led to afk, whence it
is, that men, who unqueftionably poffefs
this intellectual power, and exhibit when
called upon every indication of it, difcover
at the fame time the traces of a procedure
which never characterifes the man of mere
underftanding? The *different manner of
operation* here evidently diftinguifheth this
laft mentioned faculty from that to which
we apply the word Difcernment, in whofe
conduct we obferve the marks of underftanding eminently confpicuous, along with
fuch as appear to be derived from fome
original wholly diftinct from it.

2. But not only is this quality different
from the former in the inftance above-
mentioned. We fhall find it to be fo in
an equal degree, when we confider Comprehenfion as fhared in common by both.

The man of Difcernment may be faid in
general to form a much more comprehenfive view of things than he who poffeffeth

judgment

judgment alone, however clear and extenfive; becaufe he takes into his eftimate,
as we fhall fee immediately, a much larger
and more diverfified feries of objects. It
ought however to be obferved at the fame
time, that as the fphere in which this faculty acts is much larger than that of the
other, fo its decifions are fometimes lefs
accurate. The reafon of this we fhall difcover upon giving attention to their procedure. The underftanding by having
fhifted and examined its objects in every
point of view, difcovers at laft fuch defects as were at firft leaft perceptible; and
thus takes into its furvey *whatever* is
finally fubfervient to its ultimate purpofe.
The difcerning faculty on the other hand
from its affinity to imagination, attracted
moft commonly by ftriking, animated, and
peculiar expreffions, is lefs attentive to general uniformity. What it obtains therefore on the part of ftrength and novelty,
it is often in hazard of lofing on the fide
of exactnefs and proportion. Thefe obfervations will be moft clearly illuftrated
by trying an example.

It

It is acknowledged univerfally, that true difcernment is in nothing more confpicuous, than in combining the various principles of action into fome *original character*; or in judging of this combination when prefented to view. There is an infinite variety of motives by which conduct may be regulated according to the fituation in which a man is placed; and in adapting a particular incident fo happily to the diftinguifhing paffion or principle as to place it in a clear and ftriking light, an author fhows himfelf moft particularly to be a penetrating judge of human nature. But while he is intent upon this circumftance, the power that enables him to do juftice to one part of a character, may at the fame time overlook another of effential confequence, and thus by difcerning only what is fuitable at the time, without attending to the mutual coherence of parts, may finifh one branch with the utmoft accuracy, while an obvious incongruity takes place among all. Thus it is that difcernment, from its energy and quicknefs, often forms an eftimate whofe defects the underftand-

ing

ing is called in afterwards to fupply. Cool
and difpaffionate thought concentrates at
laft in one point of view whatever hath a
tendency to eftablifh an hypothefis, or to
determine an opinion. But in either of
thefe cafes an eye immediately fixed upon
particular objects, of whatever importance,
will overlook at the time circumftances
that reflection may afterwards fuggeft, but
which could not have been then recollected
without fuppofing that two powers of the
mind, whofe offices we have feen to be
different, fhould felect at the fame inftant
objects of various natures; and fhould act
with an uniformity that is incompatiable
with their diftinct modes of operation.

3. We obferved as a proof of the fuperior comprehenfion of the faculty we are
contemplating here, that it takes in a much
larger and more diverfified feries of objects
than that of reafon confidered by itfelf.
The proof of this remark will lead us to
take notice as the laft inftance of the difference betwixt thefe of the different natures
of the objects felected by them. Here we
muft acknowledge, that while the man of
penetration

penetration (in the fenfe given to that term in this work) judges of every point that is examined by the underftanding, he is attentive to, and is qualified to decide on others of which the difpaffionate reafoner takes not cognizance. This laft indeed, judgeth with great juftnefs and propriety of its own ufual operation on the human mind, in the fame manner as a man who hath been long accuftomed to obferve the feveral expreffions of his own countenance in a mirror, will be ftruck with the fame, or even with fimilar characters in that of another. A *difcerning* judge of mankind, is equally qualified when he fuppreffeth the influence of imagination on his decifions, to judge of this matter as coolly as the reafoner who traceth up effects deliberately to their caufes; and by obferving in what manner his own judgment operates when tried in various circumftances, will form an adequate idea of the principal characters by which it is diftinguifhed. Of every other means by which the reafoning faculty is rendered confpicuous, we may in the fame manner pronounce, that this intellectual

lectual difcernment is peculiarly qualified
either to judge of, or to exercife it. It is
otherwife with regard to the underftanding, when we come to examine the more
peculiar province of that power whofe
offices we are employed in contemplating.
A man of deep penetration, and ftrong
fenfibility, may reafon folidly and calmly
on fubjects that demand to be laid open
by clofe argumentation; becaufe a very
fuperior fhare of the power that employs
this medium to effectuate its purpofe, enters into his character. But is the abftracted reafoner, whofe feelings perhaps
are weak, and his paffions fubjected to the
controul of reafon at all times, able to
detect with the fame perfpicacity the caufes
of actions lying remote in the heart, and
indicating certain powerful emotions with
which he is wholly unacquainted?—Certainly not.—" Why?" Becaufe he hath
here no principles upon which to proceed.
He cannot in this, as in other inftances,
judge from *comparifon,* becaufe having
never been fenfible of the effect himfelf,
which he is incapable perhaps of having
strongly

ftrongly excited, he has recourfe in vain to
his own mind for any caufe that may determine his judgment.   In this cafe likewife he cannot difcover the original principle by any procefs of ratiocination, however accurate.   The effects of the paffions
muft be *known* in order to be defcribed;
and the feelings of a fufceptible heart are
not to be laid open by any procefs which
the underftanding carries on; but are
painted by him who hath *experienced* their
influence.

From thefe remarks we may difcover
the reafon for which the obfervations and
the precepts of many philofophers on thefe
laft fubjects, are confidered as cold and
uninterefting.   A man of fenfibility rejects with indignation the rules which he
who appears to have no paffions himfelf,
lays down very calmly for reftraining their
excefs.   It is the *difcerning mind* (as it
may juftly be denominated) which enters
thoroughly into this matter, and counter-
acts moft powerfully the influence of the
paffions by drawing a picture from experience of the manner in which they operate

rate on conduct. In this character the underftanding and imagination concentrating their energy, the latter renders him to whom it belongs fufceptible of ftrong impreffions from the objects that pafs around him; and the former directs him to caft off thofe only which are of importance, as well as to combine their caufes with other principles that give confiftency to the whole.

Hence we may trace to its original the difference betwixt the view which Ifocrates, and that which Homer prefents of human nature. Let us take an example from each, as this will illuftrate the preceding obfervations. The epiftle of the former, infcribed to Demonicus, confifts principally of admonitions that regard his conduct in life. He defires this young man particularly " to try to obtain a conqueft over " thofe things by which it is unworthy to " be held in fubjection; fuch as riches, " anger, pleafure, and pain. This con- " queft, fays he, you will obtain with " regard to the firft, if you confider the " acquifition of wealth rather as a mean

" to

" to encrease your glory, than to form a
" mass of useless treasure. You will sub-
" due anger if you always acquit yourself
" to the person who hath given offence,
" as you would wish him in similar cir-
" cumstances to do to you. Your desires
" you will hold perfectly in subjection, if
" you reflect properly how unbecoming
" it is, that he who commands others,
" should himself be the slave of appetite
" and pleasure. You will in the last place
" rise superior to the shock of adversity,
" if you compare your own calamities
" with those of others, and remember at
" all times that you are a man *."

These

---

* Υφ᾽ ων κρατεισθαι την ψυχην αισχρον, τουτων
εγκρατειαν ασκει παντων, κερδες, οργης, ηδονης,
λυπης· Εση δε τοιντος, ει κερδη μεν ειναι νομιζης δι᾽ ων
ευδοκιμησεις, αλλ᾽ μη δι᾽ ων ευπορησεις· Τη δε Οργη
αν παραπλησιως εχης προς τνς αμαρτανοντας, ωσπερ
αν προς σεαυτον αμαρτανοντα, και τνς αλλνς εχειν
αξιωσειας. Ευ δε τοις Τερπνοις αναισχρον υπολαβης,
των μεν οικειτων ΑΡΧΕΙΝ, ταις δε ηδοναις ΔΟΥΛΕΥ-
ΕΙΝ. Ευ δε τοις Λυπηροις, αν τας των αλλων
ατυχιας επιβλεπης, και σεαυτον ως ανθρωπος, υπομιμ-
νησκης. ΠΡΟΣ ΔΗΜΟΝΙΚ. Many of the Pytha-
gorean

Theſe advices will be juſtly denominated judicious. But they are indeed " the ſug-

---

gorean philoſophers, whoſe writings have reached the preſent times, lay down cold and general rules of the ſame kind with the former; which, though perfectly juſt and rational, can have no influence on practice. Καλον επι παντι το ΙΣΟΝ, Υπερβολη δε και Ελλειψις μοι δοκεει, ſays an ancient ſage (Democritus) of great eminence. Who diſputes the truth of this obſervation, or who receives benefit from knowing it? The ingenious Theophraſtus, in his piece entitled ΗΘΙΚΟΙ ΧΑΡΑΚΤΗΡΕΣ, purſues a very ſimple method in treating of the paſſions; but one that is much more likely to be of uſe. Proceeding upon the maxim that

Vice is a monſter of ſuch frightful mien,

As to be hated, needs but to be ſeen ;   POPE.

he goes no farther than giving a plain but full deſcription of the perſons in whom certain vices predominate; and of the effects by which the character may be known. Εκθησω δε σοι (ſays he to his friend) κατα γενος οσα τε τυγχανει γενη τροπων τυτοις προσκειμενα, και ου τροπου τη οικονομια χρωνται. In proem. Our author's plan is, in other words, to preſent to men in general a juſt picture of their faults and vices ſo clearly and forcibly drawn as that each may ſelect his own amidſt an aſſemblage ſo promiſcuous; and by ſeeing its deformity may be enabled to correct it. Such a repreſentation required knowledge of the human heart, and has obviouſly a ſtronger effect than any general admonition.

" geſtions

" geſtions of a mind at eafe." What effect
would they produce upon the angry man,
the mifer, the voluptuary, or the head-
ſtrong ?—Whether fuch general and unappropriated maxims would work any permanent effect upon practice, let the perfons who may be fubject to thefe paffions
pronounce.—Let us next confider in what
manner Homer hath treated this fubject.

That it is the purpofe of the Iliad to
expofe the fatal confequences that arife
from the indulgence of anger, is known to
every man who hath any acquaintance
with that work. We are not here to fhow
how this author acquits himfelf in attacking the prefent paffion, as a POET; but
how he fucceeds in his purpofe confidered
as a philofopher, and a man of difcernment. The ninth book of this admired
work (which perhaps has lefs than any of
the others of purely poetic beauty) affords
a ſtriking example of the prefent kind.
In the various addreffes made to Achilles
by thofe who propofed to moderate his
anger, obferve the means that are applied
for this purpofe !—Ulyffes recalls to his
                                        memory

memory the parting advice of his father Peleus, that he ought above all other things to reprefs *this* paffion*; after having attempted to kindle every latent fpark of commiferation in the heart of this hero, by a pathetic detail of the miferies of his country †. He tries to fet one paffion in oppofition to another in his mind; and to overcome his refentment by awaking the powerful ftimulus of ambition ‡.

But in order to fet the pernicious effects of this blind fury completely before us, Achilles, whom the eloquence of Ulyffes

---

* Ω πεπον, η μεν σοι γε πατηρ επετελλατο Πηλευς
Ηματι τω οτε εκ Φθιης Αγαμεμνονι πεμπε·
Τεκνον εμον, καρτος μεν Αθηναιη τε και Ηρη
Δωσουσ' αικ' εθελωσι, συ δε μεγαλητορα θυμον
Ισχειν εν ςηθεσσι· ΦΙΛΟΦΡΟΣΤΝΗ ΓΑΡ ΑΜΕΙΝΩΝ.
                                        ΙΛΙΑΔ. ι.

† —— Εκτωρ δε μεγα σθενει βλεμεαινων
Μαινεται εκπαγλως, πισυνος Διι, ουδε τι τιει
Ανερας ουδε θεους, κρατερη δε ε λυσσα δεδυκεν·
Στευται γαρ νηων αποκοψειν ακρα κορυμβα, &c. ib.

‡ —— συ δε αλλους περ παναχαιους
Τειρομενους ελεαιρε κατα ςρατον, οι σε θεον ως
Τισους' η γαρ κε σφι μαλα μεγα κυδος αροιο, &c.

could not move from his purpose, is next
attacked by that of Phœnix, his tutor, his
friend; whose age is respectable, and
whose tears stream as he speaks.   Let any
reader compare the arguments that are
brought here against the indulgence of re-
sentment, with the *judicious* advice of the
philosopher, and judge which of the two
best understood human nature*.   The former writes like a man of good sense†;

---

* It would have run this part of the work into unneceffary length, to have mentioned the characters by
which the addrefs of Phœnix is particularly diftinguifhed.   The reader will find thefe, with every other
eloquent beauty that occurs in this book, pointed out
with great propriety in the notes of Mr. Pope's tranf-
lation.

† Quintilian affigns, with his ufual accuracy and
difcernment, the various fpecies of argumentation by
which reafon obtains its purpofe.—" Effe quædam
reor (fays he) in omni genere probationum communia.
Nam nec ulla quæftio eft quæ non fit aut in re, aut in
perfona: nec effe argumentorum loci poffunt, nifi
in iis quæ rebus & perfonis accidunt.   Eaque aut
per fe infpici folent, aut ad aliud referri.   Nec ulla
confirmatio nifi ex antecedentibus, aut ex confequen-
tibus, aut ex repugnantibus.   Et hæc neceffe eft, aut ex
præterito tempore, aut ex conjuncto, aut ex fequenti
petere." Inftit. lib. iv. c. 8.

whofe

whofe own paffions were cool and duɛtile, and who formed a judgment of all others by himfelf. The latter, on the contrary, is a *penetrating* judge of his fubjeɛt, deeply acquainted with the *heart* of man, and with the moft powerful motive by which it is aɛtuated *.—To what caufe ought this ftriking difference, fo confpicuous in the prefent inftance, (and of which an intelligent reader may meet with many fimilar examples) to be afcribed?—Not furely to mere fuperiority of underftanding in the laft; for of this faculty both Ifocrates, and other authors who lay down rules for the conduɛt of life, are acknowledged to have poffeffed a very eminent fhare. Befides, it is unqueftionably certain, that this intelleɛtual power often diftinguifheth in an high degree minds that are yet difqualified to prefent fuch a piɛture of the human heart as Homer hath here exhibited.

---

* " Ingenium *celeres* quidem motus ad excogitandum acute, & quædam intelligentiæ alacritas oftendit. Judicium vero fapiens animi *Mora*, & matura inter res plures eftimatio oftendet." Strad. Proluf. i Orat.

Is

Is it then to imagination that this effect
is to be afcribed?—Surely no man ever
fuppofed that this power confidered feparately from the other, can be the parent
of thofe expoftulations that fo powerfully
imprefs the mind; and of that *defign* which
appears in the arrangement of various
means, rendered fubfervient without decli-
nation to an ultimate purpofe.   It follows
then, that " there is a mental power dif-
" ferent in its manner of operation, in its
" extent of comprehenfion, and in its
" choice of objects, from both thofe whofe
" offices we have formerly examined; and
" to this it is that we have here applied
" the defignation of the FACULTY of
"-DISCERNMENT *."

Since

---

* Should it be deemed neceffary to trace the difference betwixt the difcerning and the inventive faculty
more particularly than hath been done in the text, we
would obferve, that as reafon is diftinguifhed from the
firft of thefe in confequence of its flow and deliberate
procedure; imagination is equally fo by its volatility,
and its views that are equally indifcriminate and fuperficial. Difcernment we have already feen, of whatever fubject it takes cognizance, is always known by
examining

Since therefore this quality differs in essential respects both from that of reason and of invention when viewed as independent of each other, as far as such a view of them can be taken, it must obviously be constituted by the union of both; of whose influence reflection will show it to participate in very different degrees. From the former it receives steadiness, solidity, a proper direction, and a power of selecting the most unexceptionable means. From

---

examining it to the bottom; and by seizing in every case such means as are most proper to obtain an ultimate end. Imagination, on the contrary, if left wholly to itself, would neither propose to accomplish any *eligible* end, nor discover perspicacity in the choice of means. When its prevalence over the reasoning power is remarkable in any instance; it will be fixed in some cases rather by the brilliance and drapery of objects, than by their importance: in others, when the prospect is more uniform, no parts will be discovered to have comparative excellence. In all cases whatever, its course, wholly different from that which the discerning mind pursues, will be excentric and irregular. Its light likewise instead of displaying parts of principal beauty or utility in a work, must lose its influence by being indiscriminately and promiscuously reflected over all.

O 3 the

the latter is derived its quicknefs, perfpicacity, and almoft intuitive perception of character and manners. By the underftanding a *penetrating* judge difcovers the purport of arguments as leading to fome principle: while by the inventive faculty co-operating in this work, its *fight is fharpened* (if that expreffion may be ufed) with regard to *particular objects*, without being impaired in the leaft degree as to general extent and comprehenfion. Thus we fee by what means the mind fixeth at once upon *decifive criteria*; and imagination with all its natural volatility is rendered fubfervient to the important purpofe either of clearing, or of inveftigating truth.

Again, when the various emotions of the heart are to be traced to their fources, as arifing from one paffion upon fome occafions, and upon others from a mixture extremely complicated *; in thefe cafes, when

---

* A confummate judge of mankind carries the fource of action here mentioned fo far, as to derive from it principally not only the actions but the opinions

of

when the ſuperior mental powers are united
in ſuch a manner as conſtitutes Diſcernment; the cauſes which fancy would have
ſcanned very ſlightly, if not wholly overlooked, will be thoroughly inveſtigated;
and teſts drawn from the ſureſt of evidences, I mean thoſe of feeling and experience, will be applied to eſtimate their
ſtability and power. It is indeed in this
laſt light, as was formerly obſerved, that
penetration is principally conſpicuous, as
mere judgment, and mere imagination,
with regard to ſuch objects, is equally deficient. For the underſtanding of an individual proceeds not beyond the ſober track
of reaſoning upon facts or principles eſtabliſhed by itſelf; or of examining the juſtneſs of ſuch reaſoning eſtabliſhed upon

---

of mankind. " Nec eſt enim in dicendo majus,
quam ut faveat oratori is qui audiet; utque ipſe ſic
moveatur, ut impetu quodam animi, magis quam ju-
dicio, aut concilio regatur. Plura enim multo homines
judicant odio, aut amore, aut cupiditate, aut iracundia,
aut dolore, aut lætitia, aut ſpe, aut timore, aut aliqua
permonitione mentis, quam veritate aut præſcripto,
aut juris norma aliqua, aut judicii formula, aut legibus."
Cicer. de Orat. lib. ii.

ſimilar

fimilar facts and principles by that of
another.   Of the paffions and affections it
judgeth philofophically by attending to
their moft ufual phenomena in life.   But
when effects are derived from thefe united
with imagination, and impelled by it *, the
man of mere reafon, however comprehenfive, being deftitute himfelf of feelings
that correfpond to fuch as this union produceth, is evidently deprived of the principles upon which an eftimate can be
formed, or an enquiry conducted.

---

* It is in this cafe that fuch a conflict of jarring
paffions is often excited, that the niceft Difcernment,
when tracing effects to their originals in fo promifcuous an affemblage, is often fcarce adequate to the
tafk of obferving the effects that arife from paffions,
with whofe ufual operation, when each is examined
apart, it is thoroughly acquainted.   It is well obferved
by a modern critic on this point.   " Entre ces obfta-
cles qui ruinent les paffions, les paffions memes ne font
pas le moindres.   Les uns combattent & detruifent les
autres : & fi l'on met enfemble un fujet de joïe & un
fujet de trifteffe, on ne fera bien fentir aucune des
deux.   Horace nous avertit que tout la licence poetique ne s'etende point jufqu'a ce melange." Beffu du
Poeme Epique liv. iii. p. 354.

II. Having

II. Having thus endeavoured to fhow in what refpects the difcerning faculty differs from the principal powers of the mind confidered fingly; and in what manner it is conftituted by their union, we come next to confider its peculiar province when it is viewed as influencing the various fpecies of Compofition. It hath been already obferved, that " when a large proportion " of the inventive is combined with a " much greater fhare of the reafoning fa- " culty, to which laft therefore it is fub- " fervient, the intellectual eye will moft " commonly take cognizance of that dif- " quifition which is directed by the under- " ftanding." It is thus that philofophical difcernment is conftituted. A fhare, on the other hand, of imagination more adequate to that of reafon in a mind diftinguifhed eminently by both, renders the influence of Difcernment more confpicuous and univerfal than in the firft inftance; becaufe " it appears in this cafe with equal advan- " tage when judging of the arts, as of " the inveftigations of fcience, and can " pronounce as properly of what is *beau-*
" *tiful*

" *tiful* in the one, as of what is *just* and
" *decisive* in the other." In these two
general lights we propose here to take a
view of this intellectual quality, as we
shall thus be able to determine its office
with precision as far as the present subject
is concerned.

1. Discernment when turned to philosophical disquisition, not only suggests to a
man the truest and happiest method of
treating his subject, as soon as he hath acquired a general knowledge of it; but it
enables him likewise to fix upon the most
decisive evidence; to adopt the most signi-
ficant illustrations; and to confirm his
hypothesis where proof is most necessary,
by observing and superseding objections.

We have already considered the understanding as the parent of exact methodical
arrangement; a criterion from which we
justly form a judgment of its clearness and
comprehension. There is, however, as
we may learn from experience, a certain
" curiosa felicitas," as it may be termed,
the art of disposition; a certain happy
manner of putting facts or circumstances
together,

together, which we never meet with but among writers of diſtinguiſhed *penetration*, in the ſenſe that is here given to that term. What is it that renders the diſcourſes of Plato on valour, friendſhip, death, immortality, &c. ſo much more agreeable than thoſe of other philoſophers who have examined the ſame ſubjects? Every reader muſt be ſenſible that this is owing in a great meaſure to the manner in which he hath diſpoſed his ſentiments on theſe ſubjects. Inſtead of attending wholly to what it may be juſt neceſſary to advance on one point, and proceeding immediately to another, this author often takes ſo large a circuit at his firſt ſetting out, that we are at a loſs to determine at what point his proceſs will terminate. By keeping the mind in ſuſpence, he in this manner irreſiſtibly fixeth its attention; and while he is ſometimes apparently negligent of cloſe methodical arrangement, accompliſheth all the ends to which it is ſubſervient; along with another important purpoſe which attention to perfect regularity contributes not to bring about.

The

The illustrious Roman orator and philosopher has wrote a treatise entitled, De
Natura Deorum, which has reached the
present times. The same subject is treated
by Phurnutus, a Greek philosopher, who
explains very succinctly, and at the same
time with much perspicuity, the various
parts of nature which the deities repre-
sented. Yet the first of these (though not
the most shining of Cicero's writings) is
universally known: the last is as much
neglected. The reason is, that the Roman,
who is formed in a great measure upon
the Athenian philosopher formerly referred to, rangeth his diversified materials in
such a manner as that these throw mutual
light upon each other; and by going out
of his way as it might seem, upon some
occasions, to bring illustrations of his sentiments, he keeps attention always awake
while a succession of pleasing ideas passeth
before the imagination *. The other, on
the

* The beautiful verses which he is supposed to have
taken from the Medea of Accius, to mention no other
proof of this kind, forms one of the most agreeable
illustrations.

the contrary, juſt diſpatcheth his buſineſs in the feweſt words, and without taking any compaſs to give a beautiful variety to his Compoſition, purſues one topic with the ſame uniform brevity, after he hath finiſhed a former.

. What ſhall we ſay of theſe writers when thus compared together?—That the laſt mentioned treats his ſubject like a man of underſtanding, who comprehends and unfolds it with perſpicuity. But the former are *diſcerning* judges of human nature, who keep in their eye the complicated qualities of which characters are formed; and in order to accompliſh a purpoſe with one of

---

illuſtrations. De Natur. Deor. lib. ii. At other times when talking of the myſterious conduct of the deity, he has recourſe, with great knowledge of human nature, to examples that were recent to his readers in order to illuſtrate his ſentiments on this perplexing ſubject. " Cur omnium crudeliſſimus (ſays he) tamdiu Cinna regnavit?—At dedit poenas.—Prohiberi melius fuit, impedirique, ne tot ſummos viros interficeret, quam ipſe aliquando poenas dare," &c. We are not here entering into the propriety or juſtice of theſe ſentiments. Our buſineſs is only to take notice of the manner in which they are laid down and illuſtrated.

theſe

these effectually, judge it proper to have
recourse alternately to each *.

2. As the faculty here examined directs
to the happiest method of treating a subject, so it fixeth likewise in the conduct of
argumentation, upon the most decisive
evidence. This end it effectuates by enabling a writer, as was formerly observed,
" *to hit upon that particular point upon*
which the bent of each argument turns, or
the force of each motive depends *."   That

it

---

* It is the same in history as in philosophy. The
man of judgment will relate facts with great perspicuity, and will accompany these with solid and edifying observations.   But there is a method of instructing
and fatiguing the mind at the same time; and where
these two accompany each other, the sphere of the
former must be very much contracted.   This happens
when there is an uniform recital of facts and observations drawn from these regularly carried on; the remarks always succeeding the narration of events peri-
odically, instead of being happily interwoven with it,
so as to grow as it were out of the action, and to be
pursued no farther than as it serves for illustration.
Among modern historians who have fixed on the same
general subject, Rapin and Hume are the historians of
England.   The first is a circumstantial and judicious
writer,

it is the peculiar province of the diſcerning
faculty to fix upon theſe points in the conduct

writer, whoſe relation of facts is both diſtinct and particular; and whoſe obſervations on theſe are uſually
juſt and natural. In peruſing his extenſive work we
find one uniform method invariably purſued. The
tranſactions are firſt related at full length. The remarks on theſe are commonly placed by themſelves
likewiſe, ſo that the reader is never at a loſs in the
narration to know what will be the ſtrain of a whole
paragraph, unmixed with incidental ſentiment or illuſtration, by caſting his eye on the margin. This ſtiff
method of procedure renders this valuable work tedious and uninteresting to readers who deſire to be entertained as well as edified in reading hiſtory, and who
neglect the *uſeful* when the *agreeable* is not united with
it. The detail of events in Hume's Hiſtory (which
taken altogether is, in the author's opinion, one of the
moſt complete performances of its kind) is much more
conciſe. But he fixeth with great propriety upon circumſtances that render us acquainted at once with the
manners of the times and with the characters of the
principal perſonages. Theſe, in conſequence of their
own importance, and of the obſervations that are happily thrown into the narration without *breaking* it,
form altogether an highly intereſting exhibition. We
are pleaſed with the hiſtorian's arrangement of ſuch
various materials, as well as with their ſelection, and
conſider the end of hiſtory as accompliſhed by the
whole. The inference deducible here with regard to
the

duct of evidence, will be obvious, when
we reflect upon what hath been already
said on its usual manner of operation. We
observed, as one of the most distinguishing
criteria of this power, that as soon as a
subject is laid down, it comprehends the
most proper manner of treating it without
any tedious process of reasoning, by *fixing
upon the points that are of principal importance.*

Upon weighing therefore the evidence by which any doubtful point is to
be established, the man of Discernment
perceives immediately, not merely the
force of one argument compared with another in bringing his proof to perfection;
but that particular one which hath peculiar energy, as conveying an idea in the
clearest and most forcible manner to the
mind. Thus it happens, that in canvassing
a question, such a man throws out at once
every thing that is frivolous, and abso-
lutely foreign to the purpose. Perceiving

the *judgment* of one writer and the *discernment* of the
other, is too obvious upon the principles laid down in
this work to be particularly insisted on.

immediately

immediately in what manner each reason
or motive may be moft powerfully enforced or applied, he bends the whole force
of his talents to the accomplifhment of
that purpofe; and in this manner hits the
point upon which the proof may be faid
to reft as being decifive of its propriety;
and which, when once placed clearly before the mind, fuperfedes the ufe of any
fubfequent enlargement. The influence
of the fuperior intellectual powers acting
in combination here is obvious. The underftanding, fharpened and animated in
its procedure, by being united with a vigorous imagination, fees at once the full
effect of an important circumftance, which
without this union it would have difcovered by a gradual and circumftantial difquifition. It rejects therefore as frivolous,
arguments whofe tendency is not fo immediately perceptible, or which lie more
open to exceptions; a while it contemplates fuch as have the moft lafting effect,
the inventive power fupplies the means of
enforcing thefe with fuitable energy, and
of rendering their influence complete.

Vol. I.   P   3. The

3. That the difcerning faculty therefore will likewife fuggeft amidft various
objects of illuftration, thofe that have the
greateft fignificance when applied to certain motives or arguments, is a point that
admits of very eafy proof. It is fancy that
invents thefe illuftrations, and it is to judgment that we owe their proper application.
This laft power never fails to felect fuch
as are moft appropriated to their objects,
when imagination prefents before it a diverfified affemblage. When this laft is
languid and enervated, its exertions, whatever ftrength the underftanding may poffefs, muft be proportionably feeble; and
while we are impreffed fuitably by the fentiments that are dictated by one faculty, we
muft at the fame time be fenfible, that it
cannot illuftrate thefe by fignificant allufions, when there is a defect in that power
from which they are derived.

Hence we may difcover the caufe for
which many excellent philofophical performances are deficient in thofe expreffive
images which give perfpicuity as well as
beauty to Compofition. The judgment of
the

the writer is confpicuous in the whole execution. But having either never received from nature any fuitable proportion of imagination, or having neglected to cultivate it, he either makes feeble attempts to imitate an excellence of which he perceives the ufe; or dropping it altogether, he mars the purpofe which he propofed ultimately to bring about. It is therefore in confequence of that union of the intellectual powers which conftitutes Difcernment, that the moft fignificant illuftrations are felected as much in philofophical as in any other fpecies of Compofition, and are applied to their correfponding originals.

4. We obferved in the laft place, that it is the difcerning faculty by which a philofopher is enabled moft effectually to perceive and to fuperfede objections to which his theory may lie open. We do not here mean to affirm that a man poffeffed of this mental quality even in the higheft degree, will be capable to detect every real, and far lefs every frivolous exception that may tend to invalidate his pofitions. Of the firft, it is undoubtedly proper that

fuch

such as have importance should be perceived and removed.   With regard to the
others, an author would take up both his
own and his readers attention to very little
purpose, who should seriously attempt to
obviate these, even supposing him to have
observed them.—But in order fully to comprehend the province of Discernment in
this sphere of its exertion, we must enter
more particularly into the subject.

The objections considered in general to
which propositions that require to be confirmed or illustrated lie open, are princi-
cipally of the following kinds.   Either
these are such as must occur to every mind
upon the first proposal of a subject, and
such therefore as it obviously suggests; or
though not thus immediately perceived,
they are seen to arise naturally from the
various subdivisions of a general plan, as
an author may take these up successively
in the course of his examination;—or,
lastly, they are of that kind which arise
from particular causes that operate within
a narrow compass, and though of the utmost consequence when strenuously urged,

would

would elude the fcrutiny of the far greater number of mankind.

Let us fuppofe, in order to exemplify thefe obfervations, that a writer takes for his fubject the paffions of human nature, and the neceffity there is for keeping them in fubjection. After having expofed the evils unavoidably arifing from an indulgence of thefe, when carried to excefs; every man will be ready to object, as foon as the means of fubduing them begin to be propofed, the weaknefs and imperfection of the human mind, which renders the language of the poet that of man in general,

Video meliora proboque,
Deteriora fequor.

This therefore is a plea which would be univerfally urged againft all his arguments, and fuch as, if paffed over without an attempt to obviate, would render his rules, however excellent and judicioufly difpofed, of no effect.

Having therefore guarded as much as poffible againft the force of this objection which ftrikes at his general plan, he pro-

ceeds

ceeds to confider the paffions as diftinguifhed feparately from each other, and to afcertain the influence, defign, and tendency of each. Here the pleas which every man is ready to urge in defence of that paffion which predominates in his own mind, will fall naturally under his confideration as objections againft the reafons that he may advance for limiting its dominion. Thefe it will be obferved are lefs univerfal than the former; and though ftrenuoufly fupported by fuch as are interefted particularly in the caufe, are however of a different kind from thofe in which all would confider themfelves as concerned in general. A man of folid and comprehenfive underftanding, as he would be immediately on his guard againft an objection of the firft kind in treating this fubject, as well as qualified to remove it, fo he would probably fuggeft with equal fuccefs many of the excufes by which the indulgence of certain paffions is vindicated, and would fhow their inefficacy. But according to the degree in which the power of a paffion or prejudice is felt by fome minds,

minds, will be the fubtlety and acutenefs with which its indulgence. is defended. For before men are fubdued fo thoroughly by their paffions, as to permit thefe to dictate a fyftem of principles fuited to their conduct, they attempt to reconcile, by every plaufible argument that reflection may fug- geft, certain deviations from rectitude, oc- cafioned by the prevalence of one paffion, to the temperate dictates of reafon; and inveftigate every motive that is brought to oppofe their defire, with a feverity that is encreafed by the ftrong inclination they feel to look upon it as irrational.

In this fituation therefore, objections different from either of the former kinds will naturally be propofed againft our phi- lofopher's own arguments, which ought on that account to arife from a thorough knowledge not only of the fubject in general, but of the nature and effects of that powerful propenfity whofe exercife he propofeth to limit. But how fhall he be enabled to carry on fuch cogent and for- cible reafoning as muft here be requifite?— Undoubtedly by being capable of placing

P 4. himfelf

himfelf, by an effort of imagination, in the circumftances of him who is ftrongly actuated by a particular paffion; and by feeling (if we may thus exprefs it) its temporary influence. Thus he will be able as clearly and forcibly to expofe the effects of particular paffions when indulged to an extreme, as by fuperfeding every objection he would moft effectually accomplifh the purpofe that is ultimately kept in view.

But by what power of the mind is this end brought about?—Not furely by the underftanding alone. For if it be neceffary that he who defcribes the effects arifing from indulged paffion, fhould place himfelf in the circumftances of a man who is ftrongly actuated by it; this faculty, whofe procedure is cautious and deliberate, would fail of prefenting fituations of this kind with fufficient ftrength and comprehenfion to do juftice to each. Men of judgment (in the proper acceptation of that term) who have themfelves very moderate paffions are furely ill qualified to defcribe an excefs which they never felt; or in other words, to do juftice to a fub-
jea

ject into which they are not qualified to
enter. Their account therefore of it could
not be fuch as would exclude the objections of thofe who more thoroughly underftood the queftion. It is, as we have
obferved, by an effort of imagination
which always gives ftrength to the paffions, that circumftances of the prefent
kind are reprefented with adequate energy.
Thefe when placed in a ftrong point of
view by it, are difpofed in fuch a manner
by the faculty of reafon which accompanies the whole likewife with fuch juft
obfervations, as carry conviction moft
powerfully to the mind. But as neither
power can accomplifh this end feparately
it muft obvioufly be effected by that influence of both, which we have fhown to
conftitute Difcernment. It is therefore this
mental power whofe nature and province
we have endeavoured to lay open; that
fuggefts often the happieft method of treating a philofophical fubject; fixeth on the
moft decifive evidence, felects the moft
fignificant illuftrations, and moft completely obviates objections.

In

In the whole conduct of this procedure we muſt obſerve, that though the concurrence of reaſon and imagination exiſting in an eminent degree is neceſſary to effectuate the purpoſes here mentioned. Yet the principal exertions are made by the former. The latter (as we ſhall ſee afterwards) though making much more ſtrenuous efforts in other departments of literature, and ſuch as obviouſly point to it as their original; yet is limited here in its range, and fixed down to the contemplation of ſuch objects only as the underſtanding admits to have propriety in the inveſtigation of truth. It may therefore be adequate to theſe ends though conferred in a very inferior degree to that with which it co-operates; and in any caſe muſt act according to eſtabliſhed and determined rules.

III. Having thus endeavoured to point out particularly the nature and characteriſtical marks of philoſophical Diſcernment, it remains only in order to complete our view of this faculty, that we conſider its influence when the reaſoning and inventive

tive powers are more adequate to each
other; or at leaft when this laft in whatever degree it takes place, extending its
furvey under the direction of judgment to
a greater variety of objects than in the
former inftance; the mind judgeth as properly of what is beautiful in the arts, as
of what is juft and decifive in the refearches
of fcience. This branch of our fubject we
fhall have occafion to difcufs fo much at
large in a fubfequent fection, when we
come to trace that combination of the intellectual powers which gives rife to the
arts of poetry and criticifm; that we fhall
only make fome general obfervations here
in order to determine the peculiar province
and importance of the faculty, whofe nature and offices we have endeavoured to
difplay. Let us then confider in what
manner he who poffeffeth a great and proportioned fhare both of underftanding and
of imagination, will form his eftimate both
of the *genius* of an author, and of the excellence or defects of a performance in
which this uncommon character is difplayed.

1. Difcern-

I. Difcernment we have already feen, is diftinguifhed by no circumftance more remarkably than its power of entering into a character, when fupplied only with flight materials, and fuch as an ordinary mind would wholly overlook. Its effects confidered in this point of view are uniform. It is the fame fagacity by which, in the commerce of life, a man judgeth of the heart or intentions of another from openings that efcape the greater number of mankind *; which, transferred to Compofition, renders him a judge of the degree in which the intellectual powers fubfift, and of their particular propenfity from fmall, and, as they might be deemed, frivolous indications. Thus it is that a difcerning critic, attentive to the firft dawning of genius, will difcover in a few loofe thoughts thrown out without much connection, the characters of an accurate or comprehenfive underftanding; and from a few ftrokes in the fame manner of pathos or of defcription, will judge of the future

---

* See fect. i. p. 11, and fect. iv.

extent,

extent, fertility, and even of the characteriftical bias of imagination. The circumftances from which a penetrating judge
will form his opinions on thefe points vary
according to the ftrength of his difcernment, and the faculty that influenceth his
decifions. Some of thefe are, the models
or patterns which a young genius felects
for imitation, the vein of reflection into
which he falls moft naturally, as either
carried on with clofe philofophical accuracy, or laying open, though without much
regularity the internal feelings and affections; the images employed for illuftration, as either drawn from remote fources,
or from the fimpleft forms of external
nature :—in fine, the expreffion of a work
as either florid, creeping, correct, or in-
flated. From thefe and other circumftances, which we need not mention more
minutely, the fuperior faculties when acting in vigorous concurrence form a judgment of the character while yet but beginning to open, which we pronounce to arife
from intellectual Difcernment.

As

As imagination muft make a ftrenuous effort in the mind that judgeth from thefe circumftances of a character, it muft be proportioned in degree to the underftanding, which laft, when greatly fuperior in this refpect, is apt to reprefs the ardor of its companion, and alter the manner of its procedure.

2. It is in confequence of a fimilar combination that we judge properly of the excellence or defects of works in which genius is difplayed. As this extraordinary character is principally faid to take place from the prevalence of effects that owe their origin to imagination; this power it undoubtedly is that feels their full force, and when united with that of reafon, enables a man to difcern their expedience in the various fpecies of Compofition. The man of Difcernment therefore, when judging of works that are diftinguifhed by ingenuity, is he who by the exercife of an imagination congenial to that of the author, is powerfully impreffed by ftrokes that have original beauty; and is qualified

to

to obſerve the heightning which this beauty receives from correſponding diction, fitneſs of illuſtration, and viewed as connected with other circumſtances from propriety of diſpoſition. A more particular account of the manner in which the diſcerning faculty operates in the extenſive field that is here opened to it, belongs more properly to a ſubſequent ſection.

We have now endeavoured to lay before the reader ſuch obſervations on the nature of this power of the mind in general, and of its more peculiar influence on the preſent ſubject in particular, as that he may judge of its manner of forming deciſions, as well as of their juſtneſs and importance. The author of this eſſay is no friend to the practice of *multiplying diſtinctions* upon every occaſion, as theſe are often ſubſervient to no other end than that of perplexing, inſtead of informing the mind, and are indeed introduced principally at many times, perhaps to bring the writer off when he is embarraſſed, or to gratify his vanity. When merely nominal, they

are

are fpecious trifles. But when they ferve
to mark that point at which objects of
fimilar natures differ effentially from each
other, they are of real utility, as they at
the fame time enable the mind to think
with precifion, and enlarge its fphere of
inveftigation. The ufe of a juft diftinction
becomes ftill more confpicuous than in this
general inftance, when the things diftinguifhed from each other are to be confidered as the caufes of various and important confequences, which laft cannot
otherwife be traced up to their proper originals. From his belief that this is neceffary in the prefent cafe, the author has
taken a larger view of the fphere appropriated to the difcerning faculty than of
any other intellectual power, and fuch as
is not *wholly* prefcribed by his fubject. He
hath fo often obferved the term *aifcerning*
applied to denominate a fimple act of the
underftanding by philofophers, and the
effects of both powers afcribed indifcriminately to one, that an attempt to lay open
their diftinct natures, provinces, and manners

ners of operation, he hopes may be of
fome ufe, if not as a full difplay of the
fubject, yet as an opinion that may be followed into a larger and more diverfified
field by thofe who ftudy the philofophy of
the Mind.

SECTION V.

Of the Ufe of Memory in Compofition.

OUR view of the intellectual powers
as employed in Compofition, would
juftly be deemed incomplete, if we do not
confider that by which ideas are treafured
in the mind, and without whofe influence
the others can effectuate no purpofe. The
importance of this valuable quality in all
cafes whatever is indeed fo obvious, that
it hath been the care of mankind in every
age to extend its influence where it is
originally vigorous, or to fupply its weaknefs where it is naturally deficient. Whether indeed we behold it as the parent of
experience, and by that means of fuch in-

vestigation as is derived from this source *,
or as a requisition particularly necessary to
such as would excel in arts that include a
compass of diversified objects †; whether
we view it as an indication of, and attend-
ant on genius ‡, or finally, when improved
to the utmost by art, as capable of being
rendered subservient to purposes the most
beneficial §;—in all these senses its various

* Γιγνεται δ'εκ της μνημης εμπειρια τοις ανθρωποις.
Αι γαρ πολλαι μνημαι τυ αυτυ πραγματος μιας εμπειριας δυναμιν αποτελουσι· και δοκει σχεδον επισημη
και τεχνη ομοιον ειναι η εμπειρια· Αποβαινει δ'επισημη
και τεχνη δια της εμπειριας τοις ανθρωποις, &c.
ΑΡΙΣΤΟΤ. Μεταφυσικ. Βιβ. Α. Κεφ. α.

† "Quid dicam de thesauro rerum omnium memoria? quæ nisi custos inventis cogitatisque rebus &
verbis adhibeatur, intelligimus omnia, etiamsi præcla-
rissima in oratore peritura?—Quamobrem mirari desi-
namus quæ causa sit eloquentium paucitatis." Cicer.
de Orat. lib. i.

‡ "Memoria autem facit etiam prompti ingenii fa-
mam, ut illa quæ dicimus non domo attulisse, sed ibi
protinus sumpsisse videamur, quod & Oratori, & ipsi
causæ plurimum confert." Quint. Institut. lib. ii.
cap. 11.

§ "Neque tamen ambigimus, quin possint præstare
per eam (Memoriam sc.) nonnulla mirabilia & por-
tentosa." Bac. de Augmen. Scient. lib. v. c. 5.

offices

offices will require explanation as a neceſſary branch of the preſent enquiry. Before, however, we conſider this faculty as
more immediately regarding Compoſition,
it will be proper to make ſome general
obſervations on its nature and effects.

1. It is commonly thought that a memory uncommonly extenſive, if it is not
incompatible either with ſolidity of judgment, or with vigour of imagination, yet
is rarely united with theſe in any eminent
degree *. This maxim however, ſupported as it is by cuſtom and prepoſſeſſion,
is one of thoſe which will not ſtand the
teſt of cloſe inveſtigation. Thus far indeed, we may allow the laſt part of it to
be well founded, that men of abſtracted
and ſpeculative minds appear often to be
abſent and inattentive to common occurrences:—the incidents about which the
buſy part of mankind are intereſted, make
but a very ſlight impreſſion on their

---

* —— in the ſoul while memory prevails,
The ſolid power of underſtanding fails;
Where beams of warm imagination play,
The memory's ſoft figures melt away.   POPE.

Q 2   thoughts,

thoughts, and are therefore foon erafed beyond the power of recollection. But this,
when properly examined, will be found to
proceed not from a defect of Memory, but
from want of attention. The fpeculatift
who found this charge brought againft
him might with great juftice retort the
accufation, by faying, that the fame defect
of remembrance which might be imputed
to him in the one of thefe provinces, would
be transferred to his accufers in the other.
Nay, in this laft cafe, the charge will fall
much more heavily upon the man of the
world (as he is called) than in the former
upon the man of fpeculation, as the former
would probably be much more deficient
in recollecting abftracted truths which he
had read with liftleffnefs, (even fuppofing
him to have comprehended thefe) or even
a ftroke of pathos which he had paffed
over without emotion, than the latter
would be in recalling to his memory
events, in which, however unimportant, he
muft after all be interefted in fome degree
as a member of fociety.

Thefe

Thefe general remarks on the power of recollection will explain to us the reafon for which it is confidered as more mechanical than any of the others, and more fufceptible of improvement from application and exercife *. To accomplifh this end nothing

---

* This confideration has given rife to thofe expedients for extending memory, which, when rightly ufed, are indeed extremely valuable, but when the underftanding is defective render a man contemptible. " Nam ingentem numerum nominum (fays the penetrating philofopher formerly quoted) aut verborum femel recitatorum eodem ordine ftatim repetere aut verfus complures de quovis argumento ex tempore conficere, aut quicquid occurrit fatyrica aliqua fimilitudine perftringere, aut feria quæque in jocum vertere, aut contradictione, & cavillatione quidvis eludere, & fimilia (quorum in facultatibus animi haud exigua eft copia, quæque ingenio & exercitatione ad miraculum ufque extolli poffunt) hæc certe omnia, & his fimilia nos non majoris facimus quam funambulorum & mimorum agilitates & ludicra. Etenim eædem ferme res funt, cum hæc corporis, illa animi viribus abutantur; & admirationis forfitan aliquid habeant, dignitatis parum." De Augment. Scient. ubi fup. From this paffage, which is worthy of its author, we may judge in what manner memory will exert itfelf when the fuperior faculties of the mind are deficient, and thus

diftinguifh

nothing is more neceffary than that a man fhould be able to transfer his attention from one fet of objects to another, not perhaps originally fo agreeable, but to which he becomes fo much reconciled by inflexible perfeverance, that what was at firft the effect of neceffity becomes at laft the object of deliberate felection. The fame motive therefore by which he was impelled to one purfuit taking place with

---

diftinguifh its effects when it is a repofitory of indif-criminate ideas thrown together without order or pro-portion; from its real utility when (though perhaps equally extenfive as in the former cafe) its ideas are properly regulated by a clear and comprehenfive un-derftanding. From its precipitance and trifling in the firft of thefe inftances, it is however fomewhat too hafty in concluding, as we are apt to do in general, that becaufe Memory may fometimes contribute to fhow the defects rather than the excellence of a cha-racter, that therefore a very large proportion of it indi-cates the weaknefs of any intellectual power whatever. This habit of drawing general conclufions from one or two particular inftances, will open an inlet to a variety of errors, and is equally unjuft in moft cafes as it would be to conclude, that every man who practifed the duties of religion was an hypocrite, becaufe a few had concealed many vices under the mafque of devotion.

regard

regard to another, the memory becomes at once a laſting repoſitory of new ideas, and is thus gradually rendered comprehenſive by an eaſy and imperceptible proceſs.

Suppoſing then this uſeful power of the mind to receive improvement more or leſs durable, in proportion to thoſe degrees of attention which different purſuits are calculated to excite, it is obvious that its principal dependence muſt be upon that faculty whoſe peculiar province it is to *arreſt attention* by energy, pathos, and vigour of deſcription.—So far therefore is memory from being impaired by ſtrength and exuberance of imagination, that the beams of this ſun ſerve to give ſtrength, expreſſion, and duration to its figures rather than to melt theſe away, (as Pope moſt poetically expreſſeth it) and its objects like diamonds of the pureſt water, reflect the ray with advantage, from which was originally derived their conſiſtence and beauty.

A very plain example will ſerve to illuſtrate the preceding obſervations. A man of taſte and judgment who is at one time entertained by the recital of a beautiful

poem

poem in the clofet, and at another by hearing an elegant and judicious fermon from
the pulpit, will perhaps (though his op-
portunities are the fame with regard to
both) remember afterwards many of the
moft ftriking paffages of the former, when
thofe of the latter are wholly obliterated.—
Suppofing however the preacher to be a
man of a character in all refpects precifely
fimilar to his own, I would afk, from
whence does it arife that his memory is
more tenacious than that of the former,
and that perhaps only in the fphere in
which he is interefted by his profeffion? It
will be acknowledged readily, that a public fpeaker will not only retain what he
has compofed himfelf and has impreffed
upon his memory by application, but that
ftrokes of eloquence, which another might
overlook, will be recollected by him, and
will form the models of his imitation. Is
it not evident that the former of thefe,
being left wholly to his own direction,
finds thofe objects make the deepeft impreffion that are illuftrated by the colouring of imagination; while the latter being
compelled

compelled to ftrike into another path, finds his powers of recollection improved by exercife in the one fphere, while thefe at the fame time are in no degree weakened in the other?—In both thefe perfons however (fuppofed to be naturally of characters precifely fimilar) the mind will retain unalterably its original bias, and though fufceptible in one cafe of more diverfified objects, yet will ftill be moft eafily impreffed by thofe on which *poetic* expreffion, or ftrength of imagery confers peculiar fignificance.

It is therefore obvious that as Memory is by no means naturally fubverfive either of judgment or imagination; fo thefe on the other hand are fo far from being incompatible with it, that this laft acquires its extent by an effort of the one, and becomes tenacious of particular objects in confequence of being accompanied by the other. In fact, nothing is more ridiculous than thofe idle, and frequently affected complaints which many perfons make fo often of their defect in remembrance. Becaufe perhaps they may have known men
eminently

eminently poffeffed of this power who enjoyed at the fame time no proportioned
fhare of fuch as are deemed more effential,
they abfurdly conclude that the united
concurrence of all is never to be expected;
and by giving up all pretenfions to that
which nature has conferred upon them,
they may in reality be difclaiming the only
quality by which they were entitled to approbation or efteem.   Such men ought to
reflect that as memory becomes comprehenfive where it is originally weak by a
fteady and refolute exertion of reafon, and
as it never fails where imagination fubfifts
in any high degree to retain thofe ftrokes
of nature and paffion of which it is the
parent; fo the man who proclaims his defect in this faculty acknowledgeth at the
fame time the want or weaknefs of the
others.

2. When from confidering the advantages of memory in general, we come to
view it more particularly as it regards
Compofition, the importance and indeed
neceffity of acquiring by the method already fuggefted as large a proportion of it

as

.as poffible will appear, whether we recollect the advantage an author receives from
being able readily to remember the fentiments of others when his thoughts are
employed on fubjects fimilar to theirs; or
when we confider the benefit incomparably
greater arifing to a man of reflection and
difcernment, from being able to recall upon
every fuitable occafion thofe fentiments to
his memory which his own experience of
mankind may have formerly fuggefted.

With regard to the former of thefe objects, let a man's natural powers in general, and that of invention in particular be
ever fo eminent, yet the knowledge of
what hath been advanced on any fubject
whatever by men of acknowledged abilities muft be highly beneficial, whether he
collects from thefe, obfervations by which
the errors of his predeceffors may be corrected, obtains patterns of imitation for
himfelf, or, finally, from hints carelefsly
thrown out without any accurate inveftigation of confequences is able to extend
the empire of Science, and lays the foundation of fome new and ingenious hypothefis.

thefis. In thefe cafes a Memory tenacious of fuch objects as had formerly arrefted his attention, and ready to fuggeft an op-pofite and correfponding train of ideas tending to confirm fome propofition of which he might have been dubious, from the writings of others; removes at once that diffidence with which the modeft and ingenuous are apt to propofe their own fentiments when thefe have the appearance of fingularity, and enables an author to purfue his refearch with confidence and fatisfaction.

A little reflection will fhow us likewife that this power has effects in every branch of Compofition that requires it to be cul-tivated with the greateft affiduity. It was obferved formerly when we were explain-ing the nature of invention, that " this " term in its moft abftracted fenfe can with " regard to the human mind have no " fignificance or propriety whatever *." Every effort of this kind, in the art of which we treat, is in fact an improvement (or an attempt to improve) on fome prin-

* Sect. iii. p. 101.

ciples that have formerly been laid down, some system embraced by our predeceffors, some truths half opened, but not accurately followed out through a train of confequences by thofe who from the imperfections of human nature, rather than from any defect of their own faculties (confidered as human) were able juft to difclofe a path to their fucceffors, without examining, or indeed difcerning themfelves the various fcenery to which it would naturally open. The firft ftep once made, every fucceeding improvement is effectuated with comparative facility. The perfons who make thefe are unqueftionably in many inftances objects of efteem, and even of admiration to mankind; but to what power of the mind is it owing that a man is able to recall at any time to his thoughts the principles, whether fimple or complicated, from which his inventions derived their origin; and by whofe influence is he enabled to follow out the comparifon betwixt caufes and their effects?—Undoubtedly he is in all this principally affifted by the faculty of recollection, by which objects are

prefented

prefented to the underftanding loofe indeed, perhaps, and forming at firft view
no very clofe or accurate combination; but
which are ftill the real, though rude materials, from whofe union arife the jufteft
and moft elegant proportions.

Every art and fcience whatever advan-
ceth to perfection by a flow and almoft
imperceptible procefs. To trace indeed
either one or other, through its various
transformations to its original draught (if
I may fo exprefs myfelf) in the mind,
however it might contribute to gratify curiofity by opening a fet of new and extraordinary combinations, yet would be
an attempt wholly impracticable, as the
origin of arts, like that of nations, is involved in impenetrable darknefs. In thefe
however, reflection will convince us that
artifts of all denominations have formed
one great body; in all nations whatever,
cemented by the moft intimate union, and
maintaining a dependence on each other
not arifing from the local influence of laws,
fafhions, or what we call national prejudices, which are at the fame time limited,
and

and perpetually varying; but from a natural conformity of fentiment and character
whofe effect is inftantaneous, and its operation univerfal. In this immenfe republic, conftituted of fo many members dif-
joined by climate, cuftom, manners, and
language, Memory is the bond or cement
by which the parts are held in connection
with each other, and a proportion is obferved to take place upon the whole. To
an improvement thus univerfal, though at
the fame time flowly and gradually carried
on, all civilized nations will not only be
found to have contributed largely at different periods, but individuals likewife derive advantage from the writings, as they
frequently do from the characters, of their
predeceffors, with whofe real utility they
are not fufficiently acquainted. Thus the
fentiments of a Greek or Roman author
when transfufed from their original, of
which a writer may have very imperfect
ideas, into a language which he thoroughly
underftands, become beneficial to him in
the higheft degree, when his memory fuggefts thefe as tending to fupport fome particular

ticular train of reflection; or when his view of a subject in consequence of this recollection is rendered comprehensive *.

Here

---

* An author of diſtinguiſhed eminence obſerves with great propriety on this ſubject, that " whatever " is very good ſenſe muſt have been common ſenſe in " all times, and that what we call learning is but the " knowledge of the ſenſe of our predeceſſors. They " therefore, who ſay our thoughts are not our own " becauſe they reſemble the ancients, may as well ſay " our faces are not our own, becauſe they are like our " fathers." Pope. This obſervation is as juſt as it is happily illuſtrated, for there is an obvious difference betwixt copying the ſentiments of the ancients, and adopting ſuch as are ſimilar to theirs. In the firſt caſe, an author by either borrowing indiſcriminately the thoughts of thoſe admired writers, or by a *ſervile* imi-tation of their *manner*, betrays undoubtedly barrenneſs of invention, and a mind afraid to venture beyond certain limits, like a novice detained by fear within a magical circle. On the contrary, a *ſimilarity* whether of ſentiment or manner in this inſtance does honour to a writer as indicating a correſponding reſemblance of character, and is to be conſidered as a proof that men of good ſenſe, in all ages, have agreed in the general tenor of their ſentiments on the ſame ſubjects, though their manner of illuſtrating theſe, the inferences deduced from general principles, their method of de-tailing a ſubject, and the expreſſion in which their thoughts are conveyed are extremely different. It will

be

Here therefore new avenues of thought are opened, an inadequate detail is corrected, enlarged ideas occur to the mind as its principal powers arrange and improve upon the objects preſented by the laſt mentioned faculty; and an individual receives innumerable benefits from this general circulation of ſentiment, while he is ignorant of the particular ſource from which theſe are derived.

The principal beauties in the art of Compoſition was it poſſible to trace theſe accurately to their originals, would be diſcovered to ariſe (at leaſt in many inſtances) from ſentiments, images, or illuſtrations which we have met with in the courſe either of our reading or converſation; but having impreſſed our minds very ſlightly at the time, are afterwards ſecretly retained in the memory unknown to ourſelves, and

---

be obſerved, that we ſpeak here of *indiſcriminate* borrowing, and of *ſervile* imitation. In other caſes (ſuch as thoſe above enumerated) the introduction of either proof or illuſtration from any writers of eminence, whether ancient or modern, is not only neceſſary but commendable.

are either recollected when our thoughts
are afterwards employed on fome fimilar
fubject as *wholly our own*; or become the
caufes (however imperceptible to us) of
our falling into a certain feries of thought,
of reafoning with juftnefs, and of painting with maftery. It is happily not poffible in the laft mentioned inftance, particularly to charge an author with *plagiarifm*
(the ufual recourfe of thofe who limping
themfelves upon the crutches of antiquity,
judge it impoffible for others to walk
without thefe) becaufe the phrafeology of
his original will not be adopted, and the
point of refemblance muft lie in fome very
minute circumftance.—In all thefe inftances,
however, as well as when fentiments tending to confirm our own opinions are openly
felected for the purpofes above-mentioned, the advantages of an improved memory need not be pointed out.

3. We proceed therefore to obferve,
that as this faculty is of great importance
by enabling an author to acquire real benefit from the fentiments of others, fo it will
appear to be of ftill greater confequence,
when

when we confider it as retaining thofe
which his own experience of. mankind
may have fuggefted to him in the commerce of. life. That knowledge of mankind which can only be acquired by long
and deliberate attention, is evidently fubfervient to no . material purpofe of any
kind, unlefs when memory is improved in
fuch a manner as to prefent (when thefe
can be turned to advantage) fuch reflections as may have arifen from various occurrences. Difcernment, with materials of
this kind laid before it, acts immediately
in its proper. fphere, when it felects from
thefe fuch as tend moft immediately either
to eftablifh a theory, or to regulate practice.
It'is true, indeed, that many events, comparatively infignificant, will be wholly obliterated from the mind; that many reflections, of no confequence to promote its
ultimate purpofe, will pafs fuperficially over
it without ever being recalled; that, in
fhort, many occurrences deemed by fome
perfons of the moft indifpenfible confequence, will be cancelled from the memory
when it is ftored with fuch ideas as may

R 2 be

be turned in this manner to real utility:
and this perhaps fuggefts the true reafon
why men of underftanding, or of penetration, are fo often judged to be deficient
in remembrance.   Common ideas, like inferior expreffions in a mafterly drawing,
are ftruck out at once from the field; but
their place is fupplied by fuch ftrong, fignificant, and animated characters as no
time can efface, and whofe arrangement
promotes the purpofe of entertainment or
inftruction, as they may be directed by the
governing power.

It will be faid, and we acknowledge with
truth, that Memory appears in all this
procefs of the fame value only as a ftore-
room, which, though capable, when it is
of proper dimenfions, to contain a large
proportion of materials, yet is neither fenfible of the value of thefe, nor capable to
regulate their difpofition with accuracy.
The utility however of this intellectual
repofitory muft be feen in the fame light
by the philofopher as that of the former
(to carry on the metaphor) is by the man
of bufinefs, as neither of thefe can pro-
fecute

fecute his trade without the poffeffion of fo neceffary an implement, and both require this refervoir to be enlarged as their various fpheres of intercourfe or experience become more extenfive and open. It is in all cafes whatever only principally requifite that in the acquifition of knowledge of whatever kind, a due attention be paid to the underftanding by whofe fuperior operation fymmetry of parts is to take place on the whole. We may, no doubt, overload the memory with a multitude of incoherent ideas, which the judgment of a writer is unable to place in any exact difpofition, as well as give the latter too little exercife where it might make a ftrenuous exertion, by too fcanty and difproportioned a fhare of materials. The end of inftruction is undoubtedly marred in either of thofe cafes, though much more effectually in the firft cafe than in the laft. Obfcurity at leaft, if not utter confufion and abfurdity, muft take place when the mind, like the body couching beneath an heavy burthen, is overpowered by conceptions half-formed, and juftling out each other;

as

as imagination can at fuch a time be impreffed but flightly by any ideas, and
judgment muft be unable to felect from
fo many difcordant objects, fuch as are beft
adapted to particular purpofes. This effect
is fometimes occafioned by making too
much ufe of the various methods by which
men have attempted to extend the power
of Memory, or to fupply its defects *.

We

---

* The illuftrious author whom we quoted above,
mentions two methods by which an artificial memory
may be acquired. The firft rule he prefcribes is that
the mind fhould be habituated to contemplate objects
as ftanding in a certain order with others whofe affinity
is moft obvious, rather than to view either of thefe
without this relation. This is what he calls *prænotio*;
and he obferves, that by fuch a perception, the man is
kept from wandering in the regions of infinity; and
if memory does not immediately prefent the defired
idea, yet it falls into the proper train of difcovering
it. The other he fuggefts, is that the mind fhould
reprefent intellectual objects rather *emblematically* than
as thefe really are, by which means becoming at once,
in fome meafure at leaft, the objects of fenfe, they
ftrike the memory more forcibly than otherwife, and
are recollected with facility. This laft method it probably was by which the Corfican, mentioned by Mu-
retus, repeated with eafe fome thoufands of words in
different languages, which had no connection with
each

We are often however grofsly deceived when we pronounce, as we are ready to do from inſtances of this nature, that the principal powers of the mind are really weak in proportion as Memory is comprehenſive. In fact, the only inference ariſing from this train of obſervation is, that no degree whatever of intellectual qualities can exempt a man from falling into errors and inconſiſtencies, when the diſproportion betwixt theſe is remarkably obvious. In this caſe the balance of the mind is deſtroyed; and though neither a compre-

---

each other, immediately after he had heard theſe pronounced; each having probably recalled to his memory ſome ſenſible object by which he had been accuſtomed to repreſent it. We have many other examples, both ancient and modern, of men ſome of them (as the celebrated Cinzas) of diſtinguiſhed genius, who have carried this art to the higheſt perfection. After all, however, the former of theſe rules is undoubtedly, by far the moſt eligible, as affording exerciſe to the underſtanding, whoſe ideas (as long as the relation betwixt objects is kept in view) will be conſtantly diſtinct and explicit: by the latter (when abuſed as in the preceding inſtance) a man will acquire memory to the ſame purpoſe as a parrot is taught language, and will be only more valuable in proportion not to the choice of his ſubjects, but the number of his words.

henſive

henfive memory, nor a luxuriant imagination, can (as we have already feen) be faid
to argue a defective underftanding, yet we
can have no furer teft of a judgment adequate to every purpofe in the province of
Compofition, than when this laft appears
to have the images of the former and the
treafures of the latter (confidered as the
parent of experience) fubfervient in fuch
a manner to fome general purpofe as that
each may alternately concur to elucidate
and confirm its principles.

SECTION VI.

Of the various Combinations of the intel-
lectual Powers in the different fpecies of
Compofition.

A Curious reader will naturally be led
to enquire from the conclufion of
the preceding fection, what is underftood
by *the balance of intellectual powers*, whether this can be gained, and what are the
methods moft expedient to acquire it.
Thefe

Thefe points, as of the moft effential importance, we fhall endeavour to obviate in
a fubfequent fection:—in the mean time
it is neceffary, before we proceed to thefe
queftions, that after having confidered
each faculty of the mind as occupying a
feparate province in the art of Compofition, we fhould take a view of all thefe
as exerting united influence not merely
on the art in general, but on the parts of
which it is conftituted, requiring a combination varied in proportion to their different natures, tendency, and defign.

1. To examine particularly every fpecies of Compofition, with regard to that
union of intellectual powers from which
its origin is derived, is not neceffary upon
the prefent occafion, becaufe fome of thefe
(however different when viewed as diftinct
branches of the art) yet have their original
in common from the fame concurrence of
faculties, varied only from each other not
in their manner of exertion, but wholly in
the degrees in which thefe fubfift. Thus
under the general denomination of poetry,
confidered in the prefent point of view,

we

we may include at the same time the various species of it as indicating universally the union of judgment and imagination, though by no means always in the same proportion; and the sister art of eloquence from which in point of original it hath no peculiar mark of distinction. Philosophy on the other hand, as a science comprehending diversified subjects, sometimes demanding an high exertion of the inventive power, and at others indicating only the existence of reason, whose proof is carried on without the aid of the latter, will require to be more particularly considered. History, fable, and criticism, (the latter more immediately as connected with taste) will fall under a separate examination, with which we shall sum up the enquiry.

It will occur very readily to a considerate mind that to distinguish with precision betwixt similar objects, to detect fallacy in an argument or opinion, when this is artfully concealed by a plausible representation, to establish criteria by which judgment may be regulated, and, finally, to exhibit in exact and perspicuous
disposition

difpofition fuch abftracted ideas as it requires the niceft perception to develope
with accuracy :—that a procedure of this
kind, when properly conducted, indicates
no common fhare of that difcernment
whofe nature and operation we have attempted to point out as far as relates to
the prefent fubject. From what hath been
already advanced on the laft mentioned
topic, we may conclude that penetration
as requifite for thefe purpofes, muft be
conftituted indeed of underftanding, but
may be exerted without any proportioned
fhare of the other qualities by which in
general we have feen it to be diftinguifhed.
The truth of this remark will be obvious,
if we confider more particularly that procefs of ideas in the mind by whofe union
the ends which it is propofed to obtain in
this branch of philofophy, may be moft
eafily and completely effectuated.

When in confequence of clofe and comprehenfive inveftigation, a theory is gradually formed, and the mind proceeds deliberately to accomplifh a purpofe remote
perhaps, and difficult to be reached as it
may

may appear at firft view; a train of intermediate ideas are gradually prefented as
its enquiry is carried on, by which its approach to this end is facilitated, and the
object of refearch is more diftinctly perceived, and is examined with greater accuracy as the diftance leffens at which it
was originally beheld. By this manner a
mind intent upon the difcovery of truth,
and fixing its whole attention upon one
purpofe, can furvey in diftinct points of
view the means as diftinguifhed from each
other, by which its aim is to be obtained,
and thus can detect fuch fallacies by
minute infpection as are neceffarily overlooked in a general eftimate however accurate and judicious. Imagination, from
what hath been already obferved on its
manner of operation, muft of all other
powers be moft unfit for a procefs of this
nature; and the difcerning *faculty* as
formed by the union of both judgment
and fancy, we have feen in general to be
characterifed by perceiving a few ftrong
and decifive criteria, or by felecting a
few effential circumftances to form its eftimate;

mate; but not by advancing regularly from óne objeɛt to another, and by conſidering ſeparately each particular part, however neceſſary to conſtitute a whole. Diſcernment therefore, will enable the phiſoſopher to obſerve the end of his ſearch as praɛticable, while it is yet at a diſtance, and may form this judgment from a train of thought which a common obſerver might deem extremely remote, and even incongruous to its purpoſe; but in the ſeleɛtion of ſubordinate parts, as well as the diſpoſition of theſe in ſuch progreſſion as leads the mind imperceptibly to the point in view by a conſiſtent and accurate procedure, in theſe points judgment is required to exert its influence peculiarly; as in all the others it ought eminently to predominate *.

---

* It was probably from conſidering judgment in this comprehenſive light that Chryſippus is ſaid to have defined it as that power by which the mind, anticipating in ſome meaſure the diɛtates of experience, acquires univerſal knowledge of the objeɛts that ſurround it. Ο δε Χρυσιππος κριτηριχ Φησιν ειναι αισθησιν και προληψιν· εςι δε η προληψις Εννοια Φυσικη των καθολυ. Διοy. Λαερτ. Ζηνω. β.δ. ζ.

Should we therefore be afked to difplay
that combination˙ of intellectual powers
which gives rife to the more abftracted
branches of philofophical difquifition, and
to point out the character which ought to
be appropriated to each, it may be replied,
that in a mind adapted to the accomplifhment of fuch purpofes, imagination ought
to be diftinguifhed beyond all other qualities by *acutenefs of perception*, and reafon
by its clearnefs and precifion *. Thus the
moft acute perception is obvioufly required
to afcertain the precife point in which two
objects, to appearance perfectly fimilar,
are diftinguifhed from each other; and
clearnefs of judgment when this diftinction is once perceived, to exprefs it with
adequate perfpicuity.—Let us try an example by which thefe remarks may be
illuftrated.—An image and a metaphor
will, at firft view, be fuppofed to convey

* Ωϛε ϰδεν ϖροϲδειται ϖραγματων αγωναϛ ϰεϰτη-
μενων, το υφιϲηϰοϛ δε τελοϛ επιλογιζεϲθαι ϰαι ϖαϲαν
την ευεργειαν εφ᾽ ην τα δοξαζομενϰ αναγομεν. Ει δε᾽
μη, ϖαντα αϰριϲιαϛ ϰαι ταραχηϛ εϲαι μεϲα, &c. Id.
Επιϰ. βιϐ. ι.

the

the ſame idea to the mind, as both of theſe are included under the general name of illuſtration. A philoſopher however, of diſtinguiſhed eminence, not only diſtin-guiſheth the one of theſe from the other, as we have already ſeen*, but clearly ſhows us of what the difference conſiſts. " An image (ſays he) differs in ſome re-" ſpects from a metaphor. When it is " ſaid of Achilles *he ruſhed like a lion,* " here is a ſtrong image employed; but " when dropping the name of the hero it " is only ſaid ſimply *the lion ruſhed,* this " is a metaphor." Thus an image is per-fect when the ſimilarity betwixt two ob-jects is diſplayed by having theſe ſepa-rately exhibited to view; whereas a meta-phor ſuppoſeth this reſemblance to be uni-verſally conſpicuous, and mentions only the ſecondary object of compariſon as in-cluding the firſt.

With the ſame perſpicacity does this great genius point out the difference be-

---

* Sect. ii.

twixt

twixt the ends of eloquence and philofophy.—" Why (fays he) do we judge the
" fphere of an orator to be different from
" that of a philofopher? Is it not becaufe
" the latter contemplates *the caufe,* while
" the former is attentive to *the effect?*
" The one tells us of what injuftice, for
" inftance, confifts; the other, to what
" perfons this character belongs. The
" one explains the nature of tyranny, the
" other illuftrates his fubject by having
" recourfe to the tyrant*." In thefe examples the union of thofe qualities which
conftitute philofophical difcernment will
be perceived, and the underftanding in
particular as rendering the moft minute
diftinctions perfectly intelligible by a happy application of examples, and perfpicuity of expreffion. Without therefore
adopting the opinion of thofe who confider
all abftracted philofophy as deprived of

---

* Διατι τον Φιλοσοφον τυ ρητορος οιονται διαφερειν,
η οτι ο μεν τι εςι αδικια, ο δε ως αδικος ο δεινα· και ο
μευ οτι Τυρραννος, ο δε οιον Τυραννις. Αριςοτ. Προβλη-
ματ. τμημ. ιζ.

folidity,

folidity *, and refinement as inconfiftent
with juftnefs of reafoning, we may furely
affirm that an underftanding, however comprehenfive, that is not able to feparate
clearly the inferior parts of its theory from
each other, is unfit for this branch of philofophical difquifition : and that imagination, in order to be accommodated properly
to fuch fubtle inveftigation, muft be directed to felect fuch illuftrations as (without
regard to fublimity, beauty, harmony or
elegance as peculiarly requifite) are fuited
with the utmoft propriety to particular
objects. Judgment, it is certain, may poffefs comprehenfion without being able to
obferve the more minute proportions of
certain parts; and imagination, extent or
fublimity without the power of tracing its
objects through every little relation, in the
fame manner as the mind that plans a

---

* La philofophie ne devint abftraite que quand
elle ceffa d'eftre folide; on s'allacha des formalitez
quand'on n'eut plus rien de real a dire, & l'on ne
s'avifa de recourir a la fubtilité que quand'on n'efpera
plus faire valoir la raifon par fa fimplicité. Rap.
Reflex. fur la Philof. tom. ii. p. 358.

magnificent ftructure may overlook the fymmetry of a flight decoration; or an eye that contemplates with wonder the extent of the firmament, may be unfit even with the aid of a microfcope to mark the various lines in the organization of infects.

II. From contemplating the evanefcent objects (as they will be deemed by many perfons) of metaphyfical fpeculation, let us proceed to confider with the fame view to the faculties of the mind, a branch of this fcience more eafily comprehended as well as univerfally interefting; I mean what may be denominated the philofophy of the heart. This noble fpecies of the fcience in queftion gives fcope alternately to every intellectual faculty, and engageth the mind in purfuits which are connected with the moft important interefts of the whole fpecies.—Before we proceed to confider that combination of thefe powers which gives rife to this philofophy, let us examine a little more particularly of what it may be faid to confift.

As an inlet to any thorough acquaintance with the human heart it is princi-

pally

pally neceſſary that we ſhould have ſtudied
the paſſions with regard to their nature,
tendency, and effects. Theſe aſſume in
the various ſcenes of human life ſo many
different, and upon ſome occaſions ſeemingly incongruous appearances, that tho'
their influence extends univerſally to every
branch of conduct or ſpeculation without
exception, yet there is no enquiry in
which the mind is more apt to be bewildered, and to fall into error than that which
this various reſearch naturally preſents to
it. The difficulty here ariſeth from the
complicated nature and affinity of the paſſions to each other, connected as theſe are
ſo cloſely as that cauſes wholly diſtinct
and remote in reality are yet apt to be confounded together when we judge from
their effects. This will be obvious to any
perſon who reflects that ambition and
avarice, pride and vanity, malignity and
envy, love and pity, with many other
combinations of a ſimilar kind, produce
conſequences ſo perfectly correſponding to
one another, that in characters principally
influenced by any of theſe, a ſeries of

S 2   actions

actions is ufually neceffary to diftinguifh
the principle that is really predominant,
from another to which it bears a refemblance. It happens indeed often that the
character is formed, and a *ruling paffion* is
obferved to be univerfally confpicuous in
confequence not of any propenfity implanted by nature on the mind with particular
ftrength, but merely from certain habits
of indulgence. By thefe a paffion weak
perhaps originally, or but moderately
powerful, hath been called out into exertion more frequently than others, and
hath thus imperceptibly acquired that predominance which it gains at laft fo completely, and difplays with fuch energy.
The inferior and fubordinate emotions of
the heart as varioufly excited by an irrefiftible impulfe, as it may be deemed, are
diftinguifhed by different denominations,
as thefe appear to be more or lefs fubjected
to the controul of underftanding *.

From

---

* This is illuftrated in the following paffage from
a philofopher a few fragments only of whofe writings
have

From the union of theſe, in which, without eradicating wholly ſuch as are painful, it is principally requiſite that a proper temperature ſhould take place on the whole *; from this union ariſeth all that variety

---

have reached the preſent times. Και καθο μεν αρχεται και αγεται ο θυμος. και α επιθυμια υπο τυ λογου εχοντος μερεος τας ψυχας, α εγκρατεια και α καρτερια αγεται τυγχανουτι. Καθο δε μετα βιας αλλ' υκ εκυσιως τυτο πρασσουτι κακια τυγχανουτι. Δει γαρ την αρετην μη μετα λυπας, αλλα μετα ηδονας τα δεουτα πρασσειν· Πυθαγορ. Αποσπασ. p. 34.

* Επειδη η τυ ηθεος αρετη περι παθεα, των δε παθεων ηδονα και λυπα υπερτατα, φανερον οτι υκ εν τω υπεξελεσθαι τα παθεα της ψυκης αδοναν και λυπαν η αρετη πεπτωκει, αλλα εν τω ταυτα συναρμοζεσθαι. id. ibid. This ſentment the author proceeds to confirm by ſome very ſtriking and appoſite illuſtrations. Thus he obſerved that in order to produce health which ariſeth from the temperature of corporeal powers, heat and cold, drought and humidity, however pernicious in the extreme, are not to be removed, but to be blended ſo properly, as that from the concurrence of all may ariſe an effect of the moſt ineſtimable importance. In the moſt inchanting of all arts likewiſe that of the muſician, thoſe ſharp or deep ſounds which a man unacquainted with the art might judge to be harſh and diſcordant, yet when juſtly modulated in ſome happily conducted air contribute to render the harmony perfect, and to heighten inexpreſſibly the ef-

S 2　　　　　fect

variety of ftrong, fignificant, and delicate
fignatures by which men are in many inftances fo ftrikingly difcriminated.   A detail therefore of thefe, as exerting feparate or united influence on the conduct of
mankind, is in fact an hiftory of the human heart; and in order to develope the
movements of this complicated machine,
the fuperior powers of the mind, united
with exquifite fenfibility and comprehenfive experience muft be kept in ftrenuous
and conftant exercife.   In order to accomplifh this purpofe thoroughly, characters
muft not only be fet in oppofition to each
other, that fhades otherwife imperceptible
may be accurately delineated; but the
paffions muft be taken feparately; their
manner of operating in different affemblages expofed; the influence of habit,
prepoffeffion, an accidental combination of

---

fect of the whole piece.   In the fame manner our author obferves that the paffions, though thefe jar indeed
and are difcordant when viewed merely by themfelves,
yet when fubjected to the controul of reafon, afford the
moft powerful incitements to virtue, and are thus on
the whole of the moft indifpenfable utility and importance.

objects,

objects, and fuch other caufes as contribute to form the variety of minds particularly, inveftigated ; and an intellectual
mirror held up to us, in this manner, in
which each individual may have an opportunity to examine his own portrait, to
judge of its likenefs, and to correct fuch
expreffions as he judgeth to be improper,
or fupply thofe in which he perceives a
defect.

1. An eloquent writer of the prefent
age obferves very juftly, that, " the under-
" ftanding and the paffions are indebted
" to each other, much more than moralifts
" are commonly willing to allow; fince
" as the former difcovers our wants, and
" their gratifications in confequence of an
" impulfe from the latter, fo thefe on the
" other hand take in a greater compafs
" and variety of objects from that know-
" ledge which is acquired by the other *."
Judgment however in the whole procefs

---

* Rouffeau. See his Differt. fur l'inequalité des
hommes.

above-

abovementioned cannot be faid fo properly
to difcover original fubjects of fpeculation,
as to compare thefe together with accuracy when they are prefented to it, and to
obferve the precife points of oppofition or
refemblance. Thus, when in order to form
fome new affemblage of qualities, the mind
recollects the various difpofition of thefe
which it obferves to have taken place pro-
mifcuoufly among men, the power by
whofe operation thefe are exhibited in
ftriking and original combinations is no
doubt that of invention: but when the
firft heat hath fubfided, the expedience or
incongruity of this affemblage; the ftrength
of particular expreffions, and the comparative merit of all, as exhibiting a juft or
defective imitation of nature; of thofe
points the underftanding feparately takes
cognifance, and its perfpicacity is properly
afcertained from the proportion of thofe
figures which have paffed before it in review.

It is indeed impoffible to behold that
faculty by which man is diftinguifhed
from

from inferior animals employed in a ſphere
more worthy of its efforts, or more juſtly
adapted to diſplay its energy and comprehenſion than what is here laid before us.
The paſſions of human nature, of whatever
denomination, conſidered as ſuſceptible of
the moſt lively impreſſions from external
objects, are brought before this ſuperior
faculty by imagination, which may be
conſidered as their parent, to be followed
through all their windings, and the effects
ariſing from each, however complicated, to
be traced up to its proper cauſe.

From ſuch a variety of paſſions, called
up for the purpoſes abovementioned, reaſon, when it is required to form juſt and
natural characters from the union of all,
proceeds in courſes extremely different,
as its deciſions are impreſſed by the power
that made ſo many objects fall under its
cognifance. In this caſe a defective underſtanding appears principally conſpicuous from the qualities of the mind, as
exceeding (if I may ſo expreſs myſelf)
their natural dimenſions, or forming a
very

very improper combination in particular
circumſtances for the accompliſhment of
any rational purpoſe. Of the firſt kind
are all thoſe paſſions which are ſuppoſed
to precipitate a man to extremes * upon
almoſt

---

* Examples of this kind, readers of a certain claſs
will find in great abundance among the writers of the
old romance; among whom nothing is more common
than for a hero to run himſelf through the body upon
receiving any piece of diſagreeable intelligence, particularly when he is jealous of the fidelity of his miſtreſs;
and to be in as little danger of death from a thruſt of
this nature as from the ſcratch of a pin. We muſt
however take care not to rank with theſe, in the preſent
point of view, ſuch writers as Spencer and Arioſto,
whoſe themes are profeſſedly allegorical, and to whom
therefore a different ſtandard of criticiſm muſt be adapted. The conduct of every author whatever with regard
to the perſons of his fable, ought to be eſtimated from
the nature of thoſe beings who are his principal actors;
and of this laſt claſs again we are required to judge, as
having a certain, probable, or merely ideal exiſtence.
In either of the latter caſes (as when giants, magicians,
or dragons and hydras are introduced) we impute no
defect of judgment to the writer, when we find his
actors diveſted of human paſſions (at leaſt of the ſofter
and more amiable kind) and actions correſponding to
the ideas excited by this deſcription, we view as conſequences

almoſt every occaſion, from whoſe effects
it becomes immediately neceſſary to invent
uncommon

ſequences ariſing neceſſarily from their introduction.
It will indeed be ſaid that the laſt mentioned authors
fall into the ſame error with the former, when they repreſent men as not only encountering, but obtaining the
victory over creatures ſo greatly their ſuperiors. But
a poet whoſe ultimate aim is to enforce the motives to
virtuous conduct by allegorical repreſentation, is undoubtedly free to make uſe of expedients without cenſure, which in an account of tranſactions among merely human agents are certain evidences of defective underſtanding. Thus therefore the invulnerable Orlando attacking fearleſly whatever beings oppoſed his intentions, and the red-croſs knight reſtored to inſtant
vigour by falling into the *well of life* after having been
wounded and overthrown by a dragon, the fell in-
chanter who purſued without remorſe or pity the virtuous lady or the hardy knight; and the knight ſtimu-
lated by the paſſion of love, who devotes ſoul and body to the ſervice of his miſtreſs; all theſe it will be
readily granted are examples in which nature is over-
ſtrained as it were, and her juſt proportions are diſ-
regarded. But without having recourſe to the manners of primitive ages, in which the paſſion of love
particularly gave occaſion to actions of the moſt ro-
mantic extravagance, it is ſufficient to obſerve that
when *the moral* inculcated by allegorical compoſition
(in the illuſtration of which the underſtanding of the
writer is principally occupied) appears not to be violated, we permit him to uſe ſuch reſources with freedom
as are moſt expedient to his purpoſe; and fix our attention,

uncommon and often unnatural methods
of deliverance. One error it will be obferved in this, as in many cafes, is the parent of another, and the invention of fome
ftrange and incredible interpofition in order to refcue fome perfonage from imminent peril, or perhaps almoft inftantaneoufly to raife him from death, is in fact a
confequence of the fame inadequate judgment by which he was permitted to be
expofed to that peril, or to be rafhly
placed in fuch defperate circumftances *.

Reafon

---

tion, not upon the probable nature of the incidents
but upon the doctrine which fo many agreeable fictions are adapted to recommend.

* The remarks made on this fubject in the preceding note, p. 191. will prevent us in a great meafure
from extending the charge brought here againft the
conduct of authors in a certain fpecies of fable to the
events that occur in the great ftandards of the Epopœa. In the Iliad, Hector, ftruck down by Ajax, is
carried from the field in a deep faint, is laid down by
his attendants at a diftance from the war, and after his
recovery is wholly unable to refume the command of
his hoft. This command however he muft neceffarily
exercife without delay, and his former vigour muft
be reftored in a moment. The poet therefore takes
advantage of the received mythology of his country.
With that mafterly addrefs for which he is fo juftly celebrated,

Reaſon when its influence predominates in the mind adjuſts the intellectual ballance with more preciſion and accuracy; and aſſigning their proper ſpheres to the paſ-

---

lebrated, he introduceth the ſupreme deity, whoſe attention for ſome time had been purpoſely called off, as turning his eyes on the chief, whoſe pains immediately paſs away. The god of health deſcends at his command, and that Hector may be enabled to fulfil his deſtiny, or rather that the great moral of the fable Διος δε τελειετο βουλη, the will of God accompliſhed, may be inculcated; he is immediately reſtored to that ſtate in which Jupiter had formerly beheld him. Here therefore there is not only a " dignus vindice nodus," becauſe a ſupernatural reſource is rendered indiſpenſibly neceſſary; but the diſaſter of Hector is brought on by no unnatural ſtraining of character; and the cauſe in which he fights is ſuch as recommends him to the protection of that power which interpoſeth for his deliverance. A brave man ſuffering in the cauſe of his country is no doubt an object in whoſe behalf Homer might ſuppoſe that being to be intereſted, who looks not with an indifferent eye upon virtue in diſtreſs. The poet however it muſt be owned was in one circumſtance peculiarly favoured by the theological tenets of his countrymen, which permitted him to ſuppoſe that the attention of Jupiter might be interrupted; as by aſcribing to him an *human paſſion*, he hath introduced the misfortune and the deliverance of the Trojan prince by a detail, ſo various, ſo rich, and expreſſive of ſuch aſtoniſhing invention as ſucceeding poets muſt admire, with a deſpair of being able ſucceſsfully to imitate.

ſions;

fions, however impetuous, permits not
the character to be marked by extravagant and unnatural expreffions of their
power.

This faculty of the mind it is likewife
that regulates the general combination of
the paffions in order to accomplifh particular purpofes. Thus from a heart in
which generofity is joined with ambition,
humanity with fortitude, and more maf-
culine paffions are tempered happily by
clemency and benevolence; from fuch an
heart we expect the forgivenefs of perfonal
injuries, the voluntary facrifice upon ur-
gent occafions of private gratification; pity
exercifed towards a vanquifhed enemy, and
univerfal benignity extending to all. Here
therefore there is that mutual conformity
betwixt the character itfelf, and the action
arifing from this temperament of qualities
which indicates the prevalence of found
underftanding. On the other hand a man
whofe judgment is inadequate to the tafk
of forming from thefe materials any juft
and accurate combination, inftead of adapting circumftances to the difplay of paffions

united

united originally for particular purpofes, will at every other time be compelled to throw fome new ingredient into the portrait of his perfons as he is directed by events. It is eafy to forfee that inconfiftency and confufion muft be the confequence of proceeding in this manner, and a motly combination of intellectual and moral qualities affembled together, or which nature amidft all her mild and variegated productions never yet afforded a model of imitation.

Thus far we have endeavoured to mark out precifely the fphere that is occupied by the underftanding, confidered as unconnected with the other powers (as far as it can be contemplated in this light), with regard to its influence on the qualities of the heart. The obfervations on this fubject have referred principally to the makers or inventors of character, becaufe it is in the writings of thefe that the branch of philofophy we are here examining is moft eminently difplayed; and from thefe therefore may be felected the moft ftriking examples. The fame power however which

in

in one mind regulates and adjufts the
paffions to each other, fo as to form upon
the whole a natural affemblage, in another
takes cognizance of this regulation as juft
or defective according to its refemblance
or diffimilarity to the ftandard of nature.
He therefore who forms the original
draught as it may be called from fuch diverfified materials, and he who judgeth
with truth and accuracy of its propriety;
differ from each other only perhaps in the
degree of intellectual merit, and in the
objects to which the fame qualities receive
a direction: in other refpects, the poet
who by the various affemblage of the paffions and affections gives ftrength, fignificance, and peculiarity to his characters;
the critic who decides of thefe with propriety from the unerring ftandard above-
mentioned ; and the philofopher who,
without regard to either, confiders their
different ends, expreffions, and tendency,
as forming objects of the greateft importance and utility in his difplay of the mind ;
thefe difcover in their various fpheres that
union of intellectual powers which qualifies

fies for this branch of inveftigation, and in particular an underftanding fitted to form juft and decifive obfervations.

2. Judgment alone however, though operating as we have feen in a very exten-five range even in the prefent branch of difquifition, yet is employed principally in the tafk of throwing into juft difpofition fuch objects as are placed before it for this purpofe. The qualification therefore in-difpenfably neceffary to effectuate the full purpofe of developing the heart is that difcernment conftituted by the fuperior powers in their moft vigorous exertion, which we have formerly endeavoured to explain and illuftrate.

If it be true (as we are taught by expe-rience) that imagination is the parent of the paffions, whofe ftrength is commonly proportioned to its exuberance and vigour, we may then conclude, that a large pro-portion of it joined to the former (whofe office we have attempted to explain) muft be conferred, when thefe fprings of human action are purfued through their di-verfified effects. A man of difcernment

obtains this purpofe without any tedious
procefs of reflection in moft circumftances,
becaufe he judgeth immediately, either
from experience or comparifon. By the
former he is enabled to recollect the influence of thefe on his own mind as acting
either feparately or in union with each
other; while by the latter he can decide in
fuch cafes as fall not within the verge of
his immediate cognifance, of the confequences arifing from any combination
whatever on the conduct of another judging in the fame or fimilar circumftances of
what he finds within himfelf.

The judgment therefore that is formed
of human nature by a perfon of this character is ufually at the fame time juft and
comprehenfive. Juft, becaufe derived from
no fecondary caufe it is the immediate refult of feeling and experience; and comprehenfive, becaufe the fubject complex, as
it is, is only fuited to the mind that furveys it, which far from depending upon
conjectural evidence, is able to form an
enlarged eftimate from thofe qualities
which nature has conferred as the means
of

of its enquiry. In all this procefs we may obferve, that purpofes are obtained by what we may call with the ftricteft propriety philofophical difcernment, which difpaffionate reafon with all its accuracy and attention muft ever be unable in any meafure to accomplifh. For, as a man of weak fancy will be difqualified to trace this power through its higheft fphere of excellence, or a man of mere judgment to follow out reafon through the labyrinth of intricate and metaphyfical deduction; fo it is equally impracticable that he whofe paffions are cold, and his fenfibility proportionably deficient, fhould be able, however high in underftanding, to trace from their effects thofe caufes as powerfully influencing the minds of others, which operate fo weakly on his own. We can indeed eafily conceive a man of this caft as qualified to lay down excellent rules for the government of the paffions, to point out the danger arifing from their indulgence, and after having defcanted on thofe topics with great juftice and propriety, to render each the fubject of fome general declama-

T 2   tion.

tion. Thus a man whofe mind was never
ftimulated by ambition, may difplay many
of the evils of which we know it to be
productive; as he in the fame manner who
has no great propenfity to practife candour,
benevolence, or friendfhip himfelf, may yet
enumerate many advantages derived from
thefe with unexceptionable accuracy. But
in fuch frigid detail (of which, was it neceffary, we might adduce many examples
from moral writers both ancient and modern) that " vivida vis animi," that piercing energy of thought, by whofe means the
influence of one paffion upon another is
expofed in fuch a manner as to ftrike out
fome peculiar expreffion which the mind
inftantly appropriates; this is wholly
wanting, and the defect is by no means
compenfated by exact difpofition, perfpicuous language, and even by what may
be deemed a more valuable acquifition than
either of the former, an extenfive intercourfe and knowledge of mankind.

In general we may lay it down as a
maxim, which will be found to hold good
with very few exceptions, that where the
mind,

mind, inftead of fearching its fubject to the
bottom, runs into loofe declamation; and
when it ought to inveftigate a *caufe*, ex-
patiates only pompoufly upon the effect;
in thefe cafes a defect of intellectual powers
is commonly indicated, or at leaft an underftanding difqualified to exhibit an adequate reprefentation of the object which it
propofes to contemplate. A man of real
difcernment not only fhifts upon all fides,
as it were, every fucceffive profpect that
paffeth before him, but for the time is
really actuated by the paffion he defcribes,
or influenced in fome meafure by the motives he enumerates. By an exertion of
the fuperior faculties acting in concurrence,
he is able alternately to examine the felf-
ifh, as well as more benevolent affections
in their various modes of operation; and
thus, by the temporary but powerful influence of thefe on his own temper,
throws out particular and fignificant criteria, whofe truth is not only acknowledged by the judgment, but felt by the
heart.

T 3

An

An admired ancient, who himself poffeffed an eminent fhare of this difcernment,
treats another author with juft ridicule
who had chofen a fubject to which he
was no way equal. The rhetorician Ifocrates introduces a difcourfe which he
compofed to convince the Greeks, that
they were more indebted to the people
of Athens than to thofe of Lacedæmon,
by faying, " That eloquence is peculiarly
" excellent, becaufe it can deprefs great
" actions, and magnify fuch as are incon-
" fiderable; becaufe it can render old
" things new, and new old." " Are you
" Ifocrates (fays the critic) going to em-
" ploy this eloquence in afcertaining the
" comparative merit of the Athenians and
" Lacedæmonians ?—Then you give your
" reader a warning not to credit a word
" you may advance on the fubject *."
What then is eloquence?—Let us hear on
this fubject a perfon deeply fkilled in the
philofophy of the heart.—" An orator he

---

* Λογγιν. περι Υψ. τμημ. λη.

" tells

" tells us has the following great ends to
" accompliſh, He muſt conciliate the
" minds of his audience by a judicious
" exordium, relate facts in a ſimple man-
" ner, confirm theſe by proof, refute ob-
" jections, and after thus influencing the
" judgment of his audience, addreſs him-
" ſelf finally to their paſſions*."—In this
laſt ſphere of his exertion every part of nature is to be animated in his diſcourſe †.—
" He is to call up the dead, to make his
" country itſelf utter an addreſs to its in-
" habitants, as to her degenerate ſons;
" every thing muſt live in his deſcrip-

---

* " In omni porro cauſa judiciali quinque eſſe partes: quarum exordio conciliari audientem, narratione
cauſam proponi, confirmatione roborari, refutatione
diſſolvi, animos moveri, &c." Quintil. Inſtitut. lib.
vii.

† " Hic orator et defunctos excitabit, ut Appium
cæcum : apud hunc & patria ipſa exclamabit, aliquem-
que alloquetur:—hic Deos ipſos in congreſſum prope
ſuum ſermonemque deducet. · " Vos inquam Albani
tumuli, atque luci, vos Albanorum obrutæ aræ ſacro-
rum populi Romani ſociæ & æquales! Hic iram, hic
miſericordiam inſpirabit; hic dicet, te vidit, & flevit,
& appellavit, & per omnes affectus trahatur*." Quintil.
lib. xii. c. 10.
* Cicer. pro Milon.

" tion:

" tion : at one time he is to fingle out,
" and addrefs the criminal; at another to
" invoke the groves and altars which he
" had pollutted. The Gods themfelves
" are to be introduced into the affembly,
" and rendered fpeakers in his difcourfe.
" Thus (fays this confummate judge of
" mankind) thus will anger, pity, and
" every paffion of what kind foever be
" alternately excited, and the heart be
" rendered fufceptible of whatever impref-
" fions it may be deemed neceffary to ex-
" cite."

This difference, or rather this oppofition betwixt the Greek and Roman author
in treating the fame fubject, ferves to illuftrate in fome meafure the preceding remarks. In the former (whofe judgment
appears not to have been found enough to
regulate the fallies of a puerile fancy) we
obferve a propenfity to general defcription,
and a filly affectation of point and antithefis, which indicate a mind able only to
take a fuperficial and undiftinguifhing review. The latter on the contrary becomes
particular in confequence of fuperior difcernment.

cernment. His mind appears to have comprehended at one view, not merely the general purpoſe of the art, but the various means likewiſe by which this purpoſe may be effectuated: he has recourſe therefore immediately to the examples ; and he ſpeaks himſelf to the paſſions of human nature while he is deſcribing the art by which theſe are excited *.

3. To the combination of qualities which we have enumerated as conſtituting excellence in this noble branch of philoſophy; we need only further add, as one adventitious but neceſſary advantage that experience which indicates a man,

---

* I know no modern philoſophical performance in which the reader will find the qualities abovementioned more ſtrikingly united, than in Dr. Smith's excellent work, entitled, the Theory of Moral Sentiments. This moral anatomiſt, inſtead of being ſatisfied with general exhibitions of his ſubject, or of running (like the Greek writer abovementioned) into looſe declamation, either ſtrikes out in a ſtyle of maſterly compoſition ſuch criteria as come home to " men's buſineſs and boſoms," and require no illuſtration ; or confirms by ſuch happily ſelected examples thoſe remarks whoſe truth is leſs obviouſly conſpicous, as (in the author's opinion) evinceth the trueſt philoſophical diſcernment.

" Qui

··· " Qui mores hominum multorm vidit,"
who has examined the various manners of
mankind. The knowledge derived from
this fource produceth effects as widely diverfified as any fpecies of what kind foever. Thus the confequence of fuch intercourfe upon a mind in which the underftanding is fuperficial, commonly is to
produce a profufion of " wife faws," (as
Shakefpeare calls them), a number of unexceptionable but uninterefting obfervations on manners and character; good
admonitions, fententious maxims, and
rules of life, whofe fitnefs and propriety
no man calls in queftion, becaufe, whether
true or falfe, they reach not the cafes of
individuals, and therefore become not the
objects of inveftigation. On the contrary
when the judgment is good, but the imagination deficient, fuch remarks as this
experience may fuggeft, however folid,
will be uniform, and calculated rather to
difplay one branch of character than to inveftigate a whole. It is therefore only
when this acquifition falls to the fhare of
a mind in which both thefe powers are
concen-

concentrated, and co-operate with each other that the heart of man will be laid open, and ſuch criteria fixed upon as develope the movements however complicated of this various machine.

It would be a matter of no difficulty to ſhow that this facility of entering deeply into the feelings of the heart diſtinguiſh principally thoſe authors who will always ſtand in the higheſt rank of eminence. Take away the various and exquiſite ſhadeings of the characters in the Iliad; the talkative experience of Neſtor, the wary circumſpection of Ulyſſes, the noble boldneſs of Diomed, the implacable rage of Achilles; the fondneſs of Priam, of Hecuba, and of Andromache, ſo juſtly varied, and ſo delicately painted; take away theſe circumſtances, and the merit of this immortal work would be no more than that of a picture, in which the moſt luxuriant drapery might adorn objects whoſe lifeleſs ſimilarity the eye would ſoon contemplate with ſatiety and diſguſt. He muſt on the other hand be a very frigid critic indeed who can ſurvey that ſeries of theſe ſo nobly

ſupported

supported through the whole of this work, and suppose the author to deserve from this detail no higher praise than that of judgment. Deep penetration, exquisite sensibility, and experience, under the direction of these, of the avenues that lead most directly to the heart, constitute, in conjunction with the most copious imagination, the character of a man capable of conducting a work of this nature. The manner in which these are separately required to operate, and the spheres assigned to each in this work, may be severally collected from the preceding observations.

III. As we have now endeavoured to trace philosophy in its most extensive sense, to its original source in the various combination of intellectual powers; let us proceed to try in this philosophical history (as it may be termed) of the sciences and arts, whether we can observe likewise in some other views of the faculties formerly referred to, the origin of that science which records the various transactions of men from the earliest periods of society.—Before, however, we enter more immediately

diately into this difquifition, it may be neceffary to ftate the difference betwixt the didactic and the narrative manner.

Hiftory, when we confider it as the means of conveying inftruction by example, muft be allowed to poffefs advantages above the didactic or philofophical manner, proportioned to the degree of influence which example exerts over the practice of mankind beyond that of cold and inanimated precept. The name likewife of a profeffed teacher carries along with it a certain idea of fuperiority, which is always admitted with reluctance; and which, joined with the circumftance abovementioned, acts as a powerful counterpoife, to the good effects of which this fcience is naturally productive. Senfible of this difadvantage, the moft eminent philofophers have, in all ages, endeavoured to compenfate it by adopting as far as the feverity of their profeffion would admit, the infinuating graces of fifter arts, in the fame manner as a man of a coarfe and difagreeable afpect will naturally defire to fupply the defect of regular features and

com-

complexional beauty, by elegant improvement and a captivating addrefs. For this
purpofe we not only find the dialogue
manner of compofition fixed upon by the
mafters of this fcience to render their doctrines at the fame time agreeable and interefting.*; but in the pourtray of fcenery †, and even in developing argument,
thefe admit, upon fome occafions, figures
borrowed from the arts of eloquence and
poetry, in whofe ufe they are neceffarily
required to be fparing from the nature of
their fubject.

What the philofopher thus obtains with
much difficulty, by calling in foreign and

---

* Of this kind every reader knows are the principal
parts of the writings of the great Roman philofopher,
as well of the Greek, whom the former profeffedly
imitated.

† Take the following defcription as an example
from the Phædrus of Plato. Η τε γαρ πλατανος αυτη
μαλα αμφιλαφης τε και υψηλη τε τε αγυυ το υψος,
και το συσκιον παγκαλον και ως ακμην ιχει το ανθκς,
ως αν ευωδεςατον παρεχοι τον τοπον· Ηγε αν πηγη
χαριεςατη υπο της πλατανυ ρει μαλα ψυχρου υδατος,
&c. There are other fine circumftances in the defcription of this fhade, in which the philofophers ie-
cline to difcourfe of eloquence.

adventitious

adventitious aid, the hiſtorian can accompliſh with much greater eaſe, as the materials which he is required to mould into
proportion are ſuch as neceſſarily awaken
attention, and engage the mind in an uſeful and intereſting procedure. This circumſtance it is that gives the narrative
manner ſo much advantage above the former. In the explication of a philoſophical
theory, a ſeries of cloſe reaſoning or of
abſtracted obſervation is carried on; and
ſentiments connected with, and ſupported
by each other, form the great objects of
the work. In hiſtory, on the other hand,
theſe as forming in ſome meaſure but ſecondary views, and required to grow out
of ſome preceding narration, arreſt the attention of a reader in a very forcible manner, and when judiciouſly introduced, make
a laſting impreſſion on his memory. Thus
it happens, that a well written hiſtory is
more univerſally uſeful than any other
work. The medium through which in-
ſtruction is conveyed, we are here diſpoſed
to contemplate with pleaſure; and while
the manners are tinctured by the examples
exhibited

exhibited in fo faithful a mirror*, a fenfible mind receives an entertainment of
the moft agreeable kind, by obferving the
various operation of qualities both intellectual and moral on the characters of
men.

Thefe general remarks on hiftorical compofition (the particular confideration of
which belongs more properly to a fubfequent fection) will affift us in afcertaining
that union of intellectual powers which is
neceffary to conftitute the perfection of fo
beneficial a fcience.

As the hiftorian therefore poffeffeth advantages from the nature of his profeffion
fuperior to thofe of the didactic author,
and as his ends may be accomplifhed with
greater facility, it will follow, that a moderate, but as nearly as poffible an equal
proportion of the powers whofe offices we
have endeavoured to point out, will be fufficient to effectuate all the purpofes to

---

* " Hiftoria illuftri appellatione donata fit, cum ma-
giftra morum nominetur, quod qui ad eam fe con-
ferunt, inftructi ad vitæ cafus, femperque inde me-
liores abeunt." Strad. Proluf. Academ. p. 45.

which

which this fcience can be rendered fubfer-
fervient. In philofophy the underftanding
is employed in the felection and difpofition
of fuch abftracted ideas as the mind draws
from having formed an accurate judgment
of its own operation, or from experience
with regard to mankind in general. In
eloquence the power of invention is eminently difplayed likewife, not only as be-
ftowing high and expreffive colour on the
objects that pafs before it, but in fixing
upon new topics of perfuafion, and prefl-
ing thefe home with that irrefiftible energy
which penetrates the heart. But in hiftory
as the judgment employed in the collation
of materials fupplied wholly by others,
exerts not an act equally ftrenuous, as
when it regulates thofe which owe their
exiftence to the mind's penetrating and
intenfe contemplation of itfelf; fo the imagination in the fame manner that works
only from facts and incidents laid before
it, from which it is not permitted to de-
viate, difplays not the fame ftrength, verfatility, and exuberance, as when employed in fpheres more juftly appropriated

to its exercife, it is with more propriety denominated the *power of invention* *.

Hiftory therefore, as it purfues a middle courfe betwixt the fpheres of philofophy and eloquence, demands a fhare of every intellectual faculty, but no fuch proportion of any feparate power as will turn the balance obvioufly to a fide.   The truth of this remark will be acknowledged moft readily, when we confider the ends which this writer is required to accomplifh.

An hiftorian then ought to poffefs a clear and folid judgment, otherwife he will not only fail of giving a due proportion to the various members of his work, but

---

* What we have faid here of eloquence may be likewife applied to poetry. " Le merite principal de l'hiftorien (fays an elegant critic) ne confifte pas comme celui de poete.   Le merite principal de l'hiftoire eft d'enricher notre memoire & de former notre jugement ; mais le merite principal de la poefie confifte a nous toucher."   Ref. Critiques fur la Poef. &c. v. ii. p 283.   Let us hear Ariftotle on the fame fubject.   Ο γαρ Ιϛορικος και ο ποιητης ȣ το η εμμετρα λεγειν η αμετρα διαφερȣσιν—αλλα τȣτο διαφερει τω τον μεν τα γενομενα λεγειν του δε οιον αν γενοιτο.   Διο και Φιλοσοφωτερον και σπȣδαιοτερον Ποιητις Ιϛοριας εϛιν· Ποιητ.

unequal

unequal particularly to the more difficult parts of his profeſſion, the defect will become remarkably conſpicuous when he is required to diſentangle truth from a multitude of obſcure and perplexing incidents, or to reconcile details of the ſame tranſaction that are ſeemingly contradictory. He ought to poſſeſs likewiſe an adequate proportion of imagination, as without this his compoſition will have too much uniformity, and he will be unable to treat the different branches of his ſubject in the manner adapted moſt properly to each. A conſiderable ſhare of Diſcernment is likewiſe neceſſary to make him improve upon a diſtant hint, when he is not furniſhed with full and digeſted materials; to aſſiſt him in examining characters to the bottom, and in painting theſe ſo juſtly as that they may appear to be inferences deduced from the narration of previous incidents.—In ſhort, that experience of mankind which is acquired by having mixed in ſociety, is requiſite to give compaſs to his views, and to render his obſer-

vations

vations on men and things fuch as characterife human nature; and, to fum up
all, ftrength, and even pathos, is upon
fome occafions neceffary to complete the
character of this writer, that he may hold
up an action eminently virtuous to the admiration, or a vicious one to the contempt
and deteftation of mankind!

From this fhort account of the various
purpofes of hiftory, and of the intellectual
powers as adapted to carry thefe effectually into execution, it muft be evident,
that though there are perhaps other departments of literature in which fome of
the fuperior faculties act in a larger fphere,
or appear in more vigorous exertion; yet
there is none more happily calculated to
difplay different kinds, as well as degrees
of excellence, by calling every faculty by
which the human mind is diftinguifhed,
fuccefsively into action. Thefe, however,
with other advantages of this noble and
inftructive fcience, will fall to be more particularly detailed, when from having viewed it in its origin, as indicating a peculiar

com-

combination of mental powers, we come to conſider it in the more extenſive light of a ſpecies of Compoſition.

SECTION VII.

Of that Combination of the intellectual Faculties which gives riſe to the arts of Poetry and Criticiſm.

AN ancient philoſopher of diſtinguiſhed name, aſſigns (I cannot ſay with what propriety) admiration as the ſource of philoſophy *. Whatever may be in this, we may ſurely, with at leaſt equal truth, judge it to have occaſioned the firſt *poetic* effuſions †, as in proportion to that degree of this paſſion with which the mind was tranſported upon having contemplated the

---

* Μαλα φιλοσοφον τυτο το παθος το θαυμαζειν. Ου γαρ αλλ.η αρχη Φιλοσοφιας η αυτη. Πλατων. Θεητ.

† Οι πρωτα μεν βλεποντες εβλεπον ματην· Κλυοντες ουκ εκουον· αλλ' ονειρατων Αλιγκιοι μορφαισι του μακρου χρονου Εφυρον εικη παντα.   Αισχυλ. Προμη.θ.

works

works of nature, muſt have been the ſublimity of thoſe divine hymns in which
were celebrated the perfections of the
author. As ſoon, therefore, as men began
to exerciſe their reaſon in tracing at the
ſame time the exiſtence and attributes of
the ſupreme mind, what we denominate
lyric poetry received its origin from a
warm imagination eyeing the more ſtupendous works of the deity, and ariſing
from theſe to contemplate their original.

Me vero primum dulces ante omnia Muſæ
Accipiant, cælique vias & ſidera monſtrent, &c.
Geor. ii. 475.

Such glorious objects as theſe a great genius naturally beholds with that high enjoyment which this power of the mind
derives from having dwelt intenſely on the
ſublime and the wonderful. This branch
of his ſubject, however, the author hath
treated at ſuch length in a former eſſay,
that it would be wholly improper to re-
ſume on the preſent occaſion, what hath
already been advanced on it *.

---

* See Eſſay on Lyr. Poet. lett. ii.

Suppofing then this high and inchanting fpecies of poetic Compofition to have
received its origin and improvement from
the caufe above-mentioned, let us try
whether from different views of the human mind as varioufly imprefled by fur-
rounding objeɛts, we can account for the
rife and improvement of thofe other
branches of this art which are confidered
as the moft important.

That defire of imitating *, which our
great critic affigns as the fource of all
poetic excellence, operates upon the mind
either inftantaneoufly as the objeɛts of
external nature are reprefented by the
fenfes, and imagination fet at work to copy
the features of fome admired original; or
it works from fuch materials as are more
gradually fupplied by refleɛtion and experience, and forms by thefe means repre-

---

* Εοικασι δε γεννησαι μεν ολως την ποιητικην αιτιαι
δυο και αυται φυσικαι· το ΜΙΜΕΙΣΘΑΙ ΣΥΜΦΥΤΤΟΝ
τοις ανθρωποις, &c. Και αρμονια και ρυθμος εξ αρχης
οι πεφυκοτες προς αυτα μαλιϛα κατα μικρον προα-
γοντες εγεννησαν την Ποιησιν. Αριϛοτ. περι Ποιητ.
κεφ. δ.

fentations

fentations of fentiments, characters, actions,
and incidents; either diſtinct from each
other, or ſtanding in connection, as beau‑
tiful and expreſſive pictures of the great
drama of human life.——To the former of
theſe very little attention will convince us,
that we owe the deſcriptive; and to the
latter the more complex ſpecies of poetic
Compoſition.

1. Imagination, when it contemplates
the objects of deſcriptive poetry, fluctuates
naturally for ſome time and wanders from
one ſcene to another before a ſeries adapt‑
ed to its original propenſity irreſiſtibly
determines its choice; but this little irre‑
ſolution in the ſelection of a ſubject ſerves
only to indicate that no accidental aſſem‑
blage of external objects, however juſtly
preſented by the ſenſes, can arreſt the at‑
tention of the mind in ſuch a manner as
to produce imitation, while the ſphere is
not juſtly preſented which it is fitted by
nature to occupy. As ſoon as this aſſem‑
blage occurs, the mind becomes ſenſible of
its ſtrength, and falling at once into its
                                              proper

proper track, furveys the objects with pleafure, and imitates thefe with facility.

This inftantaneous perception, however,
of the fphere adapted naturally to its
choice, we are not to fuppofe exifting in
the mind independently (as fome philofophers feem to think that all inftantaneous perceptions do) of the faculty of
reafon *. This power approves without
                                    any

---

* When clofely examined, I am perfuaded that no
philofopher ever meant to confider inftinct (as it is
termed) and reafon as intellectual powers *really* diftinct from, and independent of each other. This diftinction however is *feemingly* made by thofe who define
the reafoning faculty to be that by which the mind acquires the knowledge of truth, in confequence of pro-
greffionary evidence ; and the inftinctive or intuitive
power is that which decides *inftantaneoufly* of the truth
or falfhood of certain propofitions, and is termed a
fenfe, from this quicknefs of perception. The following obfervations are thrown together to prevent readers
from mifapprehending the meaning of either term,
and to fhew that no diftinction of this kind can poffibly fubfift.—It is undoubtedly a truth, as clear as
any mathematical axiom whatever, that of two objects
wholly diftinct from each other, we can conceive
either to exift feparately. If, therefore, there are
truths of any kind which this inftinctive or intuitive
                                    power

any regular feries of argument of a choice
adapted with propriety to the character;
but

---

power of the mind perceives without the aid of reafon,
it will follow, that there are propofitions fo obvious
as to be approved by a mind in which this faculty
does not exift.	Let us take then the fimpleft of thefe
propofitions, that two and two make four;—and fuppofe it reprefented to a perfon not difordered in underftanding, but wholly deprived of that faculty;
would this intuitive truth be inftantly perceived by
fuch a perfon, or would any idea be conveyed in con-
fequence of repeating it?	No man furely will affert
that there would.	It will perhaps be faid, that there
is in this reafoning a petitio principii; fince reafon is
here without proof fuppofed to perform the office of
this *common fenfe,* and the example we have adduced is
one in which both being annihilated, a mind cannot
properly be faid to have exiftence.	But we fhall be
convinced, with a little attention, that the power
(whatever defignation we apply to it) by which we
deduce effects from a caufe, or inveftigate a caufe from
its effects, is in no other refpect different from that
fenfe (as it is called) by which we perceive the truth of
the fimpleft axiom, than as in the former inftances
it makes an exertion, which in the latter is unnecef-
fary.	We have mentioned one propofition purely in-
tuitive.	Let us try another, to comprehend which,
fome degree of reafon muft be neceffary.	At a very
confiderable diftance from the fhore, I obferve a
fmall fpeck, fcarce to be diftinguifhed from a cloud,
and about whofe nature I remain for fome time uncer-
tain.

but it approves in confequence of difcerning this propriety, in the fame manner as
the

---

tain. Common fenfe it will be faid, or inftinct, is the
power by which (having once difcovered that this is
a fhip) I know its real to be different from its apparent
magnitude, while yet at a diftance. Though this is
far from being felf-evident to me in any fenfe of the
word whatever; yet let us for once fuppofe it to be fo.
As the fhip draws nearer, and the fails, mafts, cordage
and mariners, are fucceffively difplayed; I become
curious to know the caufe for which it moves in a particular direction. Here an effect is immediately traced
up to its caufe, though the procefs is indeed abundantly
obvious. For as foon as it is known that the fhip is
moved upon the water, by the wind operating in any
way whatever, it will follow that its direction muft be
determined by that of the wind; and as foon as the
caufe fhall ceafe to operate, the effect (i. e. the motion)
arifing from it muft fubfide likewife. This is, indeed,
fomewhat more complex than the propofition that two
and two make four:—yet I will leave any reader to
determine, whether a perfon incapable of underftanding the former of thefe truths, would have any diftinct
idea conveyed to his mind by the latter.—Will it be
faid that it is inftinct or common fenfe, which equally
takes cognizance of both propofitions? I fhall then be
glad to know at what point this intuition ftops, and
where reafon begins. Does it trace effects from any
particular caufe? or, vice verfa, a caufe from its
effects?—Inftinct is then furely not different from
reafon; and is ufed only to exprefs the fimpleft exertion

the eye which decides of minute proportions from an accurate infpection of fome
particular

---

ertion of that faculty. Is it again ufed to fignify that
fenfe by which the mind perceives the truth of certain
propofitions which are termed felf-evident, becaufe,
without any confideration of caufe or effect, thefe are
the immediate objects of internal fenfation, in the
fame manner as external appearances are of the
fenfes?—It hath been already fhewn, that where the
power which traceth the relation betwixt an effect and
a caufe ceafeth to operate, this inftinct immediately
fubfides along with it ; and as neither of thefe can
exift feparately, they muft in fact be the fame.—Was
it neceffary to purfue this thread of argument ftill further, we might obferve that as this inftinct, or common
fenfe, cannot by any operation be diftinguifhed from
reafon when confidered as an internal perception, on
the one hand, fo neither on the other has it the leaft
connection with, or dependence upon thofe external
organs of perception which we denominate the fenfes.
The eye of an ideot will prefent to him a tree, a horfe,
or a wall, as diftinctly as that of a wife man ; his ear
in the fame manner will be impreffed by founds. Sup-
pofe him to be deprived of either of thefe fenfes, the
remaining four will ftill be diftinct from each other,
and external objects will operate as ufual upon their
various organs. But does any fuch diftinction as this
take place betwixt reafon and inftinct? When we
take away the power which inveftigates caufes and
effects, does that remain which perceives the truth of
a geometrical axiom in the fame manner as hearing
when

particular obje4, obferves with eafe that harmony which arifeth from a general correfpondence of parts in fome magnificent ftruᶜture. The laft of thefe decifions therefore, may with equal propriety be fuppofed to take place without the inter-

when the fight is removed, feeling when we are deprived of both ; and any of the five, when the others are obliterated ? The contrary of this we have already evinced.—Upon the whole, this diftinᶜtion can only be made by thofe who have not attended properly to the various operations of reafon. It may require a long procefs of evidence to render a propofition obvious to me, whofe truth another man may perceive and acknowledge as foon as it is laid down. But does it follow from this, that the faculty of my mind which takes cognizance of this truth is *effentially different* from that which perceives it of his ?—Surely not. His underftanding in confequence either of its fuperior comprehenfion, or of having been long accuftomed to a certain ftrain of obfervation, may immediately fupply the intermediate procefs by which an end is obtained ; but it is ftill the fame power aᶜting in one inftance with rapidity, and in the other proceeding with coolnefs and circumfpeᶜtion, by which both are conduᶜted to the fame period. This remark holds equally of every propofition whatever. Intuition, as diftinguifhed from reafon, is that power by which a mind is fuppofed to have before it, at one view, the whole feries of caufes and effeᶜts, and in this fenfe it can only be predicated of the Supreme Being.

pofition of fight or feeling, as the other
without that of underftanding.

Led in this manner at laft into its proper train, imagination falls immediately
to work, to copy fuch draughts as have
made upon it the moft lively and forcible
impreffion. But imagination left to itfelf
would form an imitation which however
ftriking, would rather prefent a refemblance of fome fcattered features.

Definet in pifcem mulier formofa fuperne,

than that of a whole proportioned figure;
much lefs a feries of thefe, reflecting mutual light upon each other, and ftanding
in the happieft combination. This harmonious concurrence of objects diverfified
from each other, to produce one effect on
the mind, and the beauty of each object
when viewed apart, arifing from the light
in which this is prefented to it, denominates that power of perceiving the jufteft
attitudes, and the moft delicate expreffions
which is known by the name of Tafte;
and whofe influence is peculiarly confpicuous in the delineation of external forms.
By this internal fenfe (as philofophers
have

have denominated it) objects are perceived
immediately to bear a certain relation to
each other, which even the superior faculties of the mind, when confidered apart,
would have been difqualified to trace; and
in the fphere of defcriptive poetry it either adjufts the illuftrations with elegance
and propriety to their correfponding originals when the work is going on; or it
qualifies the reader, though perhaps unable
himfelf to execute with correctnefs and
maftery, to judge with the utmoft precifion of this correfpondence, and to feel
with exquifite fenfibility the effect arifing
from it. The objects of this quality, and
the powers by whofe combination it is
conftituted, we fhall foon have occafion to
detail at more length;—its influence on
this branch of the fubject, it is juft fufficient to have mentioned.

As it is therefore neceffary that a defcriptive poet fhould be capable of perceiving remote connections, and of imitating
beauties of which few are qualified to take
cognizance; fo the effect arifing from the
union of the reafoning and inventive faculty,

culty, will be as confpicuous in this, as in
any fphere whatever. Thofe moral obfervations in particular, which are judicioufly
made to grow out of a defcription of the
external beauties of nature; and which, in
confequence of the pleafing fcenery that
foothes and delights the imagination, convey inftruction to the mind at the moft
favourable moment; difcover the writer's
judgment by the juftnefs of their difpofition, and the confiftency they give to his
performance; his imagination, by the
beauty of that vehicle in which thefe are
conveyed; and his tafte, by an happy felection of the fitteft words, and a train of
fentiment carried precifely to that point
where the mind, gratified but not fatigued,
returns with pleafure to the principal fubject.—Nor is it an inconfiderable or common fhare of thefe combined qualities by
which excellence in this branch of poetry
is conftituted. The wild, the fublime, and
the magnificient in nature, indicate not,
when painted in the richeft and moft appropriated colours, more grandeur of imagination, and juftnefs of perception, than
the

the purpofes which thefe may be made to ferve by infpiring great and exalted conceptions of the Author of nature; or by raifing the thoughts above little and tranfitory objects to the contemplation of fuch as are noble and eternal; thefe laft difcover the compafs of an enlightened underftanding, operating in ,a fphere at once dignified and comprehenfive. Even in the fport and paftime of fancy, when the fimpleft beauties of rural fcenery are delineated by her pencil, and the fimpleft occupations are afcribed to the inhabitants, a fhare of judgment much more confiderable than we are apt to fuppofe is neceffary to render the images, fentiments, and expreffion juft fuch as the fubject requires; and an exquifite internal perception of genuine beauty to diftinguifh elegance from rufticity, and to feparate a fimple from a florid or infipid imitation.

II. From this detail of the intellectual powers as combining to accomplifh thofe purpofes to which a juft difplay of external nature may be rendered fubfervient, let us follow the mind in the more ab-

VOL. I.   X   ftracted

ftracted contemplation of its own internal operations, and obferve the effects that moft naturally refult from it. By confidering in this manner the paffions and affections of mankind in diftinct points of view, we fhall comprehend moft readily that union of the nobler faculties by which thefe are happily imitated, and exhibit ftriking reprefentations of character and fentiments.

1. As the objects of our fenfes vary their appearances at different feafons, and prefent to us afpects extremely remote, if not feemingly incongruous, upon many occafions; the human mind in the fame manner, that great object of all our refearches, when guided at one time by reafon, difturbed at another by paffion, and driven at a third by a precipitate and irrefiftible impulfe to fome irrational conduct, receives expreffions as diverfified in every refpect as the former, and will make impreffions not lefs various and lively upon an attentive examination. To effectuate by means of thefe the great purpofe of conveying inftruction, is equally the ultimate

mate aim of the philofopher and the poet, who in the higher branches of his art unites the ends of philofophy with the more agreeable ones of his own profeffion. The means however by which thefe accomplifh the fame general purpofe are very different, and ferve to indicate that concurrence of the mental powers by which each of thefe (the laft in particular) ought to be diftinguifhed:

Let us fuppofe two men with both thefe characters contemplating the human mind in the earlieft period of fociety; with the view of ftudying attentively its different phænomena, and of inftructing mankind by their obfervations. The one obferving many effects arifing from the fame general principles varioufly modified, whofe feeming incongruity perplexeth him at firft, attempts, as the beft method of eradicating the moft pernicious, to inveftigate the caufe from which each derives its origin. By accomplifhing this purpofe he fuppofeth juftly that he will at the fame time difcover the beft means of procuring happinefs to himfelf, and of communicating

X 2   this

this ineſtimable benefit to mankind in general.   Our philoſopher therefore engageth from theſe motives in the ſearch of
truth, and in conſequence of a knowledge
of the human mind, acquired by accurate
obſervation, and rendered comprehenſive
from experience, becomes qualified to eſta-
bliſh rules of conduct, and to fix ſociety
by laws that indicate thorough acquaintance with the human heart upon a ſolid
and permanent foundation.   Here then
we obſerve the origin of moral inveſtigation.   But by what method ſhall theſe important ends be brought about ?   Should
we put this queſtion to our philoſopher,
he would undoubtedly reply;—" I confi-
" der man as an intelligent and rational
" agent, whoſe judgment it is neceſſary to
" convince by evidence before motives of
" any kind can operate on his practice.
" To his judgment therefore I appeal, and
" having firſt detected the cauſes of his
" errors by a clear and accurate inveſtiga-
" tion; I endeavour to lay before him
" ſuch rules of conduct as are adapted moſt
" properly to remedy his defects, and to
                                    " aſcer-

" afcertain to him the possession of such
" objects as promise him real and perman-
" ent felicity *. Of the accuracy of this
" investigation, and of the importance of
" those motives by which new principles
" are enforced; of these circumstances rea-
" son must finally decide; and I have no
" other merit than that of presenting to
" this power such consideration as may
" determine its choice to the greatest advan-
" tage."—Such would be the language of
our philosopher on this subject.—Let us
next attend to the practice of the poet, acting in the higher spheres of his profession
with the same general purpose as the for-

---

* By some such method as this it must undoubtedly be that philosophy is said to perform the wonders
which have been ascribed to it. The story of Socrates is well known : Cicero gives us another example of
the same kind, if not a still more striking one. " Stil-
ponem Megaricum philosophum acutum sané hominem
& probatum illis temporibus accepimus. Hunc scribunt ipsius familiares & ebriosum & mulierosum su-
isse, neque hoc scribunt vituperantes sed potius ad lau-
dem: vitiosam enim naturam ab eo sic edomitam &
compressam esse doctrina ut nemo unquam vinolentum
illum, nemo in eo libidinis vestigium viderit." Cicer.
de Fato.

mer,

mer, but fixing on expedients to accomplifh it extremely different *.

He likewife, we fhall fuppofe, obferves
the dangerous confequences of indulging
the paffions, and as his own have probably greater ftrength than thofe of the
former, he will be ftruck more forcibly
with the neceffity of reftraining thefe within proper limits.   He falls to work therefore with this great end kept conftantly in
his eye; and having obferved the manner
in which the paffions operate on the characters of mankind, he throws off fuch
refemblances by lively and ftriking imitations as tend to render virtuous conduct
the object of attachment; and vicious practice, of deteftation.   For this purpofe he
either fhows the pernicious tendency of
vice by that ftain which it throws upon
characters the moft dignified and exalted;
or he points out the excellence of virtue

---

* Ου πεισομεθα Ησιοδι (fays an able critic) επειδαν
τινες τοιυτυ γενους τελευτησωσιν ως αρα οι μεν δαιμονες
αγνοι επιχθονιοι τελεθουσιν. εσθλοι, αλεξικακοι φυλακες
Sυντων ανθρωπων. Πεισομεθα μεν ουν. ΕΡΜΟΓΕΝ. περι
ΕΥΡΕΣ,

by

by the luſtre it ſheds on perſons diſtinguiſhed by no ſuperiority of intellectual
powers: he holds up a faithful mirror to
mankind in general*; and by preſenting
examples which all are qualified to contemplate with impartiality, corrects the bad
conſequences of that ſelf-love which commonly renders us partial to ourſelves.

Our poetical inſtructor attends likewiſe
in this ſublime ſphere of his profeſſion, to
ſuch ſtrokes as make the moſt immediate
and laſting impreſſion on the heart. Theſe
he judiciouſly contrives to preſs with irreſiſtible energy, and to excite the emotions
ariſing from all by varying the circumſtances in a natural and happy manner from
diſtreſs to proſperity, thus at the ſame

---

* Δια των πεπραγμενων τ8 διασκευαζοντος οφειλοντος
πλατυναι το πραγμα μονον. ου μεντοι γε 8τε αιτιαις, 8τε
λογισμοις τοσ8τον 8τε αλλω τινι επιχειρηματι αλλα
μον8 τω τροπω. Διασκευαζεται μεν γαρ παντως εκ τι
των της περισασεως. Και ο τι δ'αν εκεινων η τω τροπω
πλατυνεται. Και μετα τ8 τροπ8, και προσωποποιας
οια εικος ην τελεισθαι εφ' εκας8 των πρατ]ομενων, και
λεχθηναι δυναμενων παρα των εμφαινομενων προσωπων εν
τη διατυπωσει. Id. p. 180.

time

time foothing the imagination, inftructing the judgment, and mending the heart, Such a procefs of obfervation as this probably gave rife to the drama and epopœa.

In this procefs nothing will ftrike a difcerning reader more forcibly than the various operation of the intellectual powers attempting to accomplifh one purpofe in the different fpheres of their exercife. He will obferve the underftanding, in one cafe, effectuating its end by the fimple medium of proof and inveftigation; in the other he will trace judgment, in that arrangement of incidents which renders thefe adapted happily to produce a certain purpofe; imagination, in their original invention, and in the glowing imagery which gives them colour and expreffion; difcernment he will perceive in thofe mafterly ftrokes by which the fhades of a character are happily contrafted with its diftinguifhing excellencies; and exquifite fenfibility in that pathos of fentiment and expreffion which the heart appears to have dictated, and

and by which the heart of the reader is penetrated.

The drama and the epopœa contemplated in this manner, as ariſing from the combination of all the intellectual powers, making ſeparately the moſt ſtrenuous exertion, will appear (the former particularly) to have called theſe into action with an energy proportioned to the ſtrength and variety of thoſe manners from which an example is to be formed. As theſe laſt therefore varied conſiderably in the more cultivated periods of ſociety from the uniform ſimplicity of its earlieſt ages, the dramatic poets diſcovered without doubt greater verſatility of mind, more knowledge of human nature, and deeper inſight into the motives by which the heart is actuated, who to the original imperfections ſuperadded a picture of the faſhionable vices and foibles of mankind, than he who conſidered man when his manners were ſimple and uniform, engaged in a leſs intricate and perplexing detail.

2. Of the firſt inventors of the drama we know little with any certainty, nor is
this

this a matter of any great confequence, as Æfchylus, the great reformer of this branch of poetry, found it in a ftate of imperfection, which clearly fhewed that in the preceding ages civilization had made but very little progrefs.[*] Manners at that time were ftrong, but uniform; and as the wants of men were comparatively few, their virtues or vices lay open to detection. That it required however both addrefs and difcernment, in every fenfe of that word, to ftrike off an exact imitation of thofe qualities will be acknowledged without difficulty[†]. The paffions of terror, anger,

and

---

[*] " Ignotum tragicæ genus inveniffe Camœnæ
Dicitur & plauftris vexiffe poemata Thefpis
Quæ canerent, agerentque peruncti fæcibus ora.
Poft hunc perfonæ, pallæque repertor honeftæ
Æfchylus, & modicis inftravit pulpita tignis,
Et docuit magnumque loqui, nitique cothurno.
                          Hor. de Art. Poet.

[†] The great ancient critic appears to have rather refined too much on his fubject when he fays that " tragedy exhibits an imitation not of men in general, " but of their actions; of the life for inftance of fome " individual, and of fuch objects as conftitute happi- " nefs or mifery: that happinefs confifts in action; " and though manners denominate the character, yet

" it

and revenge, though thefe may be detected with greater facility, and perhaps pourtrayed in all their appearances with lefs
difficulty than fuch as are concealed behind
the mafque of hypocrify, or are contracted
by an intercourfe with the diffolute and
luxurious part of mankind; yet when
confidered as exerted in particular circumftances, or combined with certain qualities
either intellectual or moral, cannot be
painted as appropriated to characters without a knowledge of the human heart ar-
guing at the fame time difcernment and
experience.

Hiftory however relates not any change
fo remarkable in the courfe of a few years
as that which appears to have been

" it is from thefe laft that we decide of man as happy
" or miferable, in which light he is principally exhi-
" bited in tragedy; that therefore a performance of
" this kind cannot fubfift without action, but may
" without an imitation of manners." See the 6th ch.
of his Poetics.—This is mere metaphyfical refinement.—It is certainly not true, that we judge of men
as happy or miferable only from their actions: thefe
difcover to us in general rather what men ought to be,
than what they really are. Their *manners* upon particular occafions, exhibit a much furer teft, and it is the
bufinefs of tragedy to take of both.

wrought upon the manners of the Athenians, betwixt the time of Æfchylus and that of his fucceffor Sophocles, who came only about thirty years behind him. This laft poet found his country men eminent for their politenefs, learning, elegance, and urbanity, of which they continued for fo many ages to fet mankind a pattern. The ftage, whofe reformation kept pace with refinement of manners in every other refpect, had now received great improvement, not only from the drefs and pronunciation of the actors, as regulated properly to the characters which each was to exhibit, but principally from the change made upon the chorus, which had formerly confifted of a promifcuous croud, whofe appearance frightened the fpectators inftead of producing entertainment; and whofe numbers occafioned unavoidable confufion *.

In

---

* Before the time of Thefpis and Æfchylus, tragedy was wholly performed by the chorus. The former of thefe, fenfible of the tedioufnefs and infipid uniformity of this defign, added to it one perfon as an actor,

In a ftate likewife fo varioufly modified as that of Athens, there arofe in confequence of the fields fucceffively opened to every paffion of the human mind, a va-

---

actor, but the difproportion ftill continued to be remarkable. An accident at laft brought about a reformation. In the reprefentation of the Eumenides, the barbarous dreffes of the chorus, which confifted of fifty perfons, frightened the women with child into mifcarriage, and the children into fits. Æfchylus, therefore, by contracting the number of perfons employed in the chorus, and by adding proportionably to the actors, rendered tragedy fo juft a reprefentation of manners and action as we fee it at prefent. To this change introduced among the perfons he fuperadded others with regard to machinery, decoration, and decorum. The former he effectuated by erecting a ftage for the actors inftead of a cart, which had formerly been employed; the latter, by cloathing them in the mafque, the bufkin, and the long robe; and the laft, (by far the moft important of all his alterations) by making his murders pafs behind the fcenes, inftead of being performed in fight of the audience. It is on thefe accounts principally that he is fo much celebrated by the ancients, Vid. Hor. ubi fup. Phil. in Vit. Apollon. lib. vi. c. 6. Vit. Æfchy. ap. Stanleium, &c. In this reformed ftate therefore Sophocles and Euripides found the theatre; and when we confider that thefe men poffeffed themfelves great natural abilities, and found the manners of the Athenian people improved to the utmoft, we fhall ceafe to wonder that their compofition appears fo much more correct and mafterly than that of their predeceffors.

ricty

riety of characters calculated peculiarly to give exercise to the invention of the dramatic poet, and from the dread of his rivals, the diversity of his subjects, and the exquisite taste of his hearers, attentive to the slightest deviation from nature and propriety, that correctness of Composition took place, which indicates a judgment matured by exercise, and maintaining its pre-eminence over the other faculties. Thus in comic representation, it became exceedingly difficult either to develope real vices shaded by a veil of the deepest hypocrisy, or to fix upon those little flaws in characters of distinguished eminence, which render an imitation so happily natural*. In tragic composition indeed the subjects

---

* The division of comedy among the Greeks into the old, the middle, and the new species is too generally known to be insisted on here at any length. In the first, criminal or ridiculous actions were not only painted in the strongest colours, but the name of the man was publicly mentioned, and an indelible stigma fixed upon his character.

Si quis erat dignus describi, quod malus, aut fur,

Quod

ſubjects continued at every period of ſociety to be of one kind, becauſe the poet
ſoar-

Quod mæchus foret, aut ſicarius, aut alioqui
Famoſus, multa cum libertate notabant.

Hor. Sat. lib. iv. ſat. 1.

In the middle comedy, which took place when the A-
thenian ſtate drew nearer to an oligarchy, this licence
was curbed, and the poet allowed to expoſe the actions,
but forbid to name the perſon. The laſt ſpecies of comedy, without regard to individuals farther than as
theſe may be delineated by the deſcription of particular
virtues or vices, conſiſted wholly of ſuch repreſentations
as exhibit a juſt picture of human life. It muſt be con-
feſſed that ſuch pieces of the celebrated Ariſtophanes
as have reached the preſent times, are for the moſt part
of the firſt mentioned ſpecies. This poet however
muſt be allowed to have performed a taſk which does
honour to his diſcernment, whatever diſcredit it may
reflect upon him in other reſpects, when he expoſed
the divine Socrates as an object of ridicule to the multitude, and gave mankind a conſpicuous evidence that
any character, how exalted ſoever, may be placed in a
ridiculous point of view, when the ſlighteſt flaw, or even
virtuous indignation carried to an extreme, is expoſed
by a man endowed with this dangerous talent. If
there was any circumſtance exceptionable in the conduct of Socrates, it appears to have been his being too
explicit on the ſubject of religion, (the moſt dangerous
of all topics) and inſtilling prejudices againſt that of
his country into the minds of his pupils, before he had
ſubſtituted ſuch principles in its room, as might coun-
terballance the bad conſequences ariſing from this proceeding.

foaring perpetually here in the region of the fublime and pathetic, finds characters fuited to his defign among the great and unhappy of all ages. But here likewife it became neceffary, that he fhould attend more clofely than formerly to the unity of his fable, to the confiftency of his charac-

---

ceeding. He had likewife fomewhat too unwarily abfented himfelf from the theatre when the comedies of that author were reprefented, which was a neglect not to be overlooked. See Rhymer's View of Tragedy, and Ælian's Various Hiftory, b. ii. c. 13. Of this circumftance in the conduct of this great philofopher, Ariftophanes, animated by the motive we have fuggefted, took immediate advantage. He intends to reprefent his eloquence as dangerous, and calculated to produce the moft pernicious effects. " He feigns there-" fore that a countryman involved in debt fent his fon " to Socrates's fchool that he might learn to cheat his " creditors. This young fellow is fo well inftructed " by the philofopher, that he goes home, beats his fa-" ther, and then proves that he had acted very proper-" ly." The end propofed here is perfectly obvious. But it is principally our prefent bufinefs to obferve, that thorough knowledge of human nature, which was neceffary to make Ariftophanes fucceed in his defign, and that fhare of penetration which is neceffary to make an author difcern amidft fo many excellencies as might overpower an ordinary mind, that little fpeck by which all may be obfcured, and the ends defeated to which thefe might otherwife be rendered fubfervient.

ters,

ters; and to the ftrain of his compofition, as preferying a juft medium betwixt bom-baft and meannefs, a ftyle equally remote from the ftiffnefs of pedantry, and the rant of declamation.

Upon the whole, dramatic poetry, con-fidered with regard to the faculties of the mind, requires principally the poet to be poffeffed of that difcernment which we have fhown to confift of the union of imagina-tion and judgment, and which requires the perpetual, and almoft equal operation of both. The former of thefe powers is required rather to be ftrong and perfpica-cious in this branch of compofition than florid and luxuriant, becaufe it is the bufi-nefs of the dramatic poet to reprefent man as a creature whom paffion, inclination, and appetite often directs in the conduct of life; and paffion never expreffeth its feelings in imagery and metaphor * : the latter

* Some modern writers have indeed found a me-thod of reconciling thefe circumftances, and of mak-ing their heroes rave in the flowing ftyle of rhetoric. How far they have followed nature in this conduct their readers muft be left to determine. The ancients

certainly

latter ought to poffefs the two qualities of comprehenfion and precifion, that it may at the fame time regulate the plan, adjuft the incidents to the characters, and direct with fuch exquifite propriety the time of throwing in thofe ftrokes which penetrate the heart as to render the whole piece emi-nently beautiful, and as nearly as poffible perfect in its kind *.   A mind capable of

execut-

---

certainly have both judged and acted in a very diffe-rent manner. The Oedipus of Sophocles, upon the difcovery of his guilt, expreffeth his defpair in the fimpleft, but at the fame time in the moft fignificant words.

Ιυ, ιυ' τα παντ' αν εξικοι σαφη

Ω Φως τελευταιον σε προσβλεψαιμι νυν, &c.
He recalls to his memory the places in which he had been educated, and every circumftance contributes to heighten his mifery.

Ιω Κιθαιρων, τι μ' εδεχου !

Ω Πολυβε, και Κορινθε, και τα πατρια

Λογω παλαια δωμαθ' οιον αρα με

Καλλος κακων υπουλον εξιτρεψατε.

Σοφοκλ. Οιδιπ. Τυρ.

* The poet quoted above, who appears to have been thoroughly acquainted with the human heart, excells particularly in this uncommon faculty of throwing out juft at the proper feafon thofe exquifite ftrokes of paf-

fion,

executing with maſtery a performance of this kind, muſt poſſeſs likewiſe that exquiſite feeling either of pleaſure or pain, which renders the author not merely pre-

---

ſion, or rather that perfect imitation of nature, by which every reader muſt be affected, becauſe the principles here wrought upon are common to all. The following verſes contain the moſt ſtriking examples of this kind I remember ever to have met with. Oedipus, reflecting on the ſtupendous ſeries of events by which he had been plunged in the blackeſt deſpair, exclaims in the agony of his thought

Ω γαμοι, γαμοι, εφυσαθ' ημας, και φυτευσαντες παλιν

Ανειτε ταυτον σπερμα και κπεδειξατε

Πατερας, αδελφους, παιδας αιμα εμφυλιον, &c.

From this ſcene his mind recoils with horror, and breaking from the thought, he wiſhes to drop into annihilation.

Ωπως ταχιςα προς θεων εξω με που

Καλυψατ' η φονευσατ', η θαλασσιον

Εκριψατ' ειθα, μηποτ' εισοψεσθ' ετι, &c.

Nature herſelf ſpeaks in all this, and it cannot be peruſed without emotion. Yet the expreſſion is perfectly ſimple. The poet had judgment enough to diſcern that ornament here would have been equally uſeleſs and diſguſting. Oedipus talks the language of a man overwhelmed with deſpair. He is hurried by the remembrance of his crimes, which are expreſſed in very few words, to the deſire of inſtant death. This ſtroke is introduced juſt at the proper ſeaſon, and from this circumſtance is derived its pathos and energy.

ſent

sent at every scene, but deeply interested in every transaction; and in proportion to the strength or weakness of that sensibility in the author, will be that eager appetite, close attention, or cool indifference with which the reader of discernment will peruse his work.

3. From the preceding observations on the intellectual powers, as variously displayed in dramatic composition, we shall be enabled to point out with greater facility that union of these which gives rise to the more complex species of the epopœa. Considered merely as a branch of Composition, authors have differed very much in their sentiments of dramatic and epic poetry; and a great judge of eminence in both has pronounced a decision in favour of the former *. His sentiments on this
subject

---

* " Le poeme epique (says an ingenious critic) est ce qu'il'y a de plus grand & de plus noble dans la poesie. C'est l'ouvrage le plus accompli de l'esprit humain.— Il (poete heroique) faut de grandes images, & un esprit encore plus grand pour les former. Enfin il faut un jugement si solide, un discernement si exquis, une si perfaite connoissance de la langue, dans laquelle on ecrit;

ſubjeĉt fall not particularly under our preſent examination. It is neceſſary only to
obſerve on this ſubjeĉt, that whatever advantages tragedy derives from the perfection of its plan, as relating to one event *,
from the ſhortneſs of its aĉtion, as calculated to arreſt attention more forcibly than
the diffuſive and various tranſaĉtions recorded by the epic poet †; from the ſimplicity of its fable, as admitting of no epi-
ſodes ‡; and finally, from the external
machinery of the theatre, the muſic, elo-
cution, and geſticulation with which its
exhibition is accompanied §; yet conſidered

---

ecrit; une etude ſi conſtante, une meditation ſi pro-
fonde, une etendue de capacité ſi vaſte que les ſiecles
entiers a peine peuvent produire un genie capable d'un
poeme epique." Rap. Reflex. Poet. p. 126.

* Ετι το ελαττονι μηκει το τελος της μιμησεως εςι.
Αρις. περι Ποιητ. Κεφ. κς.

† Το ανθρωπτερον ηδιον η πολλω κεραμενον τω χρονω.
Λεγω δε οιον ει τις του Οιδιπυν θειη τα Σοφοκλεους εν
επεσιν οσοις η Ιλιας. Id. ibid.

‡ Ετι ηττον μια οποιασυν η των εποποιων· Σεμειον δε·
εκ γαρ οποιασυν μιμησεως, πλειυς Τραγωδιαι γινονται.
Ibid.

§ Επειτα διοτι παντ' εχει οσαπερ η Εποποια· Και

Y 3   γαρ

ed simply as indicating a certain combination of intellectual faculties, and requiring these to be exerted either with comparative strength or variety; epic poetry has in these respects the advantages of this, and indeed of every species of composition whatsoever *. This truth will be rendered more obvious from the following considerations.

1. We have already seen that the most distinguishing ingredient of genius, the power of invention, displays in the drama rather strength and perspicacity than richness and luxuriance, because it admits not in any eminent degree of those glowing colours which are naturally and success-

---

γαρ τω ΜΕΤΡΩ εξεσι χρησθαι, και οτι ε μικρου μερος την μουσικην και την οψιν εχει, δε ης τας ηδονας επισαυται εναργεστατα. Ibid.

* " La presence de la divinité & le soin qu'une cause si auguste doit prendre de l'action, oblige le poete a faire que cette action soit grande, importante, & conduit par des princes, & par des rois. Elle oblige aussi de penser & de parler d'une maniere relevée au dessus du commun des hommes, & qui egale en quelque sorte les personnes divines qu'il introduit. C'est a quoi sert le langage poetique & figure & la majesté du vers heroique." Boffu du Poeme Epique, liv. i. p. 19.

fully

fully employed to render narration animated, or to diſplay in the happieſt attitudes the various objects of external nature. Eloquence in the ſame manner
(which derives its origin from a ſimilar
combination of the powers of the mind)
confines this power principally to the invention of topics of perſuaſion, and to the
office of conveying theſe with pathos and
energy to the heart. Philoſophy and hiſtory exclude its incidents; but epic poetry
affords the moſt unlimited range to this
faculty in whatever point of view its exertions may be ſurveyed. Thus as the parent of picturefque and beautiful imagery,
the whole compaſs of objects, whether of
nature or of art, that fall within the ſphere
of human inveſtigation lie promiſcuouſly
open to its uſe. As the poet varies his
ſcenery in the courſe of his narration; as
by ſhowing his principal perſonages in various lights he excites alternately in the
minds of his readers admiration, terror,
pity, indignation, or diſtreſs; he may
heighten every ſucceſſive proſpect by ſig-
nificant and appropriated illuſtrations, and

obtain

obtain by thefe means every purpofe to
which the *poetic* art in the trueft fenfe of
that epithet can be rendered fubfervient.
Thefe advantages the epic poet derives
from carrying on an uniform narration
of events, inftead of affuming always,
like the dramatic writer, the ftyle of converfation, which (as we have already feen)
contracts the range of imagination, and
prefents to it a lefs diverfified feries of objects. Here too the bard has an advantage over the hiftorian, even in his own
fphere of narration, becaufe the latter is
confined to the fimple detail of facts, on
which it is neither neceffary nor proper
that he fhould frequently throw the glowing colours of the faculty we are contemplating; whereas in the work of the former thefe are confidered as indifpenfably
requifite.

2. When we again take a view of imagination as inventing an endlefs variety
of new and furprifing incidents, the epic
poet is here likewife eminently diftinguifhed by the ufes he may make of this faculty
above all other writers whatever: while

an

an author is confined by the rules of the drama to a fhort fpace of time, and to incidents, however furprifing, yet tending without the leaft digreffive circumftance to bring on the principal cataftrophe; here, on the contrary, every figure of this miniature appears extended to its full proportion. The greatnefs of the action renders a confiderable length of time neceffary to complete the defign, and in the conduct of the fable, every event within the verge of poetic probability may with propriety be introduced. Unanimity and difcord, wifdom and folly, ftrength and weaknefs, anger and friendfhip, war and love, thefe with all the paffions of human nature, wrought into characters, and difplayed alternately in a feries of events conftantly diverfified, attract the attention of the reader as powerfully, and render him almoft as deeply interefted as if every part of the bufinefs was really his own, and his happinefs or mifery was connected with the event.

Add to all this the beauty of thofe inchanting epifodes, which relieve the mind

of

of the reader so agreeably, after having followed out for some time the principal branches of the fable; and the rich and various machinery which fancy is here at liberty to contrive with the utmost licence, and to paint in the most animated colours; and with these advantages in its favour, there is perhaps no other sphere whatever in which imagination may display its power of inventing incidents in an equal degree. This advantage is indeed universally allowed to epic poetry, even by those who consider the dramatic as upon the whole a more perfect species of Composition *, and it is therefore unnecessary to insist on it any longer.

Those sentimental beauties likewise, which in consequence of their novelty, or

---

* Thus Aristotle, in a passage quoted above, acknowledges that the plan of an epic poem is more complex than that of the drama, and that several tragedies might be made of one. It is somewhat odd that our great critic should adduce this circumstance in proof of the excellence of dramatic above epic poetry, as the complex nature of the fable in the latter naturally calls into exercise the intellectual powers in more various combinations, and when properly executed discovers an higher share of merit.

peculiar

peculiar delicacy are ſuppoſed to derive
their origin from the power of invention,
may here be introduced with the greateſt
propriety. Accordingly in the ſtandards of
the epopœa the moſt delicate expreſſions
of parental tenderneſs *, of filial gratitude †,
of inviolable friendſhip ‡, and of conjugal
felicity §, are every where to be met with.
Thoſe moral reflections on human life,
which tend to ſoften and mend the human
heart, are cloathed in ſuch ſtriking colours
as to make a laſting impreſſion on the memory ‖; and the events perpetually varying, pour upon a contemplative mind a
ſeries of ſuch inſtructive obſervations, as

---

* IΛIAΛ. ζ. l. 466. OΔΥΣ. π. paſſ.

† OΔΥΣ. ubi ſup. Æneid. lib. ii. l. 707.

‡ IΛIAΔ. ζ. l. 120, &c. Θ. l. 93. κ. 242, &c.
Æneid, lib. v. l. 294.

§ IΛIAΔ. ubi ſup. OΔΥΣ. ψ. paſſ. Æneid. 2.
711. 738, &c.

‖ How beautiful in this kind is the following image
in Glaucus addreſs to Diomed,

Οιη περ Φυλλων γενεη, τοινδε και ανδρων.

Φυλλα τα μεν τ᾽ ανεμος χαμαδις χεει, αλλα δε Θ᾽ υλη
Τηλεθοωσα Φυει. εαρος δ᾽επιγιγνεται ωρη.

Ως ανδρων γενεη, η μεν Φυει, η δ᾽αποληγει. IΛIAΔ. ζ.

render

render this work when properly conducted not lefs ufeful than entertaining.

3. Of imagination, as employcd in the invention of *human* charaƈters, fo much hath been faid that it would be fuperflous to infift on this branch of the fubjeƈt at any length. It muft however be acknowledged that the mythology of the ancients gave advantages to the epic bard in drawing the charaƈters of his *celeftial* perfonages, of which he is in a great meafure deprived by that more perfeƈt fyftem of revealed religion, whofe laws permit not imagination to blend oppofite qualities together in fuch a manner as to form piƈturefque and original reprefentations. Homer appears to have availed himfclf of all the benefits derived from the religion of his country: and by an happy intermixture of the qualites of the divine with the frailties of the human nature, has rendered his deities by far the moft beautiful and entertaining perfonages of his fable *. By thefe

---

* Our incomparable Milton has chofen a plan of all others beft calculated to fupply the defeƈt arifing neceffarily

theſe means he poſſeſſeth the peculiar advantage of painting many original characters
without violating the rules of *poetic*
probability. This benefit aroſe from the
practice of the ancient poets, who (as no
ſyſtem of revelation took place) were left
at liberty to invent ſuch a plan as imagination preſented at random; and ſuccceed-
ing bards, provided they did not over-
throw the ſyſtem of their predeceſſors,
might employ their divinities in ſuch actions as diſplayed in their full extent that
union of diverſified qualities which fancy
had aſſigned them. In order to render
this repreſentation complete, as an imitation of characters, the gentler and more

---

ſarily here from the nature of our religion. His devils
however, give by no means that inchanting variety
to the Paradiſe Loſt, which the heathen deities give to
the works of Homer and Virgil. Theſe laſt blend
promiſcuouſly the virtues, the weakneſſes, and even
the vices of human nature in the character of their divinities; whereas Milton, in painting his celeſtial combatants, was confined to the firſt; in deſcribing their ad-
verſaries, to the laſt mentioned qualities, but was no-
where at liberty to unite both, in ſuch a manner as
forms that imitation which the *human* mind delights to
contemplate.

amiable

amiable female qualities are blended even
with the foibles and weakneffes of that fex
among the goddeffes, who act a principal part in the work. Thus, as the fcene
varies to heaven, earth, or hell, whofe
powers are all interefted in the cataftrophe,
attention is kept always upon the ftretch
by contemplating objects perpetually diverfified, and the fubject admits by thefe
means an extent and compafs of invention
fuperior in every refpect to that which is
difplayed in any other branch of the art.

2. While the imagination thus has fcope
in the epopœa to difplay all its exuberance
and verfatility, a fphere equally extenfive is
opened to the underftanding which is required to operate as univerfally, and with
an energy proportioned to the former.

This truth will be rendered fufficiently
obvious, if we obferve, that the preferva-
tion of the unities in the epic fable, the
adjuftment of its parts to each other in
fuch a manner as to form upon the whole
a proportioned as well as diverfified feries
of objects ; its incidents judicioufly adapted to excite, but never to fatigue attention ;

tion; and its epifodes confidered as connected with the ultimate aim of the work,
and interwoven in fuch a manner as to fet
off the principal figures to the greateft advantage; thefe are ends effential to the
very exiftence of this high fpecies of compofition, and it muft be immediately obvious that each is acquired by fome exertion of the underftanding.

Judgment therefore is here required to
be at the fame time fedulous and unembarraffed; clear and comprehenfive: fedulous, becaufe the clofeft attention is neceffary to give every member of the work
its due proportion and confiftence; unem-
baraffed, that amidft the diverfity of materials, the mind may felect with eafe fuch
upon occafion as are fitted juftly to its
purpofe; clear, that every character may
be uniformly difcriminated, and that every
illuftration may correfpond to its object;
and comprehenfive, that it may be equal
to purpofes fo widely different, and effectuate each with the fame maftery and correctnefs. An artift who follows out a
fimple plan with adequate ability naturally
claims

claims our esteem and approbation; but we bestow a much larger share of both on him who brings grace and proportion out of an exhaustless variety of materials; who shapes into form, a figure consisting of the most complicated ingredients, and with a sagacity attentive to the minutest circumstance, renders every movement subservient to the ultimate purpose of his work.

As judgment therefore may display its extent and comprehension in the external machinery and mechanism of the epopœa, so it may discover true philosophical precision in the discussion of those questions, whether moral or political, that take their rise from the characters, events, and transactions of the work. Arguments will here be stated and enforced, objections will be proposed and refuted, expedients suited to the manners of the persons, and calculated to shew the points in which these last are discriminated will be fixed upon as the detail becomes complex and interesting; and doctrines of the most extensive utility, with regard to the conduct of life, may be
either

either formally unfolded, be ornamented
with imagery, or be inculcated as the mo-
rals of some beautiful allegories, as time
and circumstances require these to be treated. It was undoubtedly in consequence
of his having taken this enlarged view of
epic poetry, as affording exercise to the
underſtanding, that the eloquent and judicious Roman poet pronounceth Homer to
have excelled the moſt diſtinguiſhed philoſophers, even in their own ſphere.

Trojani belli ſcriptorem — relegi —
Qui quid ſit pulchrum, quid turpe, quid utile,
    quid non,
Plenius & melius Chryſippo, et Crantore docet.
Horace.

A noble and appropriated eulogium, not
leſs honourable to the *judgment* of the *critic* who could apply, than to the genius of
the poet who could deſerve it.

3. Diſcernment of the moſt exquiſite
kind, as reſulting from the union of the
ſuperior faculties the epic poet may evince
likewiſe in the higheſt degree, by varying
the expreſſion of *one* quality according to

the combination in which it is placed*;
by obferving the inftant at which the mind
is fufceptible of almoft any impreffion; and
beyond all other indications, by throwing
out thofe little ftrokes of nature, imperceptible to a fuperficial eye, which command the immediate acknowledgment of
a feeling heart, not by language but by
tears.

. III. The two higher fpecies of fable (the
dramatic and epic) we have now confidered particularly, as indicating a certain
union of the intellectual powers, and we
have endeavoured to point out, not only
the general offices appropriated to thefe in
the departments above mentioned, but the
peculiar qualities by which each may be
diftinguifhed. Before we conclude our
obfervations on this branch of the fubject,
it may be proper to examine with the fame
view to the faculties of the mind, fome
kinds of fable, inferior indeed to the former with regard to the *variety* of *talents*

---

* See fect. iii.

required

required for their production, but demanding an high degree of fuch as are indifpenfably neceffary for this purpofe, and giving occafion to difplay no inconfiderable
proportion of all.

Among the writers who excel in this
clafs, the firft rank will undoubtedly be
affigned to thofe who have attempted to
follow out the wanderings of the human
heart, and to delineate the firft impreffions
made upon a fufceptible mind by interefting objects, as well as the manner in which
it feels when infenfibly familiarized to
their appearance. An author who is capable of exhibiting with propriety a character of this kind, who adapts circumftances to the affections which he propofeth to excite, and paints thefe fo happily
when excited, as to imitate nature in her moft
delicate fignatures, poffeffeth an high
fhare of philofophical excellence, and fhows
that exquifite fenfibility as exifting in his
own mind, which he pourtrays fo juftly
in that of another. Here indeed the imagination difplays no fublimity, or exuberance, as the characters are not of that

Z 2   exalted

exalted caſt which require theſe to be exerted: but that inſtantaneous perception of
certain attitudes, which diſcernment ultimately derives from imagination, that
correſpondence of which every man is ſenſible betwixt the action and the feeling
giving riſe to it in one heart, and excited
by it in another; theſe circumſtances denominate taſte in the moſt eminent degree,
and that deep inſight into human nature,
which experience may indeed improve, but
cannot poſſibly confer.

In this kind of fable Mariveaux, Crebillon, and we may add, our late ingenious countryman Sterne, in his Sentimental
Journey, excel all other writers whatever,
and their excellence (diſplayed in one
ſphere only) is altogether peculiar and inimitable. The Marianne of the firſt mentioned author is a character truly exquiſite
in its kind, in which however, unleſs the
reader feels the ſentiments themſelves, it
is impoſſible to adduce examples. A heart
fluttering alternately with love and vanity,
touched with the lighteſt trifles, burſting
with paſſion, melting with tenderneſs,

actuated

actuated by impreſſions purely feminine, and having the nobleſt qualities ſhaded by a few foibles which render her ſtill more the object of affection; this is the portrait here preſented to us, and it is drawn in ſuch a manner as that the hand of a maſter appears in the execution. In that beautiful piece of Crebillon, where the waverings of a young heart unacquainted with the nature of its own ſenſations are touched with the niceſt diſcernment, the reader of taſte, for to him only theſe works are addreſſed, will find the conduct of a man thrown into life, with ſuſceptible paſſions, and a ſmall ſhare of experience, as happily expoſed as the female character of the former. The merit of the Engliſh writer, in the work we have referred to, lies in his happy talent of exciting the tendereſt and moſt affecting ſenſations from the moſt trifling occurrences. With no uncommon depth or compaſs of underſtanding, this author is diſtinguiſhed by a copious imagination, and an eminent proportion of the qualities of the heart. His diſcernment, therefore, which as a

Z 3

philo-

philofopher is neither extenſive nor accurate, yet as a moral painter is exquiſite,
and, when employed in its proper ſphere,
never fails to hit upon ſtrokes of nature
the moſt expreſſive, and upon motives of
powerful and irreſiſtible energy.

A more moderate ſhare of all the qualities above-mentioned is diſplayed upon
ſome occaſions in the invention of fables,
by which a variety of familiar characters
are exhibited either in new and well
adapted circumſtances, or with ordinary
qualities, in ſuch combination as render
the whole in ſome degree original. The
former of theſe ends is obtained when the
mind is agreeably led through a ſeries of
incidents, happily calculated to throw light
upon the principal character, and tending
to ſhow it in every ſeparate point of
view;—the latter, when its oddity is of
ſuch a kind as to render it uncommon
without being falſe or unnatural *. Examples

---

* Was I upon this occaſion to characteriſe our two
moſt celebrated modern noveliſts, I would venture to
aſcribe the firſt kind of merit to Richardſon, and the
laſt

amples of both kinds the reader of curiofity will meet with in the Gil Blas of Le
Sage, the Tom Jones and Amelia of

---

laft to Fielding. The Clariſſa of the former is in no
reſpect original. She appears adorned with an aſſemblage of virtues, and of intellectual endowments,
which it is to be hoped we ſhall frequently meet with ;
only in order to have the force of an *example,* theſe are
raiſed conſiderably beyond the common level. Conſidering this then as the author's intention, nothing
can be more admirably concerted than the incidents
by which every diſtinct excellence is called ſucceſſively
into action. Firmneſs, vigilance, circumſpection,
united with all the gentler and more amiable female
qualities, appear in the *trial* ; while reſignation, fortitude, forgiveneſs of injuries, and all the virtues of
the chriſtian, are nobly exemplified in the *cataſtrophe.*—
The *Adams* of Fielding on the contrary, ſtrikes us
wholly in the light of an original, ariſing not like that
of Falſtaff or Don Quixote, from extraordinary qualities exerted in a manner wholly new and ſurpriſing ;
but from a combination of ſuch as are indeed more
common, but marked with *one defect* that throws an
air of ridicule and oddity on the whole. This defect
is a total want of the knowledge of mankind The
incidents of the piece are fewer, and the plan leſs complicated than that either of Clariſſa, or even of the ſubſequent productions of Fielding :—but the character
is marked with *little ſtrokes* which render it *truly comic,*
and there is ſcarce a ſingle inſtance in the whole work,
in which the originality either ceaſeth to appear when
it ought to be conſpicuous, or is carried beyond
nature.

Fielding,

Fielding, the Roderic Random of Smollett, and a few other English novels which appear to stand in the same rank of excellence. If we meet not in these with those exquisite strokes of nature and passion which characterise the former, the defect is, however, abundantly compensated by characters well supported, and happily discriminated; by incidents such as we see constantly falling out, but connected so as to form a rational entertainment, in which probability is seldom violated; by a faithful picture of human life in all its diversified appearances; and by a knowledge of mankind, which to some readers may in a great measure supply the loss of a limited acquaintance, and a defective education.

It will immediately be perceived that a large proportion of the intellectual powers is required to produce a masterly performance in this branch of Composition. Perhaps, however, upon the whole, judgment is displayed in it more conspicuously than imagination. The invention of incidents (in which the last of these is principally

cipally employed here) is by no means characteriftical, as we have already feen, of the moft eminent degree of this faculty. The judgment which rangeth thefe fo juftly as to employ the different perfons in fuch fpheres of action as are beft calcu-lated to fhow their *peculiar qualities* to advantage, muft be uncommonly compre-henfive and accurate. The Adams of Fielding would have appeared to no ad-vantage had he been wholly converfant with perfons in very low life, or with fuch as were entirely on a level with himfelf. But the lady, the waiting maid, the hofts, the 'fquires, the parfons, and the juftices, with whom he is alternately and moft ju-dicioufly contrafted, contribute feparately to finifh the character, until the figure is fet before us completely proportioned.

Penetration likewife, as employed to develope the fecret motives from which the actions of men derive their origin, the ingenious novellift will difplay to great advantage in the artful arrangement of his incidents; in the ftrokes that mark his characters; in the judicious felection of

fuch

fuch topics as make the moft lafting impreffion on the heart; and in contrafting
the perfons of his fable in fuch a manner
as may moft happily expofe vice, detect
hypocrify, and render prefumption, affectation, or arrogance, the objects of ridicule.

We fhall conclude this branch of the
fubject by obferving, that Rouffeau and
Richardfon have carried this fpecies of
fable to its utmoft perfection. Thefe writers have the peculiar merit of having introduced into a love-tale, calculated one
fhould think principally to give the mind
a little tranfient entertainment, all the
graces of captivating eloquence, and the
noble maxims of a fublime philofophy.
No branch of the moral character hath
been left unexplored by thefe excellent
authors, in whofe writings (particularly in
thofe of the laft) the entertainment derived from narration is fo juftly blended
with the improvement acquired from convincing and perfpicuous deduction, that
we are at a lofs to determine which of
thefe ends is moft effectually promoted.

There

There never perhaps, was a female cha-racter more highly finished than the Eloisa of Rousseau, which is in all respects more particular and appropriated than either the Clarissa or Grandison of Richardson. It is, indeed, a perfect picture of nature, finished with the most exquisite taste, and in which not even the flighteft and moft delicate shading is deficient. We alter-nately admire, in this inchanting portrait, an happy mixture of tendernefs and fenfi-bility, love and refolution, enthufiafm and reafon, virtue and weaknefs, with a capa-city of receiving and of communicating the moft voluptuous fenfations, which fhow us all together that height of excel-lence of which this fpecies of Compofition is naturally fufceptible.

If, however, the Englifh writer is infe-rior to his rival in this invention of cha-racter, an impartial reader will allow him perhaps the advantage in the number and variety of his incidents, the precifion and compafs of his philofophy, the ftrength and pathos of his eloquence. In this laft quality perhaps no writer ever excelled

him

him of whom we are treating. The eloquence of Rousseau is sometimes sublime
and elevating *; often deeply pathetic †;
on many occasions rich, luxurious, and
inchanting ‡.   But the power of *harrow-
ing up* the soul with woe and horror; of
cleaving the heart with pity and anguish;
of dissolving the mind in that sublime melancholy which exalted genius can alone
either feel or communicate;—these seem
to be the provinces of Richardson, in
which he is wholly original and inimitable.

We have been particularly attentive to
display that union of intellectual powers
which is necessary to perfection in the species of fable here considered, as our remarks on this subject may be of some use

---

* See particularly his noble address to the Atlantic
Ocean, upon which he was going to launch with
Anson.

† His letter from the rocks of Meillerai, is wholly
in this strain.

‡ The letter supposed to have been written in
Eloisa's closet before the moment of enjoyment, and
that succeeding the full accomplishment of his desires,
are full of this luxurious description.

to

to authors of this denomination; and I do
not remember to have feen any regular
attempt made to lay open the principles
upon which a branch of Compofition fo
univerfally popular, and fufceptible of
fuch high improvement, ought to be
conducted.

IV. Having now confidered the various
combinations of the mental powers, with
regard to the other fpecies of Compofition,
it is only further neceffary that we fhould
obferve the degree of influence which thefe
exert in the fphere of criticifm.

This noble art when viewed as extending univerfally to all branches of learning,
and to every fpecies of Compofition, will
be found to give exercife in fo many ways
to the faculties of the mind, that a detail
of their various combinations in every art
and fcience to which the rules of criticifm
are applied, would carry us into unneceffary length, without effectuating any purpofe that may not be obtained by taking a
more general view of the fubject. Confidering therefore criticifm as exercifing
univerfal dominion over the two great em-

pires

pires of art and fcience, we fhall endeavour to fhow what compafs of intellectual
powers is required to conftitute the general character of maftery in this art; and
in what degrees the great objects above-
mentioned require thefe powers to be
exerted.

1. It requires but fuperficial acquaintance
with this fubject to make us fenfible that
a *great and fublime imagination* is by no
means neceffary to form a mafterly critic.
A man poffeffed of this talent in a very
high degree, will not only be apt, without
conftant circumfpection, to permit its dictates too frequently to influence decifions
with which it is no way connected, but
(as a late ingenious critic obferves very
juftly of Longinus) he will be always afpiring rather to *imitate* the beauties of his
original, than to point thefe out with that
appropriated character which tafte united
with judgment will feldom err in confer-
ring. The two laft qualities ought therefore to be confidered as peculiarly and
effentially requifite to critical excellence.
The firft in its *greateft extent* does by no
means

means abfolutely difqualify a man for occupying this fphere:—in a *moderate* proportion, as the parent of *tafte,* it is wholly
indifpenfable.

, That power which we denominate Tafte
- in criticifm (as far as the arts are concerned) is difcernment corrected by judgment *in the ufe,* as it is guided by imagination in the *original perception* of its
objects. It will be obferved that we make
ufe here of the term *perception* rather than
that of *felection* or *choice*, which arifeth,
as we fhall fee afterwards, from another
caufe.

1. That imagination only is employed
in the original perception of the objects of
criticifm, will be obvious, if we reflect by
what power of the mind it is that a man
becomes immediately fenfible of certain
exquifite beauties, or perhaps material defects in the fine arts, wholly imperceptible
to a common obferver. That it cannot be
judgment which directs us in this matter
is unqueftionably evident from this fingle
circumftance, that even where a very fuperior degree of this faculty takes place, we

. often

often find the perfons poffeffed of it not
only unable to difcover objects of this kind
themfelves, but to relifh thefe in any meafure when pointed out to them by others.
A kind of *artificial tafte* (if I may ufe that
expreffion) is indeed formed among fuch
men by application and experience; but it
generally goes no further than to render
them judges of external fymmetry and
proportion. The rough outlines of a
figure, or the conformity which a work
bears to certain general laws eftablifhed
either by reafon, or derived from habit,
will attract the attention of fuch critics
very ftrongly, and as the underftanding
when thoroughly acquainted with a fubject, and uninfluenced by any other power,
feldom errs in its decifions, a judgment
will be formed of thefe objects with great
accuracy and precifion. But of the effect
arifing from a certain happy expreffion in
the execution; of a figure as rendered not
merely proportioned, but intenfely animated by an affemblage of well adapted
circumftances; of one exquifite ftroke, contrary perhaps to common rules, and to be

con-

contemplated wholly as an object of admiration, which prefents a form immediately
to the eye with peculiar and inimitable
beauty; of thefe a faculty accuftomed
wholly to clofe inveftigation takes no cognizance itfelf, and is apt to regard as fport
and trifling what it is unable to comprehend.—In fhort, judges (as they may affect
to be ftyled) of ·Compofition who are directed wholly by the underftanding, will
form an eftimate in many inftances equally
inadequate as that of the mathematician I
have fomewhere read of, who perufed the
Æneid with maps of the countries mentioned in that work, and admired the author only as an excellent geographer.

As the perception therefore of the objects of Criticifm in the arts depends not
upon judgment, it muft neceffarily arife
from fome other power of the mind; and
this it is obvious can only be that power
which being the parent of thefe in the
artift, can alone take cognifance of them
in the perfon who furveys his performance.—" Imagination (as an elegant critic
" obferveth) dwells upon an agreeable ob-

Vol. I.   A a   " ject

" ject with delight, arrays it in the most
" beautiful colours, and becomes ena-
" moured of its own creation. Taste
" catching the contagion from fancy, con-
" templates the favourite object with equal
" transport, by which means it acquires
" and improves its sensibility: it be-
" comes more susceptible of pleasure, and
" more exquisitely acute in its sensa-
" tions *."

In order however to accomplish these purposes, we are not to judge (as was formerly observed) that an *eminent* share of imagination is indispensably requisite. In fact, however strange the remark may appear, it is yet certain that Taste (when the mind is employed not in judging, but in execution,) is often found to be most defective in those authors who are allowed to possess a superior share of that faculty from which it is more immediately derived. Shakespeare and Young, among our own writers, and Dante and Ariosto among those of a foreign nation, afford

* See Duff's Essay on Original Genius, sect. iv. p. 67.

such

fuch pregnant examples of the truth of
this obfervation, as renders any further
illuftration of it unneceffary. It is not our
intention to infinuate that thefe authors
were really deftitute of Tafte, as it enables
a man to relifh the moft exquifite beauties, and to judge with the utmoft precifion and accuracy of the productions of
others. It will appear perhaps upon examination, that men of this fuperior order
are often deficient in *execution* themfelves,
when they are yet capable of deciding,
with a difcernment rarely to be met with,
of the conformity betwixt a general ftandard and particular modes of imitation.

We have already feen the invariable
connection that takes place betwixt imagination and feeling, or fenfibility. In
proportion to the degree in which the one
takes place, will be always the poignancy
and edge of the other. In eftimating the
general merit, or even in being impreffed
by particular beauties or defects in the
work of another, it is obvious that this
fenfibility muft be lefs exquifite, and con-
fequently the mind more cool and difpaf-

fionate

fionate, than when its powers are intenfely animated by the fervor with which this faculty in its greateft vigour contemplates the object of its more immediate refearch. In the firft cafe, the mind poffeffing the power upon which the perception of thefe objects depends, can examine them at leifure, and can judge of them either by the general laws of Compofition, by their tendency to promote a particular purpofe, or by that train of intermediate ideas with which thefe ought to ftand in connection. But the cafe is altogether different in this laft fituation. A ftrong imagination, wholly engroffed by the greatnefs of its conceptions, becomes inattentive to fuch cirftances as appear to be inferior, and dwelling with tranfport upon fome favourite idea, is rendered incapable of producing uniformity and proportion on the whole. Tafte in this cafe becomes vitiated by the exuberance of that power to which it owes its origin, and thus the fame faculty that invents the theory, appears unequal to the tafk of carrying its principles into execution.

From

From thefe obfervations it is, we pre-fume, fufficiently obvious that a moderate portion of imagination is only requifite for accomplifhing the purpofes to which Criticifm (in the arts) is rendered fubfervient. Difcernment in this cafe, if it does not enter fo deeply upon fome occafions into the nature of a fubject as in the other, is yet truer, more confiftent, and lefs apt to be mifled in its eftimations by whim and fingularity.

In order however, to accomplifh the purpofes above-mentioned, it is neceffary that critical penetration fhould be invariably corrected by judgment *in the ufe* of thofe objects whofe perception depends upon the power of invention *. The man of mere fancy, whatever fhare of it he may poffefs, will always err, not indeed in the difcovery of objects, but in the fe-

---

* " Nos quid in quaqua re fequendum cavendum-que fit, docebimus (fays an admired ancient) ut ad ea *judicium* dirigatur. Præcipuum igitur, ne quod effici non poteft aggrediamur : ut contraria vitemus, & communia: ne quid in eloquendo corruptum obfcurum-que fit, referatur oportet ad fenfus qui non docentur." Quintil. de Inftit. Orat. lib. vi. cap. 6.

lection

lection of ſuch as are moſt proper upon
particular occaſions, in that juſt arrangement of inferior parts which renders a
whole proportioned and confiſtent, and in
that judicious application of examples by
whoſe uſe a theory ought to be illuſtrated *.

The

---

* In the noble work of Longinus, whoſe vivid imagination and exquiſite taſte were not always regulated
by the dictates of an unbiaſſed underſtanding, we meet
in ſome inſtances, with ſuch trivial criticiſm as the
ſpirit in which other parts of that performance is conducted, would by no means lead us to expect. Thus
he at one time cenſures Herodotus, and at another
Theopompus, for little inaccuracies which a writer
of ſuch ſuperior diſcernment ought perhaps to have
overlooked. The former of theſe in deſcribing a tempeſt ſays, Τυς περι το ναυαγιον βρασσομενους εξεδεχετο
τελος ΑΧΑΡΙ. Thoſe who ſuffered ſhip-wreck had
an unhappy exit. This word ΑΧΑΡΙ (unhappy) the
critic cenſures as not equal to the greatneſs of the cala-
mity. He is no doubt in the right. But where a
deſcription is otherwiſe ſublime (as Longinus acknowledgeth this to be) and wrought up with even divine
magnificence, is it worth while for a man capable
himſelf of imitating the ſublimity whoſe original he
developes with ſuch unqueſtioned diſcernment, to cull
out a circumſtance ſo comparatively inſignificant?
This is rather in the ſpirit of Anaxarchus, or Bentley,
than in that of an author whoſe work otherwiſe evinceth that

He

The attainment of this laſt end requires
more immediately a conſtant and ſtrenuous
exertion

He is himſelf the great ſublime he draws.   Pope.
We may here obſerve tranſiently, that an epithet may
ſometimes have impropriety when referred to ſome
particular circumſtance in a complicated deſcription,
whoſe beauty is yet ſuch upon the whole, that no
reader of taſte would chooſe its poſition to be altered, or
would ſubſtitute another in its room.   In that ſublime
deſcription of the tempeſt, in which Æneas had ſuffered ſo greatly, the bard repreſents Neptune as rouzed
at laſt by the war of elements, and ariſing to calm
the agitated ocean.

    Interea magno miſceri murmure pontum
    Emiſſamque hyemem ſenſit Neptunus, &c.
Every reader of the leaſt ſenſibility muſt be ſtruck with
the majeſty of his deportment.

            ————— *graviter commotus*, & alto
Proſpiciens, ſumma *placidum caput* extulit unda. Æn. i.
A critic, however, might no doubt, find ſome incongruity betwixt the idea ſuggeſted by " *placidum
caput*" which repreſents his countenance as *ſerene*, and
that implied in the words "*graviter commotus*" which
ſhow him to have been agitated by anger.—But does
not a criticiſm of this kind rather give pain than pleaſure to an ingenuous mind, by ſhowing that all human excellence is comparative and imperfect?—Would
any reader of taſte diſplace here the word " *placidum*"
ſo characteriſtical of that *ſerene majeſty* in the midſt of
univerſal uproar which *ought* to diſtinguiſh the monarch
of the ocean, on account of this little impropriety?
Unqueſtionably not.—But let us return to Longinus.—
            A a 4   Our

exertion of the underſtanding. Some general idea may be obtained by any man
of

Our ingenious critic after having cenſured Herodotus,
falls next upon Theopompus. He tranſcribes at
length a paſſage from that hiſtorian, where he mentions the preſents that were offered to the king of
Perſia upon his conqueſt of Egypt. He is offended
with this enumeration, becauſe inſtead of riſing from
leſſer objects to greater, Theopompus cloſeth his account with deſcribing what he calls " the furniture of
a kitchen."—Cauſſin, a writer of ſome ingenuity, has
condemned Longinus ſeverely for this cenſure, and
Bayle, in his lively manner, approves of his animad-
verſions.—" Longinus (ſays Cauſſin) is flat here and
" ſevere to no purpoſe. It was the buſineſs of a faith-
" ful hiſtorian, to take notice of the reſpect that was
" paid to the king of Perſia by the meaner claſs of
" his ſubjects; and if Longinus has taken ſuch an
" averſion to bacon, why (ſays our critic) does he not
" fall out with his deſied Homer, who deſcribes with
" ſo much ſimplicity the cookery of his princes."
Cauſſ. de Eloq. ſacr. & human. lib. i. c. 20. This
laſt hint Bayle looks upon as a home puſh, and gives
up Longinus as inexcuſable. See his Dict. Critique,
&c. art. THEOPOMPUS. But with ſubmiſſion to both
theſe gentlemen, there is more plauſibility than truth
in this reaſoning. Our excellent critic's principal
quarrel with the hiſtorian here, is not ſo much with his
account of the laſt mentioned circumſtances, as with
its being miſplaced. Εκ των υψηλοτερων επι τα τα-
πεινοτερα αποδιδρασκει δεον ποιησασθαι την αυξησιν
εμπαλιν

of tolerable imagination, of beauty or deformity, incongruity or proportion in one
object; and examples may be applied with

εμπαλιν, &c. Περι Υψ. τμημ. μγ. " He finks (fays
he) from great to ignoble objects, againſt the known
rule of conducting a climax." Longinus is certainly
right in this judgment. But the cafe of Homer is no
way parallel. When his princes are employed in
cookery no fuch *climax* is attempted. Magnificent
objects are not, as in the detail of Theopompus, blended
heterogeneouſly with fuch as are comparatively mean
and fordid :—all is uniformly fimple and natural. In
order to render Homer as culpable as Theopompus is
here, Cauſſin ought to produce fome paſſage from the
Iliad or Odyſſey, in which the poet fums up fome detail of magnificent prefents, with an account of freſh
and falted provifions. The fault therefore here is not
that the critic is too fevere, but that his example is
unappropriated. Longinus had cenfured Herodotus in
two paſſages quoted from that author, for fpoiling a
defcription otherwife fublime, not by introducing an
improper circumftance, but by making ufe of an ill-
adapted expreſſion. He quotes the above mentioned
paſſage from Theopompus, as containing an error of
the fame kind. But the fault attributed to the former is not confpicuous here. The words in this laſt
example are fuited with fufficient propriety to the fubject. In the firſt, one unlucky epithet deſtroys the
effect of a noble defcription. One therefore is a little
inadvertency in the fhading of the piece; the other
indicates a defect of judgment, or at leaſt of tafte, in
the painter.

fufficient

sufficient perspicuity to render this idea
clear and even forcible. A house for instance, a tree, or a river, may be described
with much propriety by a poet; and the
critic may with propriety likewise select
this description to exemplify some observation on descriptive beauty in the art.
But in all this process though both are
exempted from censure, neither do we
consider the former as displaying any eminent share of imagination, nor the latter,
in his application of it to a certain purpose,
uncommon sagacity and reach of understanding. It is when the subject becomes
complicated in one case by the happy intermixture of various objects reflecting
mutual light upon each other (the morn-
ing ray for instance trembling on the
bough, glimmering through the casement,
or illuminating the plumage of the little
tribes that sport on the undulating wave);
in the other, when some peculiarly happy
imitation arising from this assemblage is
instantly perceived, and *the cause* assigned
from which its significance and impression
ultimately arise;—it is in these cases that
the

the genius of the painter appears in the
moft animated light, and the fagacity of
the critic in its utmoft perfection. When
the mind, on the contrary, forms only ge-
ral theories, or even catcheth the idea of
poffible excellence, without being thus *particular* in the application of examples, we
either confider the judgment of the critic
as fuperficial, or are embarraffed by an
uninterefting and unappropriated detail.

The truth of thefe remarks will be rendered ftill more confpicuous, when we apply what hath been here advanced to the
faculties of the mind.—Man, confidered as
a being whofe actions derive their origin
from the combined influence of various
principles, would furely be defcribed in a
very inadequate manner by that moralift
who fhould trace (with whatever accuracy)
only one intellectual power, or one paffion
through its effects on human life; when
we know that the fimpleft character exhibits an affemblage greatly diverfified of
both. As the philofopher therefore difcovers the ftrength and compafs of his
own underftanding by that precifion with
which

which he explores the influence of this
power on paffions that obftruct its operation, fo the critic in the fame manner difcovers true fagacity in his profeffion who
obferves in what the excellence of this difquifition confifts, and adapts an example
thus complicated to the illuftration of his
own hypothefis.   The paffions in this laft
inftance, like the external objects of which
our fenfes take cognifance mentioned in
the former, may be contemplated feparately without much difficulty, and the
effect of each on human character may be
pointed out with unexceptionable accuracy,
by a man whofe philofophical merit is inconfiderable.   But in both cafes, we can
have no furer proof that the judgment of
a critic poffeffeth depth and folidity, than
when we find his obfervations confirmed
by examples in which the beauty is not
general, or referred to one object ; but
arifeth from a diverfified, though natural
combination.   Difcernment is here feen
to be guided by imagination in the perception of objects whofe ufe is prefcribed
by the underftanding.

II. Criticifm

II. Criticifm, when confidered more particularly with regard to fcientifical refearch, will render ftill more confpicuous our obfervations on thofe important offices which are exercifed in this province by the reafoning faculty. In philofophy we have already feen, that as judgment directs the author in the choice of his fubject, in the method of conducting it, and in the juft proportion of its parts to each other*, fo it is judgment likewife by which the critic is enabled to form an adequate eftimate of the execution. That exquifite difcernment, fo neceffary in *the arts* where imagination perceives fuch objects as reafon enables us to put to their proper ufe, is not effentially requifite to characterife the philofophical critic, becaufe the theory of which he is to judge, having been formed originally by the underftanding, its inventor; fancy can have no extenfive influence in con-

---

* Το γαρ ψευδος εν Συνθεσι αει· ενδεχεται δε και διαιρεσιν φαναι ταυτα. Το δε ῾ΕΝ ποιουν τυτο Ο ΝΟΥΣ εκαςου. ΑΡΙΣΤΟΤ. περι Ψυχ. βιε. Γ. κεφ. Ε.

ducting

ducting its examination. That we may
have a clear view of this fubject, it will
be proper to enquire what the critic in the
prefent cafe is principally required to have
in view.

The general plan of a philofophical work
is then only complete (as we have already
fhewn) when it is diftinct, connected, and
comprehenfive of the fubject *. A writer
who obtains thefe points is properly no-
minated judicious, becaufe it is unqueftionably by an effort of the underftanding that
materials are arranged in fuch a manner as
to form a whole that is proportioned and
confiftent. Even the *invention* of thefe in
this fcience we have fhewn to arife from the
fame faculty; and we have diftinguifhed
by particular criteria this kind of invention from that which is either derived from
another power of the mind, or from the
union of both. An excellence or defect in

---

* ΔΙΑΘΕΣΙΣ (fays the great philofopher quoted
above) λεγεται του εχουτος μερη ταξις, η κατα τοπον, η
καθα δυναμιν, η κατα ειδος. θεσιν γαρ δει τινα ειναι ωσπερ
και το ονομα δηλοι η Διαθεσις. ΜΕΤΑΦΥΣ. βιε. Δ.
κιφ. ιθ.

this

this difcovery or difpofition falling under the cognifance of an intelligent judge, will give him occafion to fhow that good fenfe (as it is called), that power of thinking with juftnefs and precifion, which fo univerfally denominates the prevalence of reafon. It is true indeed that a man of *difcernment*, in the proper fenfe of that word, may difplay this quality to great advantage in fuch a difquifition; but it is equally certain that a decifion perfectly accurate, and founded on the jufteft principles, may be pronounced on the invention and difpofition of materials in a philofophical enquiry by a perfon whofe powers of imagination are inadequate to thofe of his underftanding.

When again we come to weigh the comparative ftrength of arguments, as carrying conviction to the mind, we muft be immediately fenfible that it is the *reafon* of mankind only to which the philofopher here appeals, and it is *reafon* only by whofe aid the truth or fallacy of thefe arguments can be detected by the critic, who judgeth of his work. Penetration, as obferving this fallacy immediately, though concealed

by

by the moft plaufible reprefentation, will
render him qualified to enter with eafe, as
well as depth and compafs into his fubject;
but reafon alone, without this quick and
almoft intuitive perception, by its fteady
attention and gradual procedure, obtains
its end at laft as furely, though not perhaps fo quickly as the former; and by inveftigating clofely every circumftance of
its detail, lays before the mind a view of
the whole refearch conceived with comprehenfion, and expreffed with perfpicacity.

Here I am aware that a very natural and
important queftion will arife. Since (it
will be faid) the underftanding alone is
adequate to fo many purpofes in this dignified fphere of compofition, what is meant
by that *philofophical difcernment*, which a
mafterly critic is faid to difcover in this
noble and inftructive fcience, and how are
its objects to be diftinguifhed from fuch
as are contemplated folely by the faculty
of reafon? This queftion is very proper,
and in anfwer to it we muft in general obferve, that the degree of difcernment (fuch

as

as hath already been delineated) which is diſplayed in philoſophical criticiſm depends principally upon the conduct of the work which it is propoſed to inveſtigate. The critical art is in this reſpect diſſimilar to others, that though referred ultimately indeed to nature and truth as its ſtandards, yet more immediately it relates to ſome work in which theſe are imitated or developed. In an examination therefore thus conducted, it is obvious that the combination of powers appearing to predominate in the mind of the critic muſt be of the ſame kind, though not perhaps equal in degree with that which characteriſeth the writer whoſe work is examined. Thus we ſhall naturally be induced to judge of the former as poſſeſſing certain intellectual qualities from the choice which he makes of his ſubject, and with a prepoſſeſſion thus far juſtly eſtabliſhed, we ſhall conſider the execution of his performance. Reaſon, we have already ſeen, takes cogniſance of the propriety and connection of arguments as ſtanding together in a natural arrangement: diſcernment

(confifting of the union of this faculty with
that of invention) directs in this fphere in
what manner thefe may be moft powerfully illuftrated, and difcovers the beft means
of enforcing each with energy and ftrength.
This laft quality therefore will always appear to the greateft advantage in philofophy, when the work criticifed contains
excellencies arifing from the fuperior
powers fometimes making a diftinct and
fometimes an united exertion, in which
cafes the critic may fhow his penetration
in a very ftriking point of view, by tracing
each kind to its original fource; and by
following out the operation of either or
both faculties fo accurately as to difcover
his own knowledge of the human mind,
and to enlarge that of his reader.

Here it is eafy to obferve that the underftanding, however enlarged and comprehenfive, can be adequate only to a few
of thofe purpofes which it is neceffary to
accomplifh, becaufe beauties derived from
an union of intellectual powers in the author
which fubfifts not in the mind of him who
attempts to judge of his work, muft either

be

be deemed equal to one important branch of his fubject, when his difcernment of others is faulty and deficient. Still however we are to remember, that as the fphere affigned to imagination is more limited in this than in any other fpecies of Compofition, a man poffeffing ftrength and folidity of judgment may employ the critical art in philofophy, with emolument to his readers, when the examination of other fubjects requiring a more complicated intermixture of mental qualities might be juftly chargeable with abfurdity and inconfiftence.

Hiftory, when regarded as a mirror in which the mind is faithfully reflected, and the real characters of men tried by the fureft of all tefts, that of their conduct in diverfified occurrences gives fcope to the difcernment of a genuine critic, as much at leaft as any literary department whatever. There are indeed a kind of drudges who pretend to appropriate this province to themfelves, whofe labours difcover critical acumen in the fame manner as a waggon-horfe jingling his bells fhows the ardour

and

and impetuofity of the hunter; and who, though ufeful in a certain fphere, are as much difqualified for others, as the former loofed from his machine would be to take the hedge or gate at a leap in purfuit of the greyhound.   Among thefe we may include the whole tribe of verbal and chronological critics, the latter of whom in particular difplay learning and application, and even the former, upon fome occafions, ingenuity in their conjectures; but neither of thefe can apply the received opinions of what conftitutes excellence or defect in the hiftorical profeffion fo juftly to the work they are examining as to evince their own knowledge of the human heart, and thus render hiftory fubfervient to its moft important purpofe, that of inftructing mankind by example.

We would not be underftood here to detract from the real merit of authors, whofe induftry has been of ufe to fuch readers as defire to have every tranfaction recorded in hiftory as clearly elucidated as poffible.   But without incurring this cenfure, we may furely obferve that he who traceth

actions

actions with accuracy up to their original caufes, however remote and apparently incompatible with their effects; who detects for inftance jealoufy, envy, pride, avarice, or ambition in the characters of men, beneath the fhading by which thefe are often fcreened from vulgar cognifance; who, with regard to intellectual endowments, fhows what conduct was directed by judgment, what by caprice, what by paffion, and what by clear and comprehenfive recollection in the perfons of whom he treats; we may obferve that this author obtains the ultimate purpofe of his profeffion effectually; and that the critic who diftinguifheth the inftances in which thefe are fuccefsfully or unhappily delineated, differs as widely from the moft exact chronologer as he who promotes the edification of mankind does from him who minifters wholly to their curiofity. A penetrating judge of human nature has an opportunity here of fhowing his difcernment in a very eminent manner *, either

by

---

* " Paulatim ad majora tendere incipit hiftoricus,

laudare

by correcting the errors of the historian
when he appears to have mistaken his
subject by entering into a close and particular examination of the objects falling under
this writer's inspection; or by supplying
his defects where the end of history may
not have been fully obtained, by collecting
either from one fact, or from a series of
transactions, remarks which render us acquainted familiarly with the personages of
history, and able to explore with philosophical precision the causes of the rise, ex-
tension, and dissolution of empire.

Upon the whole therefore, when we
consider the critic as required in some
branches of his profession to distinguish
faults from real beauties amidst a group of
indiscriminate objects; to observe the delicate and almost imperceptible shades by
which these approach to, and almost unite
with each other; to be able in others to

laudare claros viros, & vituperare improbos, quod non
simplicis utilitatis est opus. Namque & ingenium
exercitum multiplici variaque materia, & animus con-
templatione-recti pravique formatus & multa inde cog-
nitio rerum venit." Quintil. lib. ii. c. 4.

investigate

inveftigate the principles of an art with the accuracy of a philofopher, at the fame time that the order and proportion of inferior parts is attentively marked; the caufes pointed which have given rife to uncommon deviations in one inftance, and cuftomary ones in another; and particular paffages referred to either by way of proof or example, in whofe choice as well as difpofition the mind perceives peculiar propriety; thefe, it muft be allowed, are offices in which various degrees of merit are rendered confpicuous, and are calculated when taken together to fhow us completely that combined influence of judgment and imagination which conftitutes difcernment in its utmoft extent.

Thus in the profecution of this curious and delicate fubject we have endeavoured to trace that union of the intellectual powers, which gives rife to philofophy, hiftory, poetry, fables, and criticifm, and to afcertain likewife, as nearly as poffible, that influence which each of thefe feparately confidered requires thefe to exert. Eloquence (in the prefent point of view)

differs

differs in nothing materially from the
higher fpecies of dramatic poetry, and, as
a branch of the moft effential importance
in the art of which we treat, it will fall
afterwards under examination. It will be
obferved in general, that there is a difference betwixt the fimple confideration of
the caufes that produce certain effects, and
that of the various manners in which each
requires thefe caufes to operate. In the
former point of view they have been already confidered; in the latter they belong
to a fubfequent fection.

SECTION VIII.

*Whether that ballance of the intellectual
powers from which the perfection of Compofition refults, can be obtained; and by
what methods we may make the neareft
approach to it.*

FROM the preceding feries of obfervation on the powers of the mind, as
varioufly employed in the art of Compofition, it is we prefume evident, that the
real

real faults, as well as inequalities which
we meet with ſo frequently in works of
unqueſtionable eminence, ariſe in moſt inſtances rather from that diſproportion
which takes place betwixt one faculty and
another, than from the poſitive weakneſs of any particular quality, as we are
apt to think upon ſuperficial inſpection.
It will therefore be univerſally acknowledged that a mind which had received
from nature a propenſity to Compoſition,
and in which the powers, whoſe functions
we have attempted to determine, are conferred in the higheſt degree, and are bal-
lanced with perfect equality, would attain
the utmoſt excellence in this art of which
human nature is ſuſceptible. Without en-
quiring whether a mind participating all
theſe advantages ever exiſted (a ſubject
foreign to the purpoſe) it will be worth
while to conſider the more obvious cauſes
by which this equipoiſe of the powers
abovementioned is obſtructed; and to ſum
up our view of Compoſition, as it regards
the faculties of the mind by laying down

ſuch

such rules as may tend at least in some measure to supply this defect.

I. Amidst that great disproportion of mental abilities, which the slightest observation will show us to take place among men, we shall find that nature, like a wife and impartial governor, has been careful to preserve a kind of equality in the whole species, by annexing particular faults or imperfections almost inseparably to the possession of such qualities as have the greatest tendency to render an individual the peculiar object of admiration and envy. Thus judgment, however exact and comprehensive, when not accompanied by imagination is cold and unanimated: its arguments convince, without amusing or exhilarating the mind; and we are apt to judge the trouble we have had in perusing its researches but poorly compensated by the instruction which these may have ultimately conveyed to us. The philosopher therefore, with all the pride of science, and of superior abilities, finds himself neglected because he is disqualified

to

to blend entertainment with utility, and thus difcovers that he is really inferior in one important circumftance, to thofe whom in other articles he might juftly regard as unable to rife to his fphere of excellence.

As the poffeffion of judgment without an adequate proportion of imagination is thus naturally accompanied with fome inconveniencies, as we fhall find much greater difadvantages almoft infeparably united with vigour, and much more with exuberance of the laft mentioned faculty. Where a man's paffions are ftrong, his feelings exquifite, and his mind fufceptible alternately of almoft every impreffion, it is obvious that his manners muft be characterized by marks of inequality, which bring him down upon many occafions to the common level of his kind *, and fully com-

---

* As there is no queftion fo clear but fome philofophers have ftudied to perplex, we find the fame bad confequences afcribed fometimes to reafon itfelf, or at leaft deduced from the weaknefs which are here derived from the prevalence of a licentious imagination, and the Deity impeached for having conferred it.
" Eam

compenfate for fuch other qualifications as
place him in a diftant and exalted region*.

In

" Eam dediffes hominibus rationem quæ vitia culpam-
que excluderet. Ubi igitur locus fuit errori Deorum?
Nam patrimonium fpe bene tradendi relinquimus : qua
poffumus falli. Deus falii qui potuit?—Si homines
rationem bono concilio a Diis immortalibus datam in
fraudem malitiamque convertunt non dare illam quam
dari humano generi melius fuit, &c." Cicer. de Natur.
Deor. c. 31. With regard to the prefent fubject we
need only obferve in anfwer to thefe objections, (which
Cicero has put in the mouth of Cotta) that reafon,
though at many times it is fubdued by the paffions,
yet in confequence of its obtaining in many other inftances the victory over thefe, and giving confiftence
to the character, is the power by whofe influence we
act with fteadinefs and recollection ; while fancy on
the other hand, as impelling the paffions, and acted
upon by thefe is the caufe, in the fame manner of inequality and inconfiftence. The one therefore only de-
viates fometimes from its purpofe from the imperfection
of human nature, whereas the other (unlefs when ref-
trained within proper limits) does fo at every time
without exception.

* Men of genius have exhibited but too many examples of the truth of this remark. The author of
the life of the celebrated Pallavicini, has very properly
illuftrated it from the conduct of that gentleman. His
words are remarkable. " Cofi è pur vano che non fi
trovi in quefta vita mortale cofa alcuna intieramente
compita ; & avenga fovente, che quelli, che poffiedono
migliore ingegno degli altri huomini riefcano nelli
proprie

In life therefore, conſidered as properly regulated by prudence, ſteadineſs, and equability, as well as in the art of Com-poſition, the point of perfection lies in the equipoiſe of theſe faculties acting with harmony, and extending their conſequences to every part of the character. In pro-portion likewiſe, as the meaſure in which theſe are conferred becomes nearer to, or more remote from this equality, will be the excellence or imperfection of that con-duct or production on which the intellec-tual powers are required to exert united influence.

Uncommon however as an union of this kind is, we ſhall find, upon reflection, that a near approach to perfection at leaſt, if not the abſolute attainment of it, is in a great degree obſtructed by a defective and injudicious ſyſtem of education. In order thoroughly to comprehend this matter, let us conſider a little the firſt train of ideas that are impreſſed upon the mind with re-

proprie attioni, con ſcandalo de' ſemplici peggiori de gli altri huomini." Opere di Pallavicin. vol. i. p. 10.

gard

gard to the subject of this essay, and let
us examine the effect of which these ideas
must naturally be productive, suppofing
nature to have laid a foundation fufficient
for bringing both the fuperior faculties to
operate with uniform and almoft perfect
concurrence.

1. It is acknowledged on all hands that
in the firft ftages of life, the inventive
power appears much earlier, and arrives
at maturity more fpeedily, than that which
obtains its purpofe by the procefs of intermediate argument *. A young perfon
therefore entering into life with as much
of both qualities as the human mind can
be judged to poffefs, will difplay the former in great luxuriance before the latter

---

* Quintilian includes Imagination under the name
of Memory, which he mentions as the firft indication
of genius. " Ingenii fignum (fays he) in pueris
præcipuum Memoria eft. Ejus duplex virtus: facile
percipere, & fideliter continere." When he mentions
quicknefs of perception as characteriftical of memory,
he obviously includes under this defignation one province of the power of invention which is employed,
as we have already fhewn, in the original perception
of the objects of criticifm. Inftit. lib. i. c. 3.

has

has arrived at its ſtrength and confiſtence *. This proceſs is perfectly natural, and ſuited to the firſt notions we form of intellectual exertion. The external beauties of creation form the firſt, and perhaps the higheſt entertainment of an ingenious and ſenſible mind †. Fancy having theſe at firſt impreſſed upon it by the ſenſes dwells for ſome time with pleaſure

---

* To this faculty, as the parent of ambition, we muſt refer the indications which the conſummate judge of human nature above referred to mentions as diſcovering genius; " Mihi ille detur puer quem laus excitet, quem gloria juvet, qui victus fleat. Hic erat alendus ambitu, &c." Ibid. " Excitabitur laude æmulatio. Nam licet ipſe vitium ſit ambitio, cauſa tamen virtutum eſt." Cap. 2.

† " Repreſentons-nous donc la naiſſance de la muſique & de la poeſie en quelque belle contrée parmi des hommes heureux & innocens. Imaginons-nous d'abord des bergers qui conduiſoient leurs troupeaux des le matin dans les plaines fleuries le long des paiſibles rivieres. Pendant le jour ils les retiroient a l' ombre des bois, & des collines. A ces heures-la jouiſſant du repos ou des grottes fraiſches, ſous l'epaiſſeur des arbres, ils entendoient le chant des oiſeaux, & ils furent imperceptiblement excitez a imiter ces fredons & ce doux ramage." De la Poeſ. et Peint. par M. Geneſt. ap. Div. Trait. ſur l'Elog. & Poeſ. vol. ii. p. 280.

upon

upon the original, and where the mind
receives a propenſity to Compoſition, proceeds either to copy theſe itſelf, or delights in the peruſal of ſuch productions
as contain the moſt perfect models of imitation. In theſe circumſtances it is obvious, that imagination gaining perpetual
acceſſions of ſtrength by exerciſe, while
the reaſoning power gains no degree of
proportioned improvement, muſt become
at laſt ſo excentric and irregular as to
overpower the other in the ſucceeding
periods of life, and perhaps to prevent
its growth, in the ſame manner as a ſtem
permitted to ſhoot beyond its proper dimenſions, or to bear too luxuriant a crop,
debilitates the whole trunk, and renders
its other productions ſcanty and deficient.

It is therefore upon the firſt plan of
education that is purſued with a mind
in which nature has infuſed the ingredients of genius, that its future character
may be ſaid to depend. Yet do we attend ſufficiently to the culture of its ſuperior faculties at a time when ſo many
                                    obvious

obvious advantages may be derived from this attention? A courfe, I am afraid, tending naturally and unavoidably to *break* the ballance of the mental powers is taken by far the greater number of mankind. The parent or the tutor who obferves in a child the firft emanations of genius (fhould he choofe to encourage its propenfities) attempts to ftrengthen his defire of knowledge, and to ftimulate his early inclination to ftudy by putting, we fhall fuppofe, into his hands books of innocent and agreeable entertainment. This conduct is furely thus far proper and judicious. Curiofity, the firft paffion that appears in the character, is by thefe means powerfully excited; and a partiality of the greateft confequence in every future period is eftablifhed in favour of particular fpecies of Compofition.

The cafe however varies very confiderably when the mind comes nearer to a ftate of maturity. Imagination, never fatiated with entertainment, and, where it is conferred in an high degree, running conftantly

ftantly into extremes, acquires, by indulgence in its irregular excurfions, a certain
wildnefs and faulty exuberance, which
reafon is afterwards employed to correct
to very little purpofe. When the laft likewife is either originally very unequal, or
by being neglected in the firft ftages of life
has comparatively received but a fmall
fhare of improvement:—in this cafe quib-
ble, antithefis, and little conceits, which
difcover falfe tafte, but are apt to ftrike
upon fancy in its age of inexperience and
error, will be marked with eagernefs,
transfufed into the firft effays of opening
genius, and a habit of deviating into bad
compofition will be eftablifhed at that period, when every habit of this kind is apt
to make the moft lafting, and therefore
the moft dangerous impreffions.

Yet what is the method ufually employed to cultivate a propenfity to this art
when it is firft perceived to take place?—
If thofe performances which tend to *pollute*
the imagination are with-held, fuch as
contribute to *extend* it by the fwifteft progreffion are fupplied with liberal indulgence.

gence. Plays, fables, poetic compofitions of the defcriptive kind, and perhaps the extravagant fictions of romance, are devoured with infatiable avidity. Memory is loaded with a multitude of undigefted incidents; and tafte is by thefe means often incurably vitiated, when it ought to be formed upon a model the moft accurate and correct.

It will perhaps be faid in anfwer to thefe remarks, that as the growth of reafon is comparatively flow, and its progrefs to maturity almoft imperceptible, it muft be difficult, if not impoffible, to bring this power to the fame perfection at which the inventive faculty arrives at any early feafon of life; and that as foon as it becomes capable to follow out the thread of argumentation, it is cultivated (in thofe at leaft who receive an academical education) by being applied to the ftudy of philofophy. But this inftead of clearing up the matter, renders ftill more inexcufable the conduct of thofe perfons who in place of attempting to ftrengthen the weaker power, add force to that which is originally predo-

C c 2 minant.—

minant.—Let us fee how this reafoning
would hold when applied to the common
occurrences of life.—A father we fhall
fuppofe has two fons, the one with a
ftrong and healthy, the other with a feeble and delicate conftitution. It is indifpenfably neceffary that by athletic exercifes,
perhaps by hardy culture, and by the ufe
of all the methods ufually employed to
render the body robuft and vigorous, the
latter of thefe fhould, if poffible, be made
as able to fupport fatigue and to combat
difficulty as the former. Would he judge
it an expedient proper to be ufed, if any
man fhould fuggeft fuch a method, to
ftrengthen by every means the firm and
durable conftitution, and leave that which
ftood in need of the greateft affiftance upon
the precarious hope that nature might at
laft make an effort in its favour? Or
granting both to be originally equal in
ftrength, but one of them advancing in
ftature and intellect much fafter than the
other, would he deem it rational to overlook him who required the moft affiduous
attention in order to preferve the original
equality,

equality, and beſtow this wholly on the other, whoſe progreſs to maturity might indeed be quicker, but by no means ſurer than that of the former, properly directed?—In circumſtances of this nature no man is at a loſs to judge of the moſt reaſonable means, and to know the method that is moſt eligible whether he purſues it or not.—Whence then, it may be aſked, ariſeth the difference betwixt the expedients made uſe of in ſimilar caſes to ſtrengthen the body, and thoſe that are applied to invigorate the faculties of the mind?—The cauſe is obvious. In the firſt mentioned caſe, reaſon receives immediate and convincing evidence from the ſenſes: in the laſt, without any information by this canal, the mind is left to form a theory for itſelf. As men therefore in general are by no means qualified for abſtracted ſpeculation, individuals are governed by the eſtabliſhed cuſtoms of the world; and thus one intellectual power is permitted to acquire almoſt unlimited dominion before an attempt is made to im-

prove

prove the other by a regulated plan of education.

Upon the hypothefis here laid down, a difcerning reader might find it perhaps no very difficult matter to trace thofe afto-niſhing inequalities which are to be met with in performances of the higheft emi-nence to their original fource, at leaft in many inftances. It appears to me unac-countable upon any other principles, in what manner authors who at one time ſhine in the fphere of fuperior excellence, at another fink into the moft puerile levi-ties. Intellectual operation when directed by judgment, is uniform and confiftent. A man who eftimates with precifion and propriety the comparative value of great objects upon one occafion, will (if his tafte is not vitiated by prepoffeffions acquired before his reafon came to maturity) dif-play the fame perfpicacity in judging of ſuch as are of lefs importance at another. But receiving a particular bias to fome fpecies of falfe Compofition, in the fame manner as a man, otherwife of good principles,

ciples, gains the habit of indulging a particular paffion, his judgment is unable to
reftrain this propenfity in the future periods of his life, and he fees the defect in
others, without being equal to the tafk of
correcting it in himfelf.

2. Thus far we have proceeded upon the
fuppofition that imagination is originally
prevalent in the mind; and we have
fhewn in what manner a wrong plan of
education tends to ftrengthen the bad confequences of which this difparity is naturally productive. It muft, however, be
acknowledged, that when reafon happens
to prefide eminently over the other powers, thefe confequences are not likely to
fall out, at leaft in the firft and earlieft
feafon of life; and in order therefore to
preferve an inequality betwixt the two
ruling faculties, thofe propenfities, which
in the former inftance are to be moderated
in the latter, may be indulged with fome
degree of freedom.

It is natural for every man who poffeffeth the leaft fpark of genius, to turn
his thoughts at firft upon works of fancy

and

and invention. A defire of this kind in a man whofe underftanding is folid and comprehenfive, but his powers of invention greatly inferior, ought to meet with encouragement, unlefs it fhould be carried obvioufly to an extreme, which will rarely be the cafe. Such a purfuit tends to invigorate and to extend as much as poffible, a faculty which it is neceffary to cultivate, and whofe original inferiority in this laft cafe, will leave no room to dread the effects that arife only from its wildnefs and luxuriance. When the real character however begins to be perceived, and the *bias* of the mind determines its choice of objects, a man poffeffing naturally no great fhare of imagination is in hazard of crufhing it altogether, by giving way to that courfe of ftudy in which perhaps he is principally fitted to excel. At this time he begins to fix all his attention upon the acquifition of folid and edifying knowledge as it may be deemed, and in the purfuit of this, neglecting that exterior polifh, and thofe beauties which are effentially neceffary to render this knowledge

fub-

fubfervient to any valuable purpofe, he becomes affimilated to writers who ought by no means to be regarded as ftandards of imitation; and fees, perhaps when too late, others fuccefsfully employed in a province which his own inattention has difqualified him to occupy.

But thefe, however material, are not the only confequences which neceffarily arife from neglecting to improve the inventive faculty when it is originally inferior to the underftanding. We have already fhown in what manner difcernment is conftituted by the union of both, and what qualities it derives particularly from a vigorous imagination *. Thefe as they muft neceffarily lie dormant, or be even annihilated in the mind, when that power upon which they depend remains uncultivated, will leave a deficiency fo obvious as not to be compenfated by the poffeffion of reafon alone in any extent we can affign to it. A reader deftitute himfelf of this penetration will obferve perhaps

---

* Sect. iv. p. 92.

only

only that a work is cold and wholly uninteresting, even when the arguments are
clear and convincing in the case we have
stated, without tracing exactly this defect
to its original. But he who is qualified
to judge of its influence on the minds of
others, from that which it exerts on his
own, will miss in such a performance those
happy illustrations which render arguments forcible as well as perspicuous; and
will observe in what instances these might
have been strongly impressed upon the
mind, by having fixed upon a few decisive
criteria, instead of having entered into
a minute and tedious detail, from which
he ariseth in some measure disgusted.

It is with the art of Composition in this
case, as with all other subjects of what
kind soever. Extreme indulgence in any
propension (especially in the first part of
life) will always have the most pernicious
tendency. We observe the effects of scho-
lastic education, even in that work which
immortalizeth the genius of Milton, as
the philosophical disquisition into which
Pope was led (probably by the contempt
he

he had for deſcriptive poetry) appears to have curbed the exertions of a genius otherwiſe inventive, ſublime, and diver‐ ſified *. Young, on the other hand, ſeems to have impaired his reaſoning powers, or at leaſt to have prevented their full exer‐ ciſe, by a conduct altogether oppoſite. His moral obſervations are often excellent; his language is highly ornamented, and he riſes often to a wonderful pitch of ſub‐ limity. But his judgment, in ſome parts of his writings, would ſeem to be equal to taſks †, in the execution of which we find it after all to be deficient. By having formed himſelf at firſt upon falſe models, his taſte appears to have ſuffered conſider‐

---

* This obſervation (if I am not miſtaken) is ſome‐ where made in an ingenious Eſſay on the Writings and Genius of Pope. He uſed to call deſcriptive poetry as abſurd a compoſition as a feaſt made up of ſauces. Eſſ. p. 51. This ſurely was not the reſult of that impartial reflection which preſerves a juſt medium in its deciſions; and had not Pope's imagination been uncommonly luxuriant, an adherence to this opinion would have rendered his compoſition ſpiritleſs and profaic.

† In the conduct of ſome of his tragedies for in‐ ſtance, and in his Univerſal Paſſion.

ably,

ably, and his reasoning, when closely examined, is commonly lame and dissatis-factory *. In short, he is an excellent painter, but a bad philosopher. His loose remarks are frequently just and striking; but his arguments want strength and propriety.

II. As we have thus endeavoured at some length to investigate the causes arising from our own conduct, by which the equipoise of the intellectual powers is principally obstructed, it is only further necessary to enquire by what methods these may be most effectually removed, and the mind fitted by nature to excel in Composition be qualified to approach as near as possible to perfection in the art.

Every man of reflection will acknowledge that the step requisite to the attain-

---

* " C'est une consolation pour un esprit aussi borné que le mien d'etre bien persuadé que les plus grandes hommes se trompent comme le vulgaire." Volt. It is making a proper use of such failings in a great genius to consider these as evidences of that *equality* which obtains upon the whole among mankind, as we have formerly observed, whether in this particular instance here adduced we have justly assigned the cause of these or not.

ment

ment of this important end, muft be taken
by detecting *the particular bias of the mind,*
to whatever objects it may be fuppofed
originally to point. This, among the variety of human characters, is in fome fituations perfectly eafy, and in others a work
requiring the greateft attention, and no
fmall fhare of difcernment. In every cafe,
however, without exception, where any
propenfity to the art of which we treat
takes place in the mind, a penetrating
judge will difcover it in the firft rude
effays, which may be properly denominated the fimple effufions of the heart.
In thefe circumftances, by comparing two
draughts on the fame fubject (the execution perhaps of a tafk) by a young perfon
endowed with this difpofition, and by another, at the fame time of life, who is
wholly divefted of it, or who poffeffeth it
in a very inconfiderable degree, he will
obferve an obvious difference either in
ftrength and propriety of epithet, comparative regularity of parts, or an eafy flow
of expreffion. The attempt of the latter
(if the fentiments and diction are not borrowed,

rowed, with little or no alteration, from
the firft book he can meet with on the
fubject) will be ftiff, affected, and the
vifible refult of application and labour.
It might perhaps be deemed chimerical
to affirm, that it could be poffible to difcover in any art but that of poetry, the
particular branch of Compofition to which
the mind hath received a bias. The mental powers muft be allowed to open at leifure in ordinary cafes, before we can pronounce with certainty upon the courfe
which thefe may be prefumed moft probably to purfue. It ought however to be
obferved, that we fhall find ourfelves much
miftaken if we fuppofe a genius for Compofition to be indicated at this time of
life merely by an inclination to reading
and ftudy. This difpofition, though it is
indeed an infeparable concomitant of the
talent we have mentioned, is by no means
an indication that it actually fubfifts.—
Though no man ever poffeffed the former
of thefe without the latter, yet we meet
with innumerable inftances of men who
can perufe with pleafure the writings of
                                    others,

others, and are yet unable to execute with grace and maftery themfelves. It is therefore, only by an attempt to execute that the exiftence of this uncommon qualification can be properly afcertained *.

Perhaps in very early life, when a young perfon begins to difcover fome degree of genius, but in fuch a manner as that it may be impoffible to eftimate the comparative ftrength and proportion of his faculties, nothing can produce an happier effect on the mind, than little tales inculcating an obvious moral, conducted in the

---

* Διο και την Ομηρου ποιησιν (fays an ancient moralift with great propriety on the fubject of fable) και τους πρωτους ευροντας τραγωδιαν αξιον θαυμαζειν· οτι κατιδοντες την φυσιν των ανθρωπων, αμφοτεραις ταις ιδεαις ταυταις κατεχρησαντο προς την ποιησιν. Ο μεν γαρ τας αγωνας και τας πολεμους των ημιθεων εμυθολογησεν· οι δε τας μυθας εις αγωνας και πραξεις κατεςησαν· ωςε μη μονον ακουσους ημιν, αλλα και θεατους γεγενησθαι. From thefe remarks he draws very juftly the following conclufion (which fhows his knowledge of human nature,) Τοιυτων ουν παραδειγματων υπαρχοντων δεδεικται τοις επιθυμασι τους ακροωμενας ψυχαγωγειν οτι το μεν νουθετειν και συμβουλευειν αφεκτεον. Εκεινα δε γραπτεον και λεκτεον οις ωρωσι τους οχλους χαιροντας. ΙΣΟΚ. προς Νικοκ.

simpleft

fimpleft method, and expreffed with the utmoft concifenefs and perfpicuity. Befides the tendency which thefe naturally have to form the heart to the love of virtue, the young reader will find his ideas clear and unembarraffed in the purfuit of fo fimple and eafy a detail, at the fame time that his defire to imitate will be greatly encouraged by having a pattern fet before him which he can copy without difficulty. By thefe means likewife an early relifh is acquired for genuine and natural beauty :—the mind, before it has obtained a fufficient degree of difcernment to feparate falfe from real excellence, will infenfibly imbibe a prepoffeffion in favour of the laft ; and its powers will gradually be called out into exercife as it contemplates pictures of human life approved upon reflection, and fuited to thofe ideas which on the firft view of things are fo naturally and unavoidably fuggefted.

As we have already feen that fancy makes its appearance fooner, and fhoots into more vigorous exertion than the faculty of underftanding, it will no doubt

be

be proper, that in thofe compofitions
which are firft perufed by young perfons
there fhould be fomething calculated to
amufe and foothe imagination. This end
may be gained by a very fimple train of
incidents. In a fhort and plain allegory
the moral appears fo obvioufly as to make
an impreffion on the judgment and the
memory even though this is almoft imperceptible and involuntary. When the
fable becomes more various and complicated, imagination is either bewildered in
the labyrinth of conjecture, and its firft
conceptions are obfcure and intricate; or
it is apt to dwell upon fuch circumftances
as are moft wonderful and remote from its
original ideas: In either of thefe cafes the
work of inftruction is at an end. He
therefore, who would form the mind to
excellence in the fphere of Compofition,
and would preferve as nearly as poffible
the balance of its principal powers, ought
to take particular care that its earlieft notions be clear, appropriated, and fully
comprehended. That compafs of ideas
which it is fitted to take in ought to be

marked with the utmoft accuracy; and
every fucceffive object to be illuftrated in
fuch a manner as that it may be accuftomed
to canvafs fubjects with attention, and to
exprefs its fentiments with eafe and perfpicuity. This ftrain of gradual and progreffive education refembles, methinks,
rural life in places diftant from the noife
of cities. All is feemingly calm and ftill.
To the eye in the early feafon of fpring,
but few traces of induftry and labour are
confpicuous. But in the mean time the
buds are infenfibly expanding with their
fruit; the fun is exerting more powerful
influence; the herbage is imperceptibly
advancing to maturity, and the bufinefs of
the field is going on.

When we follow the mind in its progreffive ftate, as a more improved and open
organization gives it a larger fphere of
exertion, we are no longer at a lofs to difcover its prevailing bias, and to determine
the particular fphere of its exercife. In
this fituation, a man of difcernment will
endeavour to follow the lead of nature as
clofely as poffible, without attempting to
                                    effectuate

effectuate too much at once. It muft be
obvious for inftance, that to engage a
young perfon of lively imagination at once
in abftracted and metaphyfical refearches ;
or to confine another, whofe coolnefs and
fagacity might fit him for thefe laft, wholly
to the reading of novels and poetry, would
be a method totally irrational, from which
no good confequence could refult. Inftead of ftrengthening the faculty of reafon in one cafe, or that of invention in
the other, fuch conduct could anfwer no
other purpofe than that of producing languor and inattention, if not difguft and
fatiety in both. Reflection will therefore
fuggeft to us that by continuing to grant
the power that is prevalent fome degree of
indulgence, while at the fame time we engage the perfon in whom an inequality is
perceived in purfuits whofe *principal* tendency is to cultivate that which is weaker,
we fhall moft probably obtain the end at
which we propofe to arrive by a well-
conducted procefs of education. In order
to exemplify this general theory, let us

con-

confider each of thefe cafes a little more particularly.

In a preceding part of this work * we have endeavoured to point out the marks by which we may afcertain the predominance of imagination. Suppofing then thefe indications to obtain fo fenfibly in any one inftance as that the mind may be apt to be too much influenced by this irregular faculty, perhaps no method can more effectually conduce to improve the underftanding, than engaging the young perfon infenfibly in the ftudy of thofe branches of moral philofophy which are moft eafily comprehended, and by being naturally fufceptible of elegant illuftration, are calculated more happily than any other fubjects to convey inftruction and entertainment by the fame canal. Our own language abounds with fo many excellent performances of this character, that the objection of being compelled to wait until we have acquired another for this end is happily fuperfeded. The philofophy of

----

* Sect. iii.

Addifon

Addifon in his Spectators and other peri-
odical eſſays, is adapted in a particular
manner to accompliſh this end. The
many natural and elegant graces that are
thrown into the profe compofitions of this
amiable writer, the harmonious ſtructure
of his periods, the variety and importance
of his ſubjects, his unaffected ſimplicity,
and that vein of inimitable humour which
is diſplayed in his principal characters;
theſe circumſtances, united with juſtneſs
and propriety of ſentiment, render the philofophy of this author fitted peculiarly to
form the taſte, and improve the underſtanding of him, whom if left to his own
direction, fancy and inexperience might
feduce into error.

By the ſtudy of the beſt writers on ſubjects relating to life and manners, the
mind is not only prepared by the moſt
gradual progreſſion for entering into fe-
verer philofophical difquifition, but its
thoughts will run in that channel of obfervation which is favourable to the exercife and to the culture of reafon. It will
by thefe means be habituated to reflect

on

on its own operations, and by attending
to fuch fentiments as relate immediately
to itfelf, will learn to correct propenfities,
or to avoid prepoffeffions, whofe confequences on the character and conduct of
others it may find particularly detailed and
exemplified. As foon as he on whom
nature hath conferred a talent for the
higher branches of Compofition, enters
thoroughly into this feries of moral obfervation, his natural defire of imitating the
models that are fubmitted to his cognifance, will lead him to attempt fomething
himfelf in a ftrain fimilar to that which
he perceives to have obtained univerfal approbation *. By every effort of this kind
(dictated perhaps originally by an ambition of excelling) the underftanding will

---

* This method the beft and moft intelligent writers
recommend, as at the fame time a teft of genius in
the art, and the beft means of its improvement.
" On ne s'exerce prefque jamais a l'eloquence par la
voye la plus ordinaire & la plus feure qu'il y a pour y
parvenir qui eft l'exercife frequent de la Compofition :
a quoy il faut s'appliquer avec quelque forte d'affiduité
pour en acquerir l'habitude : car rien n'eft egal a
l'avantage qu'on en reçoit." Rap. Reflex. fur l'Eloq.
p. vi.

acquire

acquire an acceffion of ftrength; and reafon will learn to judge of its objects with
fuperior accuracy, compafs, and precifion.
There is a very great difference betwixt
that improvement which may be obtained
by taking a remote and diftant view of
inftructive fubjects, though perhaps as
particular as the diftance will permit, and
the benefit acquired by bringing a certain
train of ideas near as it were to the mind,
and by endeavouring as much as poffible
to transfufe their fpirit into a copy. In
the firft cafe whatever advantage is gained
muft be the refult of leifure and application. But in the laft, the mind, like the
eye furveying attentively a variegated profpect, will follow out openings that are
imperceptible at a diftance, until it difcovers the objects for which thefe were
contrived:—imperfections in the general
defign, as well as beauties that efcape common obfervation, will become confpicuous:—in fhort, new avenues of fentiment
will be gradually difclofed:—and the man
accuftomed to purfue a thought through
all its confequences will proceed to form

a theory

a theory for himfelf in one cafe, as he lays
out an original draught of cultivation and
policy in the other; indebted only to his
inftructors for the firft general, principles
upon which the work is conducted.

To the perufal of works of this nature
by perfons of the character we have delineated, we may add the ufe of fuch critical performances as tend to form a correct and elegant tafte in the different
branches of the fine arts *; as well as to
give exercife to the underftanding by ac-
cuftoming it to accurate and particular inveftigation. The felection of various examples by which a theory is illuftrated in
thefe productions, will agreeably amufe
the imagination of a young genius, and
emulation will be excited in favour of fuch
beauties as the writer finds it moft eafy

---

* I mean here that kind of criticifm (to adopt the
language of an eminent writer) " quæ auctores cum
cæteris fcriptoribus qui eadem tractant comparat; ut
per hujufmodi cenfuram ftudiofi & de librorum delectu
moneantur, & ad ipfam lectionem eorum inftructiores
accedant. Atque hoc ultimum, eft criticorum tanquam cathedra, &c." De Augment. Scientiar. lib. vi.
p. 422.

to

to imitate *. The blemifhes likewife that are to be met with even in the moft approved ftandards of Compofition, appear in a much more ftriking light when fet in oppofition to their excellencies in a critical examination, than when we furvey the work as a whole, and are inattentive to the fource from which inaccuracies proceed, even fuppofing that we have obferved thefe fuperficially. Care however ought to be taken that the performances of this caft. that are put into the hands of inexperienced readers may neither be too philofophical, nor fuch as dwell upon minute and trifling imperfections. A man poffeffed of exuberant imagination will probably in early life be too lively and volatile to enter with attention into the difquifition of the former; and the latter will either cramp his genius too much by rendering him timid and diffident, or will difcourage him altogether by producing

---

* " Nam crefcit cum amplitudine rerum vis ingenii (fays an author of difcernment) nec quifquam illuftrem orationem facere poteft nifi qui caufam parem invenit." Dial. de Caufa Corrup. Eloq.

abfolute

abfolute defpair of obtaining perfection in
the art. Mere philofophers, and men of
mere fancy, are commonly the worft critics
imaginable. The one writing wholly
from the head is only able to execute the
mechanifm of his work, and is difqualified
to apply his own rules with propriety;
while the other throws out the reveries of
a heated imagination without coherence,
meaning, or proportion.

We muft again have recourfe to the
laft mentioned amiable writer, as one of
the fitteft in every fenfe to form the mind
in the earlieft ftages of human life. There
is not perhaps in the works of any critic
whatever, an happier mixture of found
judgment, and of temperate imagination,
than in the effays which Addifon has left
us on the fubject of Criticifm. His Critique on the Paradife Loft (however a few
fuperficial readers, incapable to think for
themfelves, and floating like feathers upon
the current of opinion, may affect to def-
pife it) difcovers true tafte, warm fenfibility, and an exquifite difcernment of
poetic beauty and defect. Deeper and
more

more philofophical difquifition may perhaps be found than the critical works of
this author prefent to us; but thefe laft,
in confequence of their temperature in this
refpect, are particularly adapted to the period we are at prefent contemplating. I
can never take up any of this admirable
writer's more ferious pieces without applying to his manner the character which
Cicero gives us of the ftyle of philofophy.—
" Mollis eft enim oratio philofophorum &
umbratilis. Nihil iratum habet, nihil in-
vidum, nihil atrox, nihil aftutum, cafta,
verecunda, virgo incorrupta quomodo *."
Perhaps Mr. Hurd's ingenious effays on
this fubject, thofe of Johnfon, and a few
of the beft French critics may be here recommended with propriety, as calculated
in a particular manner to improve the
judgment of a young genius, and to form
his tafte to correctnefs and perfpicacity.
He will be taught by thefe means to think
with precifion, to decide upon fure principles; and having once learned to diftin-

* De Orat. lib.

guifh

guifh betwixt genuine beauty and that which hath only its appearance, he will acquire an early habit of imitating the one of thefe, and of avoiding the other.

Should any other courfe of reading be thought neceffary to complete the fyftem of education that is proper at this period for the improvement of the underftanding, we would venture for this purpofe the ftudy of natural hiftory. A judicious performance on this copious and interefting fubject, hath indeed an obvious tendency to call out all the powers of the mind into fucceffive exertion, and is calculated beyond all others to excite and to gratify that curiofity which is ftirred up in a reflecting mind by objects conveyed to it by the canal of fenfation. As no theme of whatever kind, contains a more diverfified feries of objects than that of natural hiftory, fo there is not perhaps any in the profecution of which more various degrees of merit have been rendered confpicuous. That part of it which relates to the generation, the fpecies, and the organization of infects, like many other fubjects excellent

lent in themſelves, and tending to produce emolument to the reader, yet hath been followed out by authors whoſe hearts perhaps were better than their underſtandings, with ſo much minuteneſs as hath expoſed both themſelves and their ſubject to ridicule. The theme however in itſelf is undoubtedly noble, as it tends to enlarge our ideas of the power and wiſdom of that Being who has not only peopled the world with ſuch inexhauſtible variety, but has with wonderful attention adapted the organs of the ſmalleſt inſect to its peculiar neceſſities, and has directed the objects around to afford it a ſucceſſion of ſuitable ſupplies.

But the circumſtances after all which a man of great imagination will principally take pleaſure to contemplate, are thoſe parts of this ſcience which lay open the grandeur, the magnificence, and the utility of the works of nature. Accordingly, we find that the birth and generation of things, the formation of the earth from chaos, the original and the employments of its firſt inhabitants, the produc-

tions

tions of feas, rivers, mountains, &c. were
the themes both of the earlieft poets and
philofophers *, infpired as it were by the
. powerful

---

* This truth will be acknowledged by all who have
any knowledge of antiquity. The bards of thefe early
days united in their own profeffion the character of
poets and philofophers, but thefe laft attempted not to
occupy the fphere of the firft. Yet their fubjects were
the fame Προτερον μεν εν ΠΟΙΗΜΑΣΙ εξεφερον οι
ΦΙΛΟΣΟΦΟΙ τα δογματα και τας λογας ωσπερ Ορ-
φευς και Ησιοδος, fays Plutarch on this fubject. Linus,
Orpheus, Melampus, Thamyras, Palæphatus, Prona-
pides, Timæus Locris, and Hefiod, authors (the two
laft excepted) fome of whofe writings are wholly loft,
and the others preferved in broken fragments, all of
them began their fongs at that period.—" Cum non-
dum divinæ religionis, non humani officii ratio cole-
batur: nemo legitimas nuptias viderat: non certos
quifquam infpexerat liberos, &c." Cicer. de Inven.
but—αμα παντ' επεφυκει " all things were jumbled
together:" and the formation of the univerfe from
this chaos was the fubject of their fongs.

Principio cælum ac terras campofque liquentes
Lucentemque globum Lunæ, Titaniaque aftra
Spiritus intus alit: totamque infufa per artus
Mens agitat molem.   . Virg.

To this inveftigation they gave the name of Theo-
gony, which (as a learned modern writer obferves)
" is a fyftem of the Univerfe digefted and wrought
" into an allegory:—a compofition made up of in-
" finite parts, each of which has been a difcovery of
" itfelf,

powerful voice of nature, and led to furvey divine wifdom in the workmanfhip
of the Deity.

" itfelf, and is delivered as a *myftery* to the initated."
Enq. into the Life of Homer, p. 99.—The philofophers treated this fubject more fyftematically, without
the images and licence of poetry. The Ægyptians
afcribed the origin of things to matter or earth * ;
Thales the Milefian, to water † ; Plato, to the four principles, fire, water, earth, and air, put together and fupported by an invifible and infinite mind ‡ ; Lucian
humoroufly, but in a fpirit truly philofophical, afcribes
the mixture of thefe elements to Venus, or the principle of love § ; and Phornutus has explained in a very
diftinct manner the offices of every deity in the generation and confervation of things, difcovering by thefe
means the important truths that are fhrouded fo effectually beneath the veil of poetic allegory ‖. As it appears, therefore, that thefe fathers of fcience who
hung out the *firft lights* to mankind dwelt fucceffively
upon the fubjects here recommended, moft of them at
periods when the *human mind* with regard to knowledge was in its infancy, and fufceptible of any impreffions whatever ; no fubjects more appofite and inftructive can be propofed to the young and inexperienced, than thofe which were originally judged fo
important, and which are productive of fuch obvious
emoluments.

* ΔΙΟΓΕΝ. ΛΑΕΡΤ. προοιμ. p. 7.
† Id. Θαλ. p. 18.
‡ Id. Πλατ. 229.
§ ΛΥΚΙΑΝ. Εξωτ. Oper. vol. iv. edit. Bafil. p. 195.
‖ ΦΟΡΝΟΥΤ. περι των θεων φυσ. paſſ.

When

- When from contemplating in this manner the earth in general and the bodies
revolving around it, we come to confider
its various ftrata, the minerals hid in its
bowels, and that inexhauftible ftore of
materials which it contains for all the purpofes of man; the underftanding engages
in an enquiry at the fame time curious,
entertaining, and inftructive. It ought
however to be obferved, that a general
fketch of thefe fubjects calculated rather to
ftimulate than to gratify curiofity, will be
fufficient in very early life to convey as
much knowledge as a judicious inftructor
will judge it expedient to communicate.
Nothing is productive of worfe confequences, particularly upon young perfons
of genius, than an attempt to lay before
them at once the whole extent of an art,
and to hurry the mind as it were before it
is arrived at a ftate of fufficient maturity
into intricate fpeculations, whofe evidence
after all may be principally conjectural
and prefumptive. That this is the cafe
with thofe who have wrote on Natural
Hiftory, is evident from the various hypo-
theſes

thefes that have been formed of the origin of rivers, fountains, and volcanos; of the caufes that give rife in particular inftances to eruptions, inundations, and hurricanes, and other extraordinary phænomena of the fame kind. The perufal of different theories on thefe fubjects anfwers only the purpofe of opening an inlet to fceptical principles; and by involving the mind in a labyrinth of doubt and error, renders it unable to range its ideas with precifion, and to exprefs thefe with perfpicuity. The method of proceeding from the fimpleft views of a fubject to more enlarged and compounded exhibitions, is exactly analogous to the manner in which we find it neceffary to proceed when young perfons are inftructed in the knowledge of thofe languages which it is judged proper to teach them, (with what expediency we fhall fee afterwards) almoft as foon as they are capable of diftinguifhing objects. That tutor, who, as foon as his pupil had learned the firft elements of Greek and Latin, fhould put into his hands Thucydides, Pindar, Tacitus, or Perfius, would furely

be cenfured as having acted in a very abfurd and irrational manner. We fuppofe
that the man, at whatever age, who is acquiring thefe languages can for a time take
in but a fmall compafs of ideas. We extend thefe gradually by leading him from
the plaineft and moft intelligible writings,
to fuch as by a more complicated conftruction of words require application and exercife to be thoroughly comprehended. By
this procefs the explication of difficult paffages becomes at laft eafy: we grow familiar with particular idioms, and are
able to transfufe thefe into a copy: we
enter without perplexity into the whole
phrafeology, and are qualified to impart
our knowledge to others by that method
which experience hath fhown to be fuccefsful with ourfelves.

By beginning therefore with difclofing
thofe works of divine wifdom that are confpicuous in the formation and exercifes of
the various claffes of infects; by defcribing
the manner in which thefe are fitted fo
admirably for the purpofes of their creation; their little arts, policy, government,
                                    fettlement,

fettlement, and excurfions, a mind endowed with any portion of genius will engage in a moft agreeable and inftructive refearch. While imagination will dwell upon the wonderful and aftonifhing in this enquiry, judgment will find its inveftigation confiderably enlarged by ftudying the manners of thefe and the defires by which they appear to be animated *; as well as by obferving particularly the marks that ferve to difcriminate either individuals of the fame tribe, or the different fpecies from each other †. Its ideas of infinite

wifdom

---

* —— communes natos, confortia tecta
Urbis habent, magnifque agitant fub legibus ævum ;
Et patriam folæ, & certos novere penates.
Venturæque hyemis memores, æftate laborem
Experiuntur, & in medium quæfita reponunt,
Namque aliæ victu invigilant, &c.

Virg. Geor. iv. l. 153.

† The divine poet, whom we have quoted above, makes a noble ufe of the employments of thefe tribes, by making thefe inculcate fome fublime maxims of philofophy.

His quidam fignis, atque hæc exempla fecuti,
Effe apibus partem divinæ mentis & hauftus
Æthereos dixere : deum namque ire per omnes
Terrafque, tractufque maris, cælumque profundum.

Hinc

wifdom will be inconceivably augmented, and its curiofity fupplied with the higheft gratification, when by advancing gradually in its enquiry it finds the whole vifible works of the Deity tending to produce the moft beneficial purpofes; and even thofe in which a fuperficial view might feem to

---

Hinc pecudes, armenta, viros, genus omne ferarum,
Quemque fibi tenues nafcentem arceffere vitas.
Scilicet huc reddi deinde, ac refoluta referri
Omnia : nec morti effe locum ; fed viva volare
Sideris in numerum, atque alto fuccedere cœlo.

Ibid. l. 219.

The genius of Virgil fhines no where more confpicuoufly than when it is thus employed in conveying
the moft momentous truths to the mind from fubjects
apparently fimple and unimportant. In this province
of genius, beyond all others, it may be faid to deferve
the denomination of *creative*, as the author in fome
fenfe exhibits an imitation of the divine mind by ftriking the unexpected light of inftruction from a theme
which at the utmoft promifes only a little tranfient
entertainment We obferve with admiration the compafs and extent of that mind which could inculcate
from the little labours of infects the omniprefence and
immenfity of God, as the vital principle fpread through
the univerfe, and the immortality of the foul which
proceeds from, and mixes at death with divine effence,
which could inculcate thefe doctrines with propriety
as growing out of its fubject, and naturally coalefcing
with objects fo apparently incongruous and remote !

point

point out irregularity, contrived upon clofer examination for ends of great and obvious importance.—Thus, by following out a digefted plan, the underftanding will be improved by a fure, though an almoft imperceptible progreffion; and the mind will acquire an habit of tracing effects to their caufes with juftnefs and accuracy, as foon as it is capable of forming an eftimate of the comparative value of the objects that furround it.

Among the many works to which this copious fubject hath given rife in our own country, there are few calculated to anfwer all the ends which it is here propofed to bring about. Derham, in his Phyfico-Theology, has indeed explained fome parts of Natural Hiftory in a very clear and fimple manner:—but his ftyle is unhap-pily fo vulgar and unanimated, that we can fcarce recommend his work (though otherwife valuable and judicious) to thofe who ftudy to improve the intellectual powers by whofe influence the mind is qualified for Compofition. Ray, Wefley, and fome others, who have wrote on the

E e 3 fame

same topics lye open to similar exceptions. The larger compilations on the other hand, either collected from books, or the result of the author's own observation and experience, are by far too abstracted and philosophical either to improve or entertain an inexperienced reader. Happily however for our present purpose, the work of an ingenious foreigner which is elegantly translated into our own language, and is almost in every body's hands, may be recommended with confidence, as having an obvious tendency to excite, as its author intended, the curiosity, and form the mind of youth. Few readers will be at a loss to know that the work referred to is that entitled Spectacle de la Nature, and contains a general view of the works of nature carried on in that method which we have recommended as most eligible in the first stages of life. The propriety therefore of recommending this work as a means to effectuate the above-mentioned purposes, must be so obvious as to stand in need of no illustration. We shall therefore only observe, that the familiar style of dialogue

dialogue which the author hath adopted in the three firſt volumes, the happy ſelection of his characters, and that air of philoſophical negligence which is ſupported through the whole, give this performance advantages in point of entertainment equal, if not ſuperior, to moſt others on the ſame ſubject *.

Having thus endeavoured to lay open that ſyſtem of education which may be moſt favourable to the cultivation of *reaſon* in a mind diſtinguiſhed by the eminent predominancy of the power of invention, it will be a much eaſier taſk to aſcertain the method by which imagination may be ex-

---

* Though we have here principally recommended the work of a foreign writer on the ſubject of Natural Hiſtory, to the peruſal of young readers, there are ſome Engliſh writers on this ſubject whoſe works may be read for the purpoſes above ſpecified with utility. Beſides a compendious and judicious treatiſe of this kind publiſhed in the Preceptor, many of Dr. Hill's pieces are curious and edifying in this branch of literature; and even Weſley, though he appears not to have ſtudied elegance of expreſſion in his ſurvey of the works of nature, yet has taken ſuch a view of theſe as may in a great meaſure be ſubſervient to the purpoſes for which this ſtudy is here recommended.

tended

tended when it is difcovered to be weak
and inferior in a ftriking degree to the
former. We may lay it down as a rule
from which there is no exception, that
where in the fpring of human life a young
perfon difcovers no very ftrong inclination
to perufe writings whofe principal end is
entertainment, and in which fancy appears
upon the whole to be predominant, that
fuch a man poffeffeth a very moderate
fhare of the power of invention. This
laft, whenever it is conferred in any confiderable meafure, will dwell upon fuch
performances with the utmoft fatisfaction,
and will fingle out from a whole not
merely the moft ftriking incidents, but
fuch as certain little circumftances imperceptible perhaps to a common obferver,
render particularly adapted to make a
ftrong, if not a lafting impreffion upon the
mind.

This propenfity, however, to perufe
books of entertainment, is fo univerfal
among mankind in the feafon of early life,
that it may be thought too general a criterion to afcertain the extent, or even the

pre-

prevalence of an intellectual faculty in an individual. In order therefore, to judge of this matter properly a man of penetration will attend to the remarks, which, after reading an ingenious and entertaining work, will occur to the mind of his inexperienced fcholar. The power of invention when obvioufly prevalent, will ftrongly indicate its predominance by making the mind felect, as capital beauties or faults of a work, circumftances that relate to incidents, colouring, machinery. The man of this caft will dwell upon the fcenery rather than the characters of fuch a performance, and paffing over the confideration of a whole as formed of members proportioned to each other, will either be inchanted with the wild and luxuriant, or will felect thofe ftrokes, however feemingly infignificant, whofe difcovery indicates exquifite fenfibility.—When thefe marks are obferved to take place, the man may with propriety be ranked among thofe in whofe mind it is principally requifite to improve the underftanding. The prevalence of this laft, on the contrary, will render the general

ral difpofition of fuch a work the object
of his attention; thoughts in whatever expreffion thefe are clothed which fhow
either acutenefs or comprehenfion, will
imprefs the memory when the moft fignificant illuftrations are no longer recollected; an impropriety in fome train of
fentiment, or in fome particular occurrence,
will in fuch a mind cancel a part of the
improvement or pleafure which might
otherwife be derived from either; and the
fitnefs of a particular part as juftly fuited
to thofe which make up a whole will be
obferved, when its beauty as an ornament
will be wholly overlooked.—In this laft
cafe, therefore, the feafon of youth fhould
not be permitted to pafs over, without
every method being taken to extend and
invigorate the powers of invention. It requires no great fhare of attention to difcover that thefe laft reflections are not fuch
as will occur upon the firft perufal of a
work to a young perfon of genius, if we
fuppofe it to be principally characterifed
by imagination. In very early life fuch a
man will be apt to feel a *perpetual fluctua-*
tion

tion of thought, (if we may exprefs it in this manner) a rapid fucceffion of new ideas crouding into the mind as his atten- tion is called off from one object to an- other; and in the midft of this internal commotion, if his thoughts are fixed by any feries of incidents whatever, that par- ticular circumftance will make the ftrongeft impreffion which a glance of reflection, imperceptible perhaps at the time, recom- mends as that which he himfelf would have felected in the fame fituation.

So indelible however are the impreffions which nature ftamps upon the mind, that with regard to the prefent fubject, in what degree foever we fuppofe a man to poffefs a talent for Compofition, he will be eafily diftinguifhed, even by a fuperficial obferver, from one who reads merely for amufe- ment, or even from a native propenfity to ftudy and obfervation. The laft of thefe as he is directed by no other motive in the reading of a work than either the enter- tainment he may receive from it at a va- cant hour, the reputation of learning he may acquire by retailing various opinions

on

on difficult and controverted fubjects, or by the neceffity he finds of fupplying his own want of original fentiment by gaining it from others, will be fatisfied with being qualified to mark out the capital beauties of a performance, perhaps with great judgment and accuracy, but without making fuch remarks as difcover any defire of imitation. The opinions therefore which thefe men form with regard to propriety of fentiment, ftrength of reafoning, or the proportion fubfifting betwixt the inferior members of a work, may be the refult of their own experience and attention;—but their remarks on the Compofition (particularly of a performance in which tafte and genius are difplayed) are ufually either retailed implicitly from the converfation of thofe who are efteemed the beft judges; or will fhow fuch little accuracy and difcernment in this matter as will leave a man even of moderate penetration at no lofs to pronounce that they are out of their fphere.—We now return to the principal fubject,

When

When, in conſequence of ſome ſuch proceſs of obſervation as we have attempted
to ſuggeſt, it hath been diſcovered that a
young perſon is poſſeſſed of a good underſtanding, but a very inferior ſhare of imagination; in order to extend this laſt faculty to ſome equality with the other, a
tutor will ſeldom err in granting a liberal
indulgence to the deſire which every man
of genius feels in his earlieſt years, to pe-
ruſe works of fancy and invention; unleſs
only when theſe (as is too often the caſe)
have any tendency to corrupt the heart.
A little reflection will thoroughly convince
us, that this method of proceeding can be
productive of no ſuch bad conſequences as
might at firſt view be ſuppoſed to ariſe
from it. The underſtanding participating
in no degree of the giddineſs and volatility
of fancy, arrives at maturity by a progreſſion not leſs ſure, becauſe it is commonly
imperceptible; and, unleſs in ſome very
extraordinary inſtances, acts not with full
force until the edge and vivacity of imagination begins to ſubſide. By ſtrength-
ening therefore this laſt when it is very
deficient

deficient, the other it is obvious can be in no degree impaired, becaufe in every work we fhall not only find fomething of which reafon is required to take cognifance, but when this power predominates remarkably, the mind will be naturally difpofed to dwell upon every object that is favourable to the improvement of its ruling faculty, rather than to take in thofe fublime effufions of genius, which are calculated almoft wholly for the meridian of tafte and fenfibility. Thus reafon will continue to improve in the prefent inftance, in whatever exercifes the mind is engaged, becaufe it will always meet with fomething adapted to this purpofe; whereas imagination may be crufhed when a man is engaged in certain purfuits which afford nothing calculated to ftrengthen or extend it.

In order therefore to bring the leading powers to a balance as nearly as poffible, when the latter is found to be weak and difproportioned, the perfon diftinguifhed by this inequality ought not only to be early accuftomed to the perufal of works

of

of invention, but his preceptor will perhaps find it expedient to point out to him
thofe *purely poetic beauties* which, deriving
their origin almoft wholly from imagination, are not of fuch a kind as he who has
received from nature a very moderate proportion of this faculty might felect for
himfelf. By thefe means as fancy begins
to extend by being kept in perpetual exercife, the mind will conceive fuch ideas of
the fublime, the elegant, the picturefque,
as well as of the correct and harmonious,
in Compofition, as it will be a vain attempt
to infufe when the judgment is arrived at
full maturity, and when tafte is no longer
fufceptible of improvement.

We may obferve further on this branch
of our fubject, that as the prevalence of
underftanding never fails to be indicated
by a certain cool and fedate manner which
is in fome meafure incompatible with the
impetuofity of imagination, fo the *paffions*
that obtain in a remarkable degree in this
laft inftance are either wholly abforbed in
the other cafe, or at leaft fubfift in a meafure much lefs perceptible. It will therefore

fore be expedient to wake the embers of thofe paffions, and to call each fucceffively into action, as a ftep indifpenfably requifite to promote any ftrenuous exertion of the intellectual powers. That we may fully effectuate this purpofe, fuch models of Compofition as are at once approved as the beft ftandards of the kind, and may be imitated with *comparative facility*, ought to be laid before the mind when its faculties are come nearer to their full growth, and when the man is able to determine the fphere in which he is particularly qualified to excel. Thus the writings of Homer or Shakefpeare will no doubt contribute to invigorate the power of invention, in the fame manner as the genius of Milton is faid to have been raifed to that wonderful pitch of fublimity at which it afterwards arrived by his being addicted to the reading of romance. But where no great portion of fancy is conferred by nature, a man may be brought to admire the beauties of poetic Compofition, and even to feel their influence, while his own confcious inferiority produceth a defpair of imitation.

As

As foon therefore as his imagination is inflamed, and of confequence his ambition excited in very early life by having ftudied the works of a great genius, and by having his principal excellencies explained, illuftrated, and rendered familiar; thefe works, as having anfwered their purpofe, may be laid afide; and the moft approved ftandards of philofophical, eloquent, or hiftorical Compofition will ferve, by being fubmitted to his enquiry, to gratify that afpiring emulation which we fuppofe to have been ftimulated by his attention to the former. By this method his mind will receive that improvement which is beft fuited to the bias and ftrength of its faculties *, and with his reafon exerting

the

---

* " A principio caveamus (fays a great genius formerly referred to, writing on a fubject fimilar to the prefent) a penfis, vel magis arduis, vel magis pufillis quam res poftulat : nam fi *oneris nimium* imponatur, apud *ingenium mediocre* bene fperandi alacritatem obtundes ; apud ingenium fiduciæ plenum opinionem concitabis, qua plus fibi polliceatur quam præftare poffit ; quod fecum trahit focordiam. In utroque autem ingenii temperamento experimentum expectationi non fatiffaciat, id quod animum femper dejicit & confundit."

the same force it might have done upon a
plan of education adapted wholly to cultivate the underſtanding; his imagination
will acquire extent and compaſs greatly
ſuperior to that which a plan of this kind
could ever have produced. If he cannot
therefore at any future period ſoar into
the region of the ſublime and the wonderful, he will learn at leaſt to expreſs his

---

De Augmen. Scient. lib. viii. p. 464. It is with
much ſatisfaction that the author finds in a work of
this great man, a rule laid down correſponding ſo
happily to that which is preſcribed in this branch of
his work. It is undoubtedly true, that a man in the
middle rank of genius with a moderate ſhare of good
ſenſe will be apt, in conſequence of that juſt way of
thinking which accompanies this qualification, to have
his hope of ſucceſs wholly depreſſed by contemplating
a ſtandard greatly beyond his reach; as he, on the
other hand, with the ſame qualities, who has confidence
enough to attempt an imitation, will be ready to ſink
into indolence when he finds his execution ſo diſpro-
portioned to the excellence of his model. Emulation,
as we formerly obſerved, may be excited by a ſtudy of
this kind more powerfully perhaps than by any other;
but in order to direct it properly when once ſtimu-
lated, authors of merit, whoſe beauties may be more
eaſily imitated, ought to be laid before a man of this
character; whoſe mind being then unbended and eaſy
will proceed in its courſe with alacrity and per-
ſeverance.

thoughts

thoughts with vigour and energy :—if his diction is feldom coloured with the glow of imagery, he will however avoid the extreme of tedious and infipid uniformity : in fhort, by having the fphere of his inventive power enlarged by a train of ideas paffing conftantly before it, in the fame manner as a feeble conftitution is rendered healthy by exercife; he may obtain the graces, though not the majefty of Compofition; and may become a correct and mafterly writer, though never a great and elevated genius.

III. As we have now attempted, in compliance with the defign of this fection, to inveftigate the caufes that obftruct the equipoife of the mental powers as far as thefe arife from a defective plan of education, and to fuggeft fuch expedients as may contribute moft effectually to prevent their confequences; it is only further neceffary that we obviate an objection which fome readers may make with regard to the difficulty of carrying the fcheme we have laid down into execution; and the real or

chimerical

chimerical value of its effects fuppofing
the plan to be fteadily purfued.

1. As to the firft, it will no doubt occur
to every man who reflects on this fubject,
that the difficulty of carrying on a procefs
of this kind, where an end of importance
is to be gained, can form no reafonable
objection (efpecially in extraordinary inftances) againft the attempt. In the prefent cafe, however, we fhall find upon examination no fuch impediments either in
difcovering the predominant faculty of
the mind, or in applying in particular
cafes the rules we have laid down, as may
at firft view be fuppofed.

The degree of attention required to find
out a talent for any fpecies of Compofition
depends partly upon that branch of the
art to which the mind hath received a
bias, and partly upon the meafure in
which this bias is obferved to prevail.
With regard to the particular kind of
Compofition, it muft be obvious, that in
whatever inftance the talents requifite to
form a poet or an orator take place, thefe
will

will make fo ftriking an appearance as to command obfervation, even fuppofing the parent to be remifs in his attention to a circumftance of this nature from indolence, or inattentive from avocation. Either of thefe will fall fo early into his natural courfe as to leave no queftion by what fpirit he is animated. It is a matter of no confequence whether the one character is, or is not miftaken for the other in the feafon of fport and paftime. It is fufficient that we know what may eafily be afcertained, that the mind is diftinguifhed by a large proportion of imagination. When this difcovery therefore is once made, by the firft effays of any kind which he throws out in the firft ftages of life, it cannot furely be difficult (fuppofing the man to whofe care fuch a perfon is entrufted, difqualified for the tafk of fuperintending his education) to find men of tafte, and of difcernment in this refpect, who will lead him into that courfe of ftudy which may be favourable to the improvement of the inferior faculty.—Again, when the mind is obferved to have acquired from nature a

F f 3

more

more didactic and philofophical character, it requires not certainly either an exten- five fhare of penetration to difcern in that cafe that *invention* is not the diftinguifhing characteriftic, nor any uncommon degree of judgment when this is known to en- gage a man in fuch purfuits as tend to open and enlarge his imagination. In either cafe it is only requifite that the fame attention which is employed to teach a young perfon the fyntax of a language, a circumftance of no great confequuace as to intellectual culture, fhould be applied either to the faculty of invention, or of ratiocination.

2. The other part of the objection which regards the *utility* of the method we have attempted to recommend, admitting it to be carried into execution, fhould it be feri- oufly propofed, will be found upon enquiry to proceed from a very defective acquaint- ance with the powers of the human mind. That thefe, confidered in general, are fuf- ceptible of the higheft improvement, is a truth not only univerfally acknowledged by the teftimony of mankind, but the whole

whole fyftem of education adopted among
every cultivated people proceeds upon it as
an eftablifhed and irrefragable maxim.
Thus as elegant manners, and an exterior
polifh of the moft agreeable nature is acquired by living in a court, and by fre-
quenting what is called *good company*; fo,
wifdom, circumfpection, courage, benevolence, the qualities of the heart as well
as thefe of the head, are found to depend
in an eminent degree upon the firft principles that are implanted in early youth;
as their exertion upon particular occafions
is directed by experience. That the time
of earlieft youth likewife is neceffary in a
particular manner for the accomplifhment
of thefe purpofes is evident, not merely
from what reafon fuggefts to us, but is
confirmed by our obferving univerfally
that when this feafon, fo peculiarly appropriated to improvement, is permitted to
pafs over without being properly employed, the mind acquires gradually a fettled
character, and its habits, whether good or
bad, become fo firmly rooted as never
afterwards to be thoroughly eradicated.

F f 4   If

If then we find by experience that the whole powers of the human mind taken together, are not only fufceptible of culture, but are even moulded into a new form by the infufion of fuch principles as are calculated to ripen and unfold them;— is it not obvious, that the fame attention which is beftowed on all, directed to ftrengthen that faculty which appears to be weakeft, will probably be fuccefsful when it is applied with judgment, and when the *crifis* is happily fixed upon, at which affiftance is indifpenfably neceffary to bring the original feeds to maturity ?— Should this reafoning be judged conclufive, no objection can lie either againft the *utility* of the plan we have laid down in the prefent fection, or the poffibility in any inftance of carrying it completely into execution. How far we have fucceeded in our attempt to afcertain the particular means by whofe ufe either judgment or imagination may be invigorated, the judicious reader muft be left to determine.

We cannot conclude this important branch of our fubject until we have made

one

one remark, which appears naturally to arife from the preceding obfervations. It is the impropriety of the method commonly taken to improve the mind when it is juft beginning to furvey and to difcriminate objects. In the ftages of infancy and childhood the care of a parent is very juftly employed to fupply the body with proper nourifhment, and to render the conftitution hardy and durable. It is chimerical to fuppofe that the mind in this helplefs ftate can receive improvement of any confequence. As foon however as it begins to diftinguifh and compare ideas, the attention of thofe employed in the work of education appears (ufually at leaft) to be occupied by circumftances *wholly foreign* to the principal end, if not in a great meafure tending to obftruct it. The boy, as foon as the natural bafhfulnefs and timidity (fo peculiar to this feafon, and fo characteriftical of genius) is brufhed off by reproof and example, is taught to prattle over a few words with a certain air of affurance, which gains him the reputation of promifing parts; and in the ftudy of

his

his native language; if his spelling and pronounciation is accurate, it is considered as a matter of no great consequence whether he understands the sentiments, allowing that these are adapted to his capacity, or whether they are such as he cannot possibly comprehend. The bias given to his mind by nature is so far from being attended to, that should imagination happen to take the lead in it, the keenness and extravagance that usually characterise it are contemplated as the criteria of uncommon genius, and are encouraged to exert themselves to the utmost. When he comes forward a little further, his intellectuals supposed to be in a state of almost total quiescence, while his body is advancing speedily in its growth, some years of the greatest importance are permitted to elapse while he is learning the grammatical part of a language, which had it been deferred a little longer he must in half the time have thoroughly understood, and his mind during this period receives no real improvement from his preceptors of any kind whatever. The study of the sciences immediately

mediately fucceeds; and having got fome general knowledge of the branches of philofophy, his literary education is judged to be accomplifhed, and he is turned over to his own direction. The amufements in the mean time of his vacant hours in which by the indulgence of his prevailing bias he undoes whatever may be inculcated at other feafons, are paffed over without notice.

By purfuing in this manner the fame track indifcriminately with all, a fyftem of education is adopted, by which, contrary to the teftimony of univerfal experience, all men whatever in point of capacity are put upon a level. A man, perhaps eminently qualified for active, but no way fitted for contemplative life, is yet compelled to embrace the latter in which his talents are wholly mifapplied; as on the contrary, a man of genius (taking the word in its ufual acceptation) hurried into the tumult of bufinefs, finds himfelf engaged in enterprifes which he cannot bring to any conclufion; and his abilities are loft to the public and to himfelf by being directed

rected to improper objects. Admitting,
however, that such a man may find (as
sometimes no doubt is the case) that his
talents have not been mistaken; yet, from
the remarks already made, it must be easy
to observe, even in this case, the confequence arising from an early and unlimited
indulgence of the *ruling* faculty acquiring
false ideas, and gaining an habit of carrying these into exercise, in consequence of an
original neglect whose effects cannot afterwards be corrected.

Some readers, I am aware, who may
admit the truth of these observations, will
yet exclaim that there is hardly any practicable remedy for the evil here complained of. " In order to rectify it (they
" will say) there must be an end of all
" public seminaries, in which the masters
" would find it an arduous task indeed, to
" distinguish, amidst an indiscriminate num-
" ber of scholars, the peculiar character of
" any single person so exactly as to pur-
" sue a particular method with him, while
" their attention is successively employed
" to gratify many wants, and to explore
　　　　　　　　　　　　　　　" many

" many characters among thofe committed
" to their charge."—But a little recollection will fuggeft the anfwer to this objection.—Though there is no individual,
however weak his intellectual powers, who
would not be benefited by fuch a fcheme
as we have attempted to fketch out in this
fection, fteadily carried into execution, and
judicioufly applied to the propenfity of his
mind;—yet in common cafes, when no
peculiar and *difcriminating* quality makes
its appearance, the attention here recommended is not neceflary. A man of ordinary parts fitted perhaps to go through
life with approbation, but difcovering no
bias to any branch of the art which we
here treat of, might indeed receive advantage by having the powers of his mind
properly balanced by an happy education,
to whatever objects thefe might afterwards
be directed; but with regard to Compofition, the neglect of that method which
we have propofed as moft eligible, could
produce no confiderable detriment. Art
may indeed *polifh* and *improve upon* the
materials of nature, but cannot *create* thefe

where

where they fubfift not originally. Thus
to communicate an idea of what conftitutes
beauty, either in painting or poetry, to a
man who is deprived of that internal fenfe
by which it is perceived, would be an attempt as ineffectual as to make a blind
man a judge of colours, or to entertain
the deaf with a concert of mufic. In inftances, on the other hand, which fall out
but rarely of thofe who difcover an early
propenfity to fome fpecies of Compofition,
we have already fhown that it is a matter
of no great difficulty either to find out
the weak fide of the character, or to adopt
a plan of education calculated to adjuft,
and to maintain the balance of the intellectual powers.

But that we may fet this matter wholly
on a proper footing, let us only take for
granted what will furely be allowed, that
men of this clafs are qualified to make
quicker progrefs than others in the ufual
literary departments; and it will only be
neceffary to defer the time when they begin to acquire the rudiments of a language
till a little later than ordinary, in order to

accom-

accompliſh the purpoſe we have mentioned. The parent, or tutor, taking advantage of the criſis at which the mind
becomes capable of improvement, will find
nothing further requiſite than to carry on
in the mean time the plan laid down in
this eſſay, or what more adapted can be
ſubſtituted in its room, till by habituating
his pupil to form ideas of correct and
maſterly Compoſition he gains ſome knowledge of excellence in the art. By this
method, when he comes afterwards to read
the performances of claſſical writers in a
foreign language, he will be able without
the aſſiſtance of his maſter to judge for
himſelf of their peculiar characters; and
having the foundation once laid by others,
will by the ſtrength of his own reflection
and experience erect a proportioned and
durable ſuperſtructure.

END OF THE FIRST VOLUME.

www.ingramcontent.com/pod-product-compliance
Lightning Source LLC
Chambersburg PA
CBHW022028110726
47901CB00006B/1683